Roger Oldfield once taught History at Great Wyrley High School, a few hundred yards from the former Edalji home. His view of the family was later transformed by his experiences working as an Advisory Teacher for Multicultural Education. Academics, journalists, authors and television programme-makers have drawn on his expertise on the Edalji family. He and his German wife have two daughters.

Outrage:
The Edalji Five and the
Shadow of Sherlock Holmes

Roger Oldfield

Outrage:
The Edalji Five and the
Shadow of Sherlock Holmes

Vanguard Press

VANGUARD PAPERBACK

© Copyright 2010
Roger Oldfield

The right of Roger Oldfield to be identified as author of
this work has been asserted by him in accordance with the
Copyright, Designs and Patents Act 1988.

A CIP catalogue record for this title is
available from the British Library.

ISBN 978 184386 601 5

Vanguard Press is an imprint of
Pegasus Elliot MacKenzie Publishers Ltd.

www.pegasuspublishers.com

First Published in 2010

Vanguard Press
Sheraton House Castle Park
Cambridge England

Printed & Bound in Great Britain

Disclaimer

The author and publisher would like to thank the following for permission to use illustrations: Staffordshire Record Office – St Mark's church, Rev. Shapurji Edalji, Enoch Knowles confession; Pauline Badger – Henry Badger, Maud Badger; Stueart Campbell - Inspector Campbell, Rev. Shapurji Edalji; National Archives – map, Great Wyrley Colliery shed, sites of outrages (adapted), George Edalji, anonymous letter; R. and M. Whittington-Egan (eds) *The Story of Mr. George Edalji* by Sir Arthur Conan Doyle, Grey House Books – George Edalji without and with glasses, 'God Satan' and 'foulmouth' letters; Staffordshire County Council - George Anson; *Black Country Bugle* – Royden Sharp drawing, cartoon drawing of outrage; Gillian Tindall, *City of Gold*, Temple Smith – Towers of Silence, Bombay, Watson Hotel; St Mark's church – Rev. Shapurji Edalji, Rev. John Compson; David Jennings - Porthcurno Telegraph Museum - St Levan church; National Maritime Museum - East India Docks; English Heritage – Gladstone; Victoria & Albert Museum – Walter Crane map; Trevor McFarlane – Edalji family; Birmingham Central Library – George Edalji letter; Old UK Photos - Portland Prison; David Thorpe – Welwyn Garden City; David Jennings – St Clement's church, Porthccurno.

Every effort has been made to contact the copyright holders and we apologise if any have been overlooked. Should copyright have been unwittingly infringed in this book the owners should contact the publishers, who will make corrections in future printings.

This book is dedicated to all the former students of Great Wyrley High School, who delighted in the exploration of early versions of this story.

CONTENTS

ACKNOWLEDGEMENTS

Dad often makes funny jokes
He also talks to strange blokes
He wants to go to Bombay
But can't afford it anyway
His job is multicultural education
He's building up another nation
If you don't watch it he'll start talking
About George Edalgie
It's in his heart
And walking.

Our younger daughter, then aged eleven, wrote these lines many years ago. Her poem reflects my family's amused tolerance whenever I 'start talking' about the Edaljis, a tolerance for which I am eternally thankful. My wife Gabi has herself found time to 'start talking' about the writing of this book, and has provided much constructive criticism, whilst our daughters Sara and Susanna have checked the proofs with cheerful persistence. There are also indeed many 'strange blokes' I have talked to. Special thanks go to my early inspiration, Michael Harley; I have not agreed with all his conclusions, but his researches revealed so many unseen possibilities within the George Edalji case. Thanks also to Roy Lewis, former Staffordshire County Inspector for History, who provided a great deal of practical support with my early research and the preparation of a work-pack for schools, and to former Police Sergeant Alan Walker, once Curator at the Staffordshire County Police Museum, whose enthusiasm on the George Edalji affair led to new lines of enquiry. I am thankful beyond words for my six years in multicultural education when, working alongside Paul Bellingham, Phil Colclough, Ian Fenn, and many others, I learnt so much about the consequences of Britain's imperialist past, and came in touch with so many great visions of 'another nation'. Nigel Tringham and Phil Emery were very generous in sharing their expertise as professional historian and writer respectively. Thanks are due above all to Stephen McGonigle, who has the Edalji family 'in his heart' too; he has given much creative advice and encouragement.

LIST OF ABBREVIATIONS

B.A.L.S.	Bolton Archives and Local Studies Searchroom
B.R.L.	Birmingham Central Library, Reference Library
C.C.A.	Canterbury Cathedral Archives
C.L.	Cannock Library
E.R.O.	Essex Record Office, Chelmsford
L.D.R.O.	Lichfield Diocesan Record Office
L.R.O.	Liverpool Record Office
O.R.O.	Oxfordshire Record Office, Oxford
P.R.O.	Public Record Office (now the National Archives)
S.C.P.M.	Staffordshire County Police Museum (transferred to S.R.O. 06-07)
S.R.R.C.	Shropshire Records and Research Centre, Shrewsbury
S.R.O.	Staffordshire Record Office, Stafford
U.S.P.G.	United Society for the Propagation of the Gospel, Rhodes House Library, Oxford
W.L.H.C.	Walsall Local History Centre
W.S.L.	William Salt Library, Stafford

INTRODUCTION: THE VIEW FROM 1953

Behind the curtains

2 June 1953. Maud's shrinking violet of a house was small, sunk deep into the remotest corner of a Welwyn Garden City cul-de-sac. Behind windows darkened by the clutter of neglected bush-growths there lurked curtains worn with age, and behind them lay George, blind, weak and helpless. Maud watched over her older brother, just as she always had, just as she had once watched over their parents in their last days, first Shapurji and then Charlotte. Horace was different: since childhood she had cared ever less for her other brother, and when recently he had been the first of the three to go there were few tears to be shed. Now, if anyone had bothered to come and peer through those shy end-of-cul-de-sac windows, they might perhaps have seen her pour George one of his last cups of tea from her china teapot.

As George lay dying in that decaying little house I was a six-year-old on holiday in Cumbria winning one of the children's categories in a Coronation Day fancy dress competition. Submerged in my father's mountaineering clothes I won because at the last minute he hung a 'Just back from Everest' placard on my enormous rucksack. This triumphant message reflected the hot news held over for the big day – another British expedition had made yet another conquest, if only of a mountain this time.

As Britain fêted its past with traditional coronation pomp from the Mall to Westminster Abbey, the world outside was moving on. Jawaharlal Nehru, who in 1907 had written home from Eton complaining about George's treatment, was now the first Prime Minister of an independent India. Soon the rest of the empire would follow India's lead, leaving the British to the slow retreat into their little islands and beliefs in former greatness. The past still lived on in the cheers of the crowds, though, as Queen Elizabeth II, weighed down by ancient crown jewels, peered out and waved from the golden carriage which monarchs had used for the same purpose since the coronations of George IV and Queen Victoria.

Maud's beloved brother died two weeks later, so soon after the unfavoured Horace. She was alone, the last Edalji in England.

I grew up knowing nothing of any of them.

I can imagine talking to you Maud. It seems easier with you and Charlotte than with single-minded Shapurji or quiet George, and Horace was so remote. Even you I missed by ten years, though: whilst I was sweating before my 'O' levels in Manchester in 1961 you were making your last visit to Great Wyrley in Staffordshire, and within months you were alongside George's grave in yours.

I first heard of Great Wyrley a decade later, when an advertisement for the Head of History post at the comprehensive school, just a few hundred yards from your birthplace, pitched me into your family's past. If only I had met you. If only I had met you this story would surely have been a little more certain about the boundaries between outrage and truth.

****

November 2004. Here I am in Freda Shimmin's immaculate converted pair of alms-houses near Peterborough. She looks 71 but is 91, the distant relative Maud named in her will – Maud could find nobody closer than the great-granddaughter of her mother's aunt's sister. I sit on Freda's sofa and she points into a cupboard on my left: 'There's Maud's teapot,' she says. I catch my breath: 'Maud's teapot?' How is it that a grown man can tingle at the sight of a china teapot? It's just three feet away, the closest I will ever get to Maud – or to George.

Freda went to Welwyn Garden City in 1962, brought back some of the treasures from Maud's chaotic family archive. This is Maud's house now. Here are her shadows. On the wall on the right are two samplers, each dominated by Turkey reds, one embroidered by her aunt in 1847,

'... Mary Sancta Stoneham
Aged seven years and a half
Ketley Parsonage...'

and one by her mother in 1850 or 1851,

'... Charlotte Stoneham
Aged Eight Years...'

On the wall ahead is a miniature of Maud's great-uncle, the Reverend Edward Bate Compson, fresh-faced and savouring his future, the man who conducted her parents' wedding. How much did they tell her about that extraordinary event?

A wedding

I imagine that on the day in question – 17 June 1874 – dozens of coal-miners labouring deep beneath the earth would have heard nothing of the cannon-fire at dawn, but the noise must surely have shaken the rest of Ketley into sleepy recollection of the unique event just a few hours away.[1] That lustreless industrial village near Coalbrookdale in central Shropshire was to celebrate a wedding without precedent in its history, or indeed in the history of most other communities in Britain at the time. The bride, Charlotte Stoneham, had lived in Ketley all her life, but the bridegroom, Shapurji Edalji, had had a much more remarkable life-path: he had been born a Parsi in Bombay,[2] converted to Christianity in his early teens, and moved to England in his twenties. Asians were unknown, still less Anglo-Asian unions, in a community in which most people had been born and bred within a few miles of the beds in which they now lay.

At Ketley parsonage, Charlotte and her family eventually rose to begin their final preparations. Charlotte's mother, Mary, and her father, the Reverend Thompson Stoneham, were at the centre of arrangements – Reverend Stoneham had been Vicar of St Mary's since it opened in 1838. He was to give Charlotte away, whilst his older daughter, Mary Sancta, was to be one of three bridesmaids. The gunfire at four had also disturbed the sleep of an array of guests from the Midlands and beyond. There were members of the Stoneham family of Essex, and of Mary's family, the Compsons of Bromsgrove. Among the Compsons were two of Mary's brothers, the Reverend Edward Bate Compson, who was to conduct the wedding, and the Reverend John Compson, Vicar of Great Wyrley in Staffordshire. As for Shapurji, support came in the form of the Reverend Reginald Yonge, Vicar of the Liverpool parish in which he was a curate.[3]

Finally Charlotte was ready, arrayed in a wedding dress made of rich white silk. On her head she wore a wreath of orange blossom, and a white veil covered her face. With her

---

[1] *Wolverhampton Chronicle*, 24 June 1874.
[2] As this is an historical work the name Bombay will be used instead of the modern Mumbai.
[3] *Shrewsbury Chronicle*, 26 June 1874.

father, her sister, and the other two bridesmaids, she made her way along the flag-bedecked path to the church. They found the churchyard packed with well-wishers, for so many people had arrived that the building itself was full. The crowd parted to let the wedding party through, and father and daughter entered the building to the smiles of a community which knew them well.

For Shapurji, waiting for the bride to walk down the aisle, this was a more lonely experience. As he stood before the two men who were to lead the service, the Reverend Edward Bate Compson and the Reverend Reginald Yonge, he could only be acutely conscious of the fact that none of his own family were present; even the best man was a vicar from a nearby parish, imported for the occasion. Indeed, Shapurji's closest relatives may still have seethed at his boyhood abandonment of the faith into which he was born.

Nevertheless, when he put the ring on Charlotte's finger Shapurji was also marrying into a new kind of security, a family well up the ladder in the Church of England. One of his new relatives, the Reverend John Compson, sitting in a pew behind the bride, was considering when he should resign his living in Great Wyrley. He was unwell and his resignation could represent a very special wedding-present, paving the way for Shapurji to succeed him and thus become probably the first person from South Asia to be appointed as the incumbent of an English living.

Local journalists wrote vivid accounts of this special moment in the history of both Ketley and Britain – one described the event to readers as being among 'the most noticeable weddings in the district for years'.[1] The reports nevertheless had virtually nothing to say about the bridegroom; there was no celebration of his claim to be the first ordained Indian clergyman in England, and one paper made no mention of him whatsoever.[2] Marriages between white and black or minority ethnic partners were few and far between in the mid-19th century, and mostly unheard of in communities outside London and other major ports such as Liverpool. Such marriages were usually frowned upon by British society at the time, as Sir Arthur Conan Doyle was to illustrate in an early Sherlock Holmes story, 'The Yellow Face', written later in the century. Here Effie Munro describes how she 'cut herself off from my race' in order to marry a black American. She also

---

[1] *Shrewsbury Chronicle*, 26 June 1874.
[2] *Wellington Journal and Shrewsbury News*, 20 June 1874.

makes it clear what many people felt about the children of mixed marriages: 'It was our misfortune that our only child took after his people rather than mine.'[1] Mixed 'race' children were widely viewed at that time with pity, as the evidence of their 'foreign parentage' was so obvious – 'the dark little face with the woolly hair of Africa curling above the smiling eyes, or the features, perhaps not so dark, with the luxuriant hair of Hindoostan'.[2] As the notion of 'scientific' racism developed during the nineteenth century it became a commonplace assumption that the mixture of 'races' would lead to physical, mental, and emotional deformities, and that the superior white 'race' would be contaminated.[3] The idealism of another Parsi from Bombay, Shapurji Saklatvala, who became the third Asian M.P. in the British House of Commons, was not shared by majority white British opinion: he married a white Englishwoman in 1907, and his dream was that their four children would themselves marry people from different nations and thus help to create a hodge-podge which would destroy nationalism.[4]

We can only guess what passed through the minds of the parishioners at St Mary's as the wedding ceremony proceeded. Certainly members of Charlotte's family did not appear to share popular ideas on race: they not only recognised Shapurji's talents (Reverend Stoneham had already invited him to preach at St Mary's) but also welcomed him warmly into the family. Their feelings were, however, clearly shaped by prevailing attitudes. Charlotte's sister, Mary Sancta, revealed this years later when she told a Birmingham M.P. 'Our friends at that time too felt as we did that Parsis are of a very old and cultivated race, and have many good qualities.'[5] Although the Stonehams were liberal for the age, Mary Sancta clearly thought of 'racial' or cultural groups as existing in hierarchy, with Shapurji acceptably high up the scale.

When the newly-wed couple departed for their honeymoon in Wales on that day in 1874 they travelled bravely forward into a future uncharted by tradition.

---

[1] Sir Arthur Conan Doyle, 'The Yellow Band', published in *The Strand Magazine*, 1893, reprinted in William S. Baring-Gould (ed.), *The Annotated Sherlock Holmes*, 2 vols, John Murray, 1968.
[2] Cited in Rozina Visram, *Ayahs, Lascars and Princes*, Pluto Press, 1986, p. 35.
[3] Barbara Tizard and Ann Phoenix, *Black, white or mixed race?*, Routledge, 1993, p. 20.
[4] Zerbanoo Gifford, *The Golden Thread – Asian Experiences of Post-Raj Britain*, Pandora, 1990, p. 222.
[5] B.R.L., 370795 (letter by Mary Sancta Stoneham, January 27 1904, in 'Papers and Documents Relating to the Trial of George Edalji on a charge of maiming horses, 1902-4', part of 'A Collection of MSS Formed by Sir J. B. Stone 1894-1907').

Ghosts

May 1971. Of course I knew none of this, Maud, when I made one of my last journeys in my first car, a moody second-hand Hillman Imp acquired three years earlier. In face of the dire environmental warnings contained in three seminal books of the period – 'Silent Spring', 'Blueprint for Survival' and 'Limits to Growth' – the car eventually went, and would not be replaced for a decade. Still, Hillman Imp did carry me into Great Wyrley for interview that day, and its maroon colour proved to match the school uniform perfectly.

There was a hiccup first. I still remember that when I turned on to Station Road from the village's spine, the Walsall Road, I missed the immediate turn to the school. I only realised this was a mistake when I went under the bridge carrying the Rugeley-Cannock-Walsall railway from north to south and found myself entering Cheslyn Hay. In those eight hundred yards between the school and the first houses on Station Street beyond the bridge, I realised later, I was ploughing through ghosts.

One of those houses on Station Street, Maud, was of course once the home of some of your parents' greatest allies at St Mark's, the Edmunds family. And when I came back across the Cheslyn Hay boundary and under the railway bridge I was yards away from the former station, used each weekday by your beloved older brother, first to get to school, then college and later work. Next came the house inhabited in 1903 by stationmaster Merriman. Then there was St Mark's vicarage, your home for the first thirty-six years of your life, and St Mark's church, with your father's shy grave hidden under the trees in the far corner of the grounds. Just before the back gate of the school there was High House farm, where your nearest neighbours on that side, the Greens, had lost a sheep and a horse in the 1903 bloodbath. Finally there was the school itself, built on the site of the former Brook House farm, with Brook House still standing beyond the school fence; here lived John Hatton in your day, for thirty years a kind of squire to your father as parson – the biggest landowner in the village and, amongst many other things, sometime churchwarden, director of the Great Wyrley Colliery Company and magistrate.

On starting work I soon discovered that those eight hundred yards were at the heart of a story which in your time had made

Great Wyrley world-famous, Maud. The sensational events of 1903 to 1907 were a godsend for a history teacher, especially when faced last lesson on Friday by thirty teenagers fizzing with thoughts of the weekend. What better attention-grabber than an account of brutal attacks on horses, cows and sheep at sites which they all knew? The Great Wyrley outrages of 1903-7 which caused you and your family such pain were still part of the local folk-memory seventy years later. Students would bring in postcard copies of a photograph of two horrifically injured horses – family inheritances from a print run of 5000 organised by one of your enterprising fellow-citizens in 1907. They would repeat the widely-held assumption that the outrages were the work of the 'Wyrley Gang', and the story that during the summer of 1903 the police used to put cotton round your vicarage home to try to prove that your older brother was breaking out at night to slash open the bellies of your neighbours' animals. I could hardly fail to profit from their fascination.

BOOK I: A DYING PONY

1. A village's tale

Hopes and horses

When I was a pit-pony driver
Just a boy all alone in the dark
In the dirt and the damp, with a smoky oil-lamp
My one grain of comfort was Spark –
There was something about that wee pony
On which I could always depend
Like the bond between shepherd and sheepdog
Or cowboy and four-legged friend.

J. R. Green[1]

First the scene had to be set, and as one class after another stared at my ever-developing slide-show we gasped together at shots of familiar local sites which had in many cases looked completely different at the turn of the 19th century. The fast-growing commuter sprawl of the 1970s was beginning to obliterate the shape of a community once scattered across a parish consisting of five straggling hamlets – Upper and Lower Landywood, Great Wyrley (which gave the parish as a whole its name), Cheslyn Hay and Churchbridge.

Amongst the photographs were old shots of St Mark's church, vicarage and schoolroom, the complex which had once acted as a main focal-point for the scattered community. When the Edalji family celebrated Christmas there in 1902, I could tell my classes, Charlotte and Shapurji, elder statespersons in the community after twenty-seven years' service, had plenty to look forward to for their children in the coming year. George, aged twenty-six, was already a solicitor (and author) of promise in the commercial heart of Birmingham, one of England's greatest cities. Horace, aged twenty-three, had left home and was set on a career with the Inland Revenue. Even Maud, at twenty, was at last during 1903 to loosen some of the constraints of life as a clergyman's daughter: it was in that year that she was offered a post as Assistant to the Kindergarten Mistress at Queen Mary's High School in Walsall.

---

[1] Poem by J. R. Green, cited in John Bright, *Pit Ponies*, Batsford, 1986, p. 104.

The majority of people in Great Wyrley and Cheslyn Hay could not even dream of such cosy futures. The miners, ironworkers, tile-makers, farm labourers, and servants whose weddings Shapurji had conducted in the first years after his arrival as Vicar of St Mark's in late 1875 had produced a generation whose prospects were only marginally better than their own. Certainly living conditions were slowly improving. There had been a gradual increase in life expectancy, partly because of the disappearance of the worst housing,, to be replaced by such solid turn-of-the-century terraces as can still be seen today on Walsall Road, Station Street and elsewhere. Indeed, several houses on today's Station Street were constructed just before or during the community's year of trauma in 1903 – and George himself drew up the conveyance for at least one, built by the Edmunds family. More new housing was appearing at Landywood, where in the years to 1914 the Harrison family built terraces for miners at their Number 3 Plant, in streets named after engagements of the Boer War (1899–1902), such as Modder River and Spion Kop.[1] Public health measures also promised greater life expectancy: Great Wyrley had acquired piped water by 1902, and water was soon to flow through Cheslyn Hay's new system – George Edalji himself drew up an agreement to buy land for £5,500 from John Hatton for Cheslyn Hay waterworks. Other facilities, such as gas lighting, were appearing; this was only slowly – there were just two gaslights on the whole of Station Road at the time that animal-slashers were creeping through the parish in 1903, though more were on the way.[2] The effect of the 1870 Education Act and the efforts of the School Board (of which Shapurji had been a member), moreover, had been to ensure that practically every member of this new generation had an education, in contrast to many of their parents who had often signed against their children's names with a cross in Shapurji's register of baptisms.

The vast majority still left school at twelve, however, and clanking steam-engines let young boys, clutching their Davy lamps and their sandwiches, down the same pit-shafts their fathers had descended for years – at the Plant colliery (half a mile down the railway line from the vicarage), at the Quinton or the Nook collieries, or at Harrison's Number 3. This last great new shaft had been sunk in 1896 at the southern end of the parish by a local dynasty of mining entrepreneurs, the

---

[1] C. H. Goodwin, *The Chase for Coal: Methodists, Miners, and Manufacturers on the Cannock Chase Coalfield, 1797 to 1929*, unpublished manuscript 1988, p. 21 (copy in C.L.).
[2] *Cannock Advertiser*, 3 January 1903.

St Mark's vicarage, 1903

St Mark's church, sometime before 1905

Kind permission of Staffordshire Record Office

Rev. Shapurji Edalji

Kind permission of Staffordshire Record Office

George Edalji as a young man

Harrisons; these magnates controlled the lives of Great Wyrley miners and their families from their house, set in 600 acres at Wychnor Park near Burton-on-Trent, and occasionally descended on the village like royalty.[1] This development gave the community a new centre of gravity, away from Gilpin's ironworks at the northern end of the Walsall Road.

Other youngsters went to toil on the land, for the Hattons of Brook House farm, the Greens of High House farm, the Stanleys of Landywood farm, for Thomas Wootton of Great Wyrley or the Bungays of Cheslyn Hay. At the Cannock end of the parish, in Churchbridge, young adolescents began lives of sweat at Gilpin's edge toolworks, beating out sickles and scythes, or labouring in associated activities. Others went off to the brickworks in Cheslyn Hay. A handful of girls went into service with the Edaljis, the Hattons, or the Hawkins.

Whatever their class, there was one thing which all members of this sprawling community had in common: a dependence on animals. Within the confines of the parish in 1903 there were less than 4,500 people but as many as 1,000 horses, ponies and cows, and enough sheep to send half the county to sleep on a nightly basis.[2] All of these animals were important, but the horses and ponies were vital for every aspect of the economic and social life of the community. Hundreds of miners, men such as Thomas Farrington and Henry Garrett, worked each day with or alongside horses and ponies, at the surface and in the darkness below. Their relationship was sometimes, but not always, like the 'cowboy and four-legged friend' romance, and miners on occasion drove their ponies with ruthless indifference in order to maintain the pace and rhythm of the production process; in 1907 William Powell, an employee at Harrison's Number 3, went before the magistrates charged with cruelty to a pony – beating and kicking it, saying he would 'either make the pony work or kill him'.[3]

Horses were essential for every sphere of work, and one local farmer, Henry Badger, great-grandfather of one of my students, made money selling on horses he had bought outside the village.[4] Through the seasons horses sweated and strained in the fields of farmers such as the Hattons, the Stanleys, and the Badgers, pulling ploughs, harrows, seed-drills, threshing

[1] C. H. Goodwin, *The Chase for Coal*, p. 17.
[2] *Express & Star*, 7 November 1903.
[3] *Staffordshire Advertiser*, 21 September 1907.
[4] Interview with Herbert Badger, grandson, 1985.

machines, corn grinders, reapers, cutters, binders, and all the other machinery of the agricultural year, or they tugged the farmers' carts along lanes and roads. At Gilpin's ironworks, the labour of horses enabled the constant flow of coal, iron, and finished goods. Dray-horses dragged heavy carts with tanks of beer down bumpy lanes to the Lord Nelson Inn in Cheslyn Hay (run by the Bungays), the Robin Hood in Churchbridge (William Hughes was landlord, and the pub had served generations of workers at Gilpin's works), the Star (where Henry Badger managed to fit the role of landlord into his busy portfolio), the Royal Oak, the Wheatsheaf, or the Swan. Horses and donkeys were keys to the business of traders such as William Brookes, grocer and postmaster, William Wynn, plumber and decorator, Jack Hart of Cheslyn Hay, who worked as a butcher in Bridgetown, and Joseph Holmes, a Cheslyn Hay grocer. Horses brought in the fire brigade to deal with fires in houses, hay-ricks, or fields of dry stubble. Horses still pulled barges in their slow progress up the Wyrley-Essington Canal or the branch of the Staffordshire-Worcestershire leading to Gilpin's works.

Although a few cars were starting to drone up and down Walsall Road, the arterial route along which much of the community straggled, for the more prosperous it was still horses which pulled the traps and carts which gave some independence from the railway system; in June 1903 the cart belonging to one couple from Walsall overturned on the way back from a visit to Elizabeth and Thomas Green of High House farm, and the woman died.[1] Some citizens used horses for sport or for military frolics; Harry Green, son of the Edaljis' neighbours Elizabeth and Thomas, had a horse he used to ride out with the yeomanry in Walsall. The wildly eccentric Cannock doctor, John Kerr Butter, who sometimes visited patients in a pony and trap trailed by his pack of Dalmatian dogs, did some of his work in Great Wyrley; for a short time he did, admittedly, try to replace his pony with a zebra from his astonishing menagerie in Cannock, but it was too frisky and he soon gave up on the experiment.[2] It was a horse which was to pull the dog-cart provided for Superintendent Bishop by the Staffordshire police force so that he could more effectively seek out the perpetrators of the awful deeds of 1903. Horses took citizens to their last resting-place at Great Wyrley cemetery, opened in 1897 after Shapurji and his predecessors had filled St Mark's churchyard with graves; for the poor, it might be a cart pulled by a tired nag, whilst for the handful of rich it might be an ornate hearse drawn by a 'black master',

---

[1] *Cannock Chase Courier,* 13 June 1903.
[2] *Cannock Advertiser,* 26 March 1976.

suitably plumed and caparisoned in ornate trappings of mourning.

Scattered everywhere in the villages of Great Wyrley and Cheslyn Hay were cows and sheep, and up the Walsall Road, down remote lanes, on narrow tow-paths, at grimy pitheads, in dank underground tunnels, in stables, sheds, fields, and factories, horses and ponies slaved and sweated, grazed, or slept.

Village of fear

Then came the sensational story. The one the students were waiting for. The story still swirling in the community memory when I first arrived in Great Wyrley. The morning of 2 February 1903. The parish awake. Chilling news. A valuable colt lying brutally slaughtered in a field near the Plant colliery on the Cheslyn Hay side of the railway line. Its belly torn across with a deep and savage cut. Joseph Holmes, a popular Cheslyn Hay shopkeeper, shaking over his loss. 'A DASTARDLY ACT AT WYRLEY', as the *Chase Courier* put it.[1]

This was just the beginning, as almost every adult born in the area still knew in the 1970s. On 10 April the parish was shaken by another attack, this time to the east of the railway. A horse owned by Ernest Thomas, baker in Landywood, was found so badly injured that it had to be destroyed.[2] Then on 2 May a cow belonging to Mrs Bungay of Cheslyn Hay was cruelly maimed in Lower Landywood.

Within two weeks the *Chase Courier* was announcing more 'SHOCKING CRUELTY AT WYRLEY'.[3] This really was the most shocking outrage to date. A horse belonging to Henry Badger, the man who was great-grandfather of one of my students, tenant farmer of the Duke of Sutherland as well as landlord at the Star Inn on the Walsall Road, had been attacked whilst grazing in a field to the east of the Walsall Road towards the northern end of the parish. The horse's wounds did not stop it moving, but they were enough to allow its intestines to drop as it tried to walk. The animal had clearly stumbled about in agony, now and again treading on its own intestines, before dropping to the ground exhausted. On the same night, a few hundred yards away on the same side of the Walsall Road, a sheep owned by Thomas Green of High House farm suffered a similar fate.

---

[1] *Cannock Chase Courier*, 7 February 1903.
[2] *Cannock Chase Courier*, 9 May 1903.
[3] *Cannock Chase Courier*, 16 May 1903.

Henry Badger, who lost animals in the outrages

Kind permission of Pauline Badger

**Henry Badger's wife, Maud, who worked with her
husband on the land and at the Star Inn**

Kind permission of Pauline Badger

On 13 June the *Chase Courier* ran the headline 'ANOTHER OUTRAGE AT WYRLEY: TWO COWS HACKED TO DEATH'.[1] The two cows, the property of the mine-owning Harrisons, had been attacked on the night of 6 June at Wyrley House farm on the east side of the Walsall Road near to the southern end of the parish. Again each animal had a long gash along the abdomen. One was already dead when found, the cut being so deep that it was disembowelled. The other was still alive, but barely.[2] Superintendent Barrett of Lichfield and Inspector Campbell, the officer working on the case in the parish from day to day, went to investigate an increasingly familiar scene.

Attacks on animals had long been a well-known rural crime. Indeed, a letter to the *Daily Telegraph* in 1907 pointed out that Staffordshire had a particularly bad record; between 1894 and 1903 the number tried summarily for malicious damage to animals was far above the average for counties and perhaps the highest in the country.[3] As the outrages went on, police and community could only speculate about motives – frustration with unemployment, disaffection with life in the mines, resentment towards the better-off farmers, blood-lust, bravado, perhaps a pub bet. Stagnation in the coal trade – by the summer some mines were only working half-time – left many local men with time and dissatisfaction on their hands.[4]

With three horses, three cows, and a sheep killed or injured in grisly fashion in Great Wyrley parish in the space of three months, the pressure on the police to stop the wanton butchery intensified. The Staffordshire force responded on 8 June by drafting in about twenty officers from all corners of the county to do special duty in the parish. Most had to stay in the village for long periods and accommodation was provided for them on a local farm. Through June, July and the first half of August they maintained their eerie vigils, often watching fields and animals through the night – though Henry Badger's granddaughter-in-law told me recently that the rumour was that the police stayed in sheds playing cards whilst they should have been out on duty.[5] Superintendent Bishop was in overall charge.

****

[1] *Cannock Chase Courier*, 13 June 1903.
[2] *The Birmingham Daily Mail*, 2 July 1903.
[3] *Daily Telegraph*, 22 January 1907.
[4] *Cannock Advertiser*, 20 June 1903.
[5] Repeated on *Heart of the Country,* ITV Midlands, 10 November 2005.

George Edalji's work routine had barely changed for years. Each day started just after 7.30 with the short climb to Great Wyrley station to catch the train for his solicitor's office in Birmingham. On the same train there was often a group of boys who travelled to Walsall Grammar School, 'a rather disreputable lot' according to one jaundiced fellow-traveller: Wilfred Greatorex, of Hednesford; Westwood, who got on in Cannock; Stanley, whose father, the local miners' trade union agent, was to become an M.P. in later years; and Quibell, son of the left-wing Vicar of Hednesford.[1] Sometimes George and the boys shared the same compartment. As a result, the fifteen-year-old Wilfred Greatorex and George had known each other by sight for three or four years.

The turning-point for both George and community came after another bloodcurdling outrage, committed during the night of 28/29 June at a spot close to the Plant colliery but between the railway and Walsall Road. At Quinton Colliery, owned by Messrs Blewitt, the shift had gone as usual that night. Police hid in the darkness in fields near the engine shed, where two of Blewitts' horses were kept when they were not at work shunting trucks along the colliery railway.[2] At 5.00 in the morning the foreman noticed one of the horses come up to a pool of water to drink, and was horrified to see its entrails hanging from its stomach. When he looked for the other horse he found it dead and completely disembowelled.[3] The alarm was raised, and as there was no hope for the injured horse it was shot. News streaked through the parish and crowds swarmed to the spot, recklessly obliterating any clues which might have remained.[4] Meanwhile George went off to work by rail as usual, this time in the same compartment as Wilfred Greatorex and his school-mates. As the train passed the gruesomely mutilated horses, George asked 'They're Blewitts', aren't they?'[5]

****

By now Great Wyrley was in a state of terror. Residents dubbed the mysterious perpetrator 'Jack the Ripper'; the real Jack the Ripper had been at work in London only a few years previously and was still in everyone's mind. Many owners of horses started to lock them up at night, even though this required extra effort after farm workers had spent a long day in the fields. At Parish

[1] *Daily Telegraph*, 16 January 1907 (J. E. Wilkes to editor); *Express & Star*, 5 September 1903; *Lichfield Mercury*, 11 September 1903.
[2] *The Birmingham Daily Mail*, 2 July 1903.
[3] *Lichfield Mercury*, 3 July 1903.
[4] *Cannock Advertiser*, 4 July 1903.
[5] *Express & Star*, 5 September 1903.

Council meetings the question of compensation for those who had lost animals was raised.[1] One suggestion was that voluntary contributions might be collected, but the Council agreed to another, namely that the County Council should be approached; the County Council was still dominated by an aristocratic clique – Lord Hatherton was chair, Sir Reginald Hardy was vice-chair, and the Earls of Dartmouth and Harrowby were members. The Council reported that it had no power to award compensation but that a reward to catch the perpetrator could be offered.[2]

Then came the twist which accelerated the Edalji family towards catastrophe. The atmosphere of mystery, fear and suspicion was suddenly intensified by the appearance of a stream of frightening anonymous letters. The first was addressed to 'P. C. Rowley, Bridgetown' and postmarked 30 June, the day after the attack at Blewitts':

> Sir,
> A party whose initials you'll guess will be bringing a new hook home by the train from Walsall on Wednesday night... he has got eagle eyes and his ears is as sharp as a razor an he is as fleet of foot as a fox and as noiseless an he crawls on all fours up to the beasts an fondles them a bit and then he pulls the hook smart across em and out their entrails fly before they guess they are hurt. You want 100 detectives to run him in red handed because he is so fly and knows every nook and corner... [3]

This disturbingly bloodthirsty letter connected the outrages with the group of passengers who travelled by train to Walsall and Birmingham. On 2 July the *Birmingham Daily Mail* provided full coverage of the outrages and the same day a rumour began to circulate in the area that one of the train passengers, George Edalji, had been arrested. George's response was to put an advertisement in local papers offering a reward of £25 for information leading to the conviction of anyone circulating rumours or anonymous letters about him.[4]

Then, on 4 July, a postcard under the signature of 'John Sullivan' was sent to Blewitt and Co. It linked the Great Wyrley outrages, Jack the Ripper and the Phoenix Park murders in Dublin with 'Irish Fenions'. Another letter, written in very different style from the first two, arrived on 8 July, seemingly from the youth

---

[1] *Cannock Advertiser*, 30 May, 4 July 1903.
[2] *Cannock Advertiser*, 1 August 1903.
[3] Cited in R. D. Yelverton, 'In the Matter of George Ernest Thompson Edalji', pp. 3-4 (copy in C.L.).
[4] *Lichfield Mercury*, 10 July 1903.

Wilfred Greatorex of Hednesford who travelled on the same train as George on schooldays:

> *Sir,*
> *My name is Greatorex and I live at Littleworth Farm. I am only a schoolboy at Walsall and I went to Rugeley first... I have got a dare devil face and can run well and when they formed that gang at Wyrley they got me to join. I knew all about horses and how to catch them best. I had never done none before till those two horses near the line at Wyrley and they said I had drawn the longest lot and said they would do me in if I funked it, so I did and caught them both lying down at 10 minutes to 3 and they roused up and then I caught each under the belly but they didn't spurt much blood... Now I'll tell you who are in the gang... there's one named Broell from Wyrley and a porter called Edgar of Wyrley Station... there's Edalji the lawyer him as they said was locked up, there's Fred Wootton from Cheslyn Hay... Now I have not told you who is at the back of them all I mean the Captain... He offered me £2 to hold my tongue yesterday and I said I would but I think its not enough so I shall split but you must settle for me to go to a ship when I have told you... if you bother me when I come off the train I will not go quiet or be locked up...*

Now it appeared that a gang was at work – and that George was a member. The envelope containing the letter was from Osborne & Son, a well-known stationer in central Birmingham. Although the letter purported to come from Wilfred Greatorex, written on a piece of paper stuck on the back of the envelope were the words: 'Your affectionate friend, Fred Wootton'.[1] Fred Wootton was one of the Great Wyrley boys who travelled to school on the Walsall line.

Littleworth Farm was in Hednesford, three miles from Great Wyrley, and the letter mentioned some of the Hednesford boys who also travelled by train to Walsall Grammar School, but the writer was clearly familiar with Great Wyrley parish and its inhabitants too, particularly with those who lived or worked in the area around the station and vicarage. The references to the 'gang' and the 'Captain' became the germ of the popular local assumption to which my students often referred – the idea that the crimes of 1903 were the work of an organised 'Wyrley Gang'.

---

[1] Cited in R. D. Yelverton, 'In the Matter of George Ernest Thompson Edalji', pp. 17-18.

Suspicion

The police came to the curious view that George was himself responsible for some of these letters. The local sources I read in 1971-2 reported briefly that he had already been suspected of writing a series of anonymous letters as a youth in the early 1890s. Now, according to this interpretation, he cleverly disguised his handwriting and tried to bluff the police by naming himself as a member of the 'gang'.

Indeed, some time after the 29 June outrage at Blewitts' and the rumours about George's involvement in the attacks the police began to keep a regular watch on the vicarage at night to try to catch this believed gang-member getting out. Then, after the arrival of the 8 July Greatorex letter, Inspector Campbell went to see George and announced, ingratiatingly, that he thought George could assist his investigation. As a result George later gave Campbell any letters which he received, though Campbell was in fact already looking for evidence which would incriminate him, however feeble: 'I was carefully taking a note of Mr. Edalji during the interview and I could see,' he reported later in court as if he had found proof of guilt, 'at the conclusion of each answer he smiled.'[1] George actually made his own suggestion during the interview – that the police should use bloodhounds to try and catch the person or persons attacking animals. He also questioned the competence of the police, and was later to suggest that this became a reason for police hostility towards him.[2] The police themselves came to the view that the guilty George welcomed any contact with the authorities because he would then know which path the investigation was taking.

Next a letter, postmarked 10 July, was sent to 'The Sergeant, The Police Station, Hednesford' with a threat which raised the stakes even higher: the recipient would be shot if he came after the writer. Although it was not signed, the content of this new message otherwise had much in common with the 'Greatorex' letter, including mention of the Hednesford boys who used the train:

> ... There will be merry times at Wyrley in November when they start on little girls for they will do 20 wenches like the horses before next March... Mr Edalji, him they said was locked up is going to Brum on Sunday night to see the

---

[1] Inspector Campbell's deposition, 3 September 1903, cited in R. D. Yelverton, 'In the Matter of George Ernest Thompson Edalji', p. 24.
[2] *Staffordshire Chronicle*, 24 October 1903.

Captain near Northfield about how its to be carried on with so many detectives about and I believe they are going to do some cows in the day time instead of at night. O I do think you a great big coward why could you not trust me and don't you be lounging about or following us when we come off the 5.39 train... what made you go to Stanley and Quibell. I never said nothing about them... I know all the toffs if I have got a dare devil face its no worse than yours nor that policeman Upton's... You bloated blackguard, I will shoot you with father's gun through your thick head if you come in my way... I will murder you if I get a thick bit of rope round my neck for it, but I don't think they would hang me but send me to sea... [1]

A further letter actually signed 'Greatorex' was sent to the police on 15 July, but another in the series, received by George himself on 23 July, was different in format from the others:

George Edalji
I do not know you, but I have sometimes seen you on the railway, and I do not expect I would like you very much, if I did not know you, as I do not like natives. But... I do not think you have anything to do with the horrid crimes... The people all about said it must be you because they do not think you are a right sort... If another horse is murdered the people will all say it was you...

A LOVER OF JUSTICE

George handed this 'Lover of Justice' letter to the police, and a few days later he sent for Inspector Campbell in order to pass on more mail from Greatorex:

Littleworth Farm...
George Edalji
I daresay you think yourself a very sharp fellow but you arnt a gentleman or you would not have put the police on my tracks as you have... I am going to tell the truth it was those 2 socialists youngsters Stanley the cub of that socialist scheming miners agent who is always making strife, a dirty fucking swine... and Quibell the cub of that ranting parson who started the report about you... Now dont do anything to Quibell as he only said what Stanley told him you go tomorrow night to Stanley and take a thick stick and

---

[1] Cited in R. D. Yelverton, 'In the Matter of George Ernest Thompson Edalji', pp. 19-21.

*give him a good hiding, never mind if you murder
him everyone will say you were quite right in
thrashing him as most people here think he and his
father are guilty of the horrid crimes everyone is so
shocked at. Be sure to go to Stanley at once as they
are going to send him to a training ship. It soon
caught on about you murdering the horses because
none of the people think you are the right sort...*
          Wilfred Greatorex

The last Greatorex communication was a postcard delivered on
5 August to George Edalji's Birmingham office. It had been
posted in Wolverhampton and the date stamp was for the
evening of 4 August: as George and Maud went on an excursion
to Aberystwyth on 4 August and only returned in the early
morning of 5 August George, on the face of it, could not have
been responsible for this postcard. It ran:

> *Sir,*
>   *Do you think it seemly for one in your position to be
> having connexion with Arthur Quibell's sister every night
> seeing she is going to marry Frank Smith the socialist.
> Rather go back to your old game of writing anonymous
> letters and killing cows and writing on walls.*
>
> *Yours respectful Wilfred Greatorex (Jnr.)*[1]

The police still believed George was writing these letters,
although if he did he was openly linking himself with the
outrages, and the night-time watch on the vicarage continued.
Out of this arrangement came the local story, repeated by many
of my students, that during this period the police tied cotton
thread round the building to try to catch George coming out.[2]

The night

For the tale of Wyrley's most famous moment we
would sometimes leave the classroom and walk the few
hundred yards down Station Road as far as St Mark's. There we
would have a look inside the church, find Shapurji's grave in

---

[1] Cited in R. D. Yelverton, 'In the Matter of George Ernest Thompson Edalji', p. 5.
[2] I never found any evidence to confirm this until the granddaughter of Ernest Stokesay
told me in 2006 that as a policeman on duty in Great Wyrley in 1903 he had been sent to
buy six balls of cotton twine from Peacock's in Walsall. According to the story passed on to
her, this cotton was used to set up the vicarage trap on at least one occasion.

the grounds, and strain to get a glimpse of the vicarage's rear bedroom windows through the trees. Then the story began.

On 17 August, George arrived back at the vicarage from work some time after 6.00 p.m. He changed into some blue serge trousers and an old housecoat, and from around 7.15 to 7.55 carried out some business with a David Hobson in the study at the vicarage.[1] He then changed from his housecoat into a blue serge coat, and walked through Churchbridge to Bridgetown, where at around 8.30 he gave some boots to John Hands, a boot-maker, for repair. The weather was dry, but it had been raining during the day and there were still some puddles.

As his supper would not be ready for another hour George took a stroll around the neighbourhood, being seen by a number of people and greeted by a few. When he got back to the vicarage he still had a little time before supper, so he walked the short distance to High House farm, the Greens' farm, but did not go in and just made his way back home. A Walter Whitehouse saw him enter the vicarage at 9.25. He went in via the kitchen, where Charlotte was busy, and eventually had his supper in the dining-room.[2] The maid, Dora Earp, who returned to the vicarage at about 9.45 after an evening off work, saw him at this time. After chatting with Charlotte and Maud he retired to bed at about 10.45 – in the room which he had shared with his father since about 1886, when Maud had been ill and her mother had taken her into her bedroom to look after her. Shapurji went to bed around 11 o'clock and saw his son at that time. As usual he locked the door before getting into bed.

Even before darkness had sunk on Great Wyrley that night, dozens of miners were already well into their night-shift under the earth. At the pit-head at the Plant colliery (owned by the Great Wyrley Colliery Company), half a mile up the railway line from the vicarage, the winding-engine periodically hissed and clanked into the stillness of the night. At intervals, wagons of coal rumbled away southwards to the furnaces of the Black Country. Elsewhere all was silent.

For miles there was no light, save for the glare from the occasional fire-bucket mounted on a pit bank.[3] Under the cover of the night, up to twenty policemen were scattered across the landscape, wandering between fields containing horses, or

[1] *Staffordshire Chronicle*, 24 October 1903.
[2] Shapurji Edalji, *The Case of George Edalji*, The United Press Association, 1905, p. 16.
[3] *The Birmingham Daily Post*, 29 September 1903.

stationed within sight of likely targets. As he peered into the dark, each officer had hours to contemplate what he would actually do if suddenly confronted by a man or men carrying a sharp weapon which had already been used on a string of animals with ruthless ferocity. At about 11 p.m. a newcomer to the whole operation, Sergeant Parsons, saw a pony in a field near the Plant colliery but on the other side of the railway from the colliery buildings. The pony seemed fine. Sergeant Parsons rejoined two other officers nearby.

Just before midnight the rain-squalls started. As the men pulled their cloaks tight and willed the dawn to come, any kind of shelter seemed attractive. For some there was the chance to sneak into the colliery and chat to the winding engineer. For others the magnet was the signal box which glowed in the night alongside the line between the colliery and the vicarage. We do not know how many surrendered to temptation that night.

The police had already dispersed when just before the sun rose at 4.50 the rain cleared. According to his later statement in court, Shapurji, troubled by lumbago was already awake. Less than an hour later, Henry Garrett, a fourteen-year-old miner on his way to work at the Plant colliery, noticed near a shed the pony seen by Sergeant Parsons the previous evening.[1] The roan-coloured animal was in a pitiful condition. Across the abdomen and the near side was a clean cut wound, exposing the bowels.[2] 'The blood was trickling from the wound,' he said later. 'Something like a lump of fat was hanging out' and the horse 'was dropping pretty quickly'. Sergeant Parsons and his senior, Inspector Campbell, were called immediately, and when they arrived they found another officer, P. C. Cooper, already talking to William Wootton, horse keeper at the colliery, who was holding the pony.[3] Inside a nearby shed there was blood on the ground, with footprints leading to and from it. Campbell and Parsons knew what they wanted to find, and they did – further footprints, which they claimed led in the direction of the vicarage, half a mile away.

---

[1] *Express & Star*, 5 September 1903.
[2] *Staffordshire Advertiser*, 22 August 1903.
[3] *Lichfield Mercury*, 11 September 1903.

Inspector Campbell (left), who led police investigations in Great Wyrley in 1903

Kind permission of Stueart Campbell

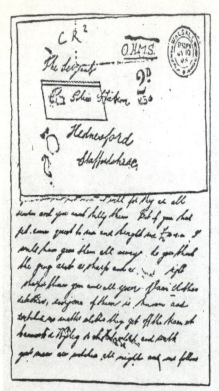
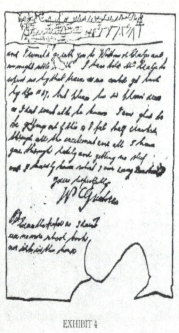

**'Greatorex' letter from the
1903 series of anonymous letters**

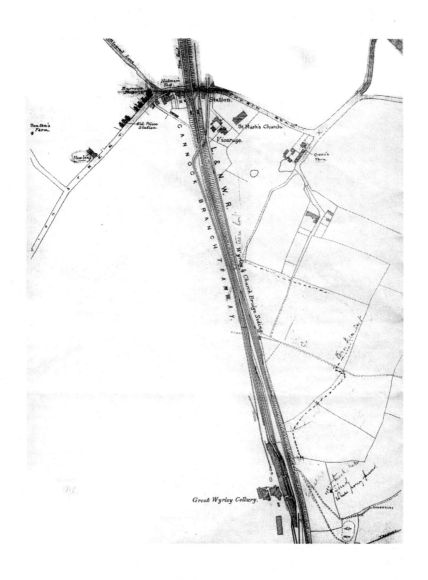

**Map showing the footprint tracks the police
alleged led towards St Mark's vicarage from the scene
of the attack on a pony
on the night of 17/18 August 1903**

Courtesy of the National Archives

**Shed belonging to the Great Colliery near to which
the mutilated pony was found on 18 August 1903**

Courtesy of the National Archives

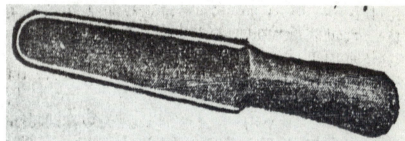

The botany spud (believed by the police to be a dagger) with which the outrages were supposed to have been committed. It has no sharp edge, and would not cut cheese.

Maud Edalji's botany trowel, examined by the police as a suspected weapon (from George Edalji's article in Pearson's Weekly, 1907)

The Edalji household was already in action. Charlotte had knocked on the men's bedroom door at 6.40 to let George know it was time to get ready to go to work.[1] George's breakfast was served by the maid, Dora Earp, who was to testify in court that he was wearing his old housecoat at this stage. Maud was also up and about when he left, just after 7.30. He got to the station, and there he was approached by a Joseph Markew, once a policeman but now an innkeeper, who announced that Inspector Campbell wanted to see him. Then Markew's uncle appeared, and George heard him say that another horse had been killed. George nevertheless insisted on going to work on his normal train.

Charlotte and Maud were still eating their breakfast, whilst Shapurji had not yet come downstairs. There was a knock on the door and Dora Earp opened it to find Inspector Campbell, Sergeant Parsons and P. C. Cooper on the doorstep. In they came, seemingly convinced that now was the Edaljis' moment of truth. Charlotte stood near the kitchen door and faced them.

The memory of the sounds and sights which followed stayed with you for the rest of your life, Maud, did they not? You heard the police arrive and you were drawn into what happened next, but however many times you replayed those memories you could not make those three men see that they were utterly wrong.

Inspector Campbell immediately demanded to see George's clothes, and Charlotte went upstairs to collect them. According to Campbell the old housecoat (not the blue serge coat used for the evening walk) was damp, and on the inner side of both cuffs it had dark reddish stains (he wanted this to be blood from the pony) and white stains (supposedly saliva). There were also, he claimed, brownish coloured hairs on the cuffs and hairs on the breast. He pointed out similar hairs on a waistcoat which Charlotte had supplied. The family flatly contradicted him. Charlotte insisted that the 'hair' on the coat was really a thread, and Maud, called by her mother from her breakfast, declared that her impression of the 'hair' was that it looked like a 'roving'. When Shapurji came downstairs Campbell pointed out two places on the coat where there were horse-hairs. Shapurji first of all denied that the coat was damp and then took it to the window, examined it carefully, and announced: 'There is, to be sure, no hair there.'

---

[1] *Cannock Advertiser*, 22 August 1903.

George's blue serge trousers were also examined and found to be damp and muddy at the bottom, whilst in the study the police found some boots which they said were damp too; the heel of one was worn down in a way which the police claimed was quite distinctive.[1]

Next they needed a weapon. 'Where is your son's dagger?' asked Inspector Campbell hopefully. Charlotte repeatedly denied that George had a dagger, despite Campbell's disbelieving 'Yes, he has,' so the Inspector tried another line 'One of you has a weapon,' he insisted, but Charlotte only offered the very unhelpful 'No he has his railway key.'[2] A new tack was called for, and P.C. Cooper, who had obviously been eyeing Maud suspiciously during the expeditions she sometimes undertook in search of wildflowers, asked what she used to collect flowers with. This line of enquiry produced no more than her botany trowel, but then the police came up with something more promising: four razors were found in a box in the bedroom used by Shapurji and George. According to Campbell, one was wet and appeared to have been used recently. He showed it to Shapurji, who, according to Campbell's court evidence, began to rub the wet off with his thumb. Shapurji was to deny indignantly that he had done this, and to insist that George, who went to the barber for shaving, did not even know of the existence of the razors.[3] For the moment, though, a razor became the weapon with which the pony had been slashed.

Only the jacket and the waistcoat, wrapped in paper supplied by Charlotte, were taken from the vicarage as evidence and placed on a police cart, though P. C. Cooper returned a few minutes later to collect the boot with the worn-down heel. Campbell and Parsons boarded a train for Birmingham, and at about 11 a.m. they arrested George at his office. Fatally, George commented: 'I am not surprised at this. I have been expecting it for some time.' This was used in court against him, but it could be taken to refer to what he saw as the longstanding animus towards him going back to an outburst of hostility to the family in a series of anonymous letters which had appeared between 1892 and 1895, made worse by the hostility aroused by his allegations of police incompetence in July.[4] He also asked the police whether the arrest had something to do with a C. A. Loxton, Clerk to Walsall Justices, who a couple of years earlier

---

[1] *Express & Star*, 21 October 1903.
[2] Shapurji Edalji, *The Case of George Edalji*, p. 34.
[3] Ibid, p. 37.
[4] *The Umpire*, 11 November 1906.

had taxed him about the appearance of offensive writing on walls in Great Wyrley; this reaction suggests a man who did not know why he was being accused. The police took him back to Cannock on the 1.27 p.m. train, and there he was locked in a police station cell.[1]

Back at the scene of the crime the colliery vet, Robert Lewis, had arrived at about 8.30 a.m. and examined the pony's wound. It was fresh, he said, done within the last six hours. There was no hope of recovery and the animal was shot by William Wootton, the horse keeper at the colliery. A section of the hide was cut from the horse by William Bruton, a horse slaughterer, and later taken to the police station on the police cart, along with George's coat and waistcoat.[2] As for the weapon, Lewis believed that it must have been curved and have had a handle offering a strong grip – the razors were ruled out by this theory.

About an hour later P. C. Cooper was on the scene with the worn boot obtained from the vicarage. By this time sightseers had appeared at the spot and, as even P. C. Cooper admitted in court: 'There were men coming to work and there were a lot of other footprints near where the horse was standing near the railway arch...' Despite the confusion, he was able to claim: 'All the footprints led towards the shed, except one which left the shed.'[3] He believed that George's boots matched these marks, and other marks leading in the direction of the vicarage – half a mile away, over grass, clover and stubble fields, over a headland where the day before grain had been cut and reapers had trampled, over a bridge above a brook, across hedges and ditches, gates and stiles.[4] Even then the trail he identified tapered out before it reached the actual vicarage. Instead of taking casts of the footprints he simply 'made impressions... with the left boot,' and measured the footmarks with 'straw and a stick'. This crude operation was the only piece of evidence which ever linked George with the scene of the crime, unless we believe that the horse-hairs appeared on George's coat because he attacked the pony.

In the afternoon Charlotte and Shapurji, convinced of George's innocence, gave a group of about a dozen police officers permission to comb the grounds of the vicarage and the church without a warrant. Watched by a gathering crowd, the

---

[1] *Cannock Advertiser*, 22 August 1903.
[2] *Staffordshire Chronicle*, 24 October 1903.
[3] Shapurji Edalji, *The Case of George Edalji*, p. 39.
[4] George Edalji, *Pearson's Weekly*, 11 April 1907.

officers used clubs to beat around the gravestones with sacrilegious abandon in the effort to find a hidden weapon.[1] Campbell and Parsons returned that afternoon to collect the trousers, which Campbell claimed in court were not in the same condition as they had been in the morning, having been thoroughly cleaned by Charlotte; Maud vehemently denied it. The two officers also collected the four razors, one of which they were to describe later as being wet.[2] They then took George's boots back to the scene of the crime to compare with the footprints again.

It was 9.00 p.m., according to some of the later accounts, when the coat, waistcoat, trousers, razors and horsehide were examined by the police surgeon, Dr John Kerr Butter, the man whose magnificent menagerie in Cannock was evidence of a passionate love of animals. So far as the blood on the coat was concerned, all he could find were two tiny stains which might have come from a nose-bleed. There was however something much more damning: he found twenty-nine hairs on the coat, and five on the waistcoat, matching the hair on the piece of hide taken from the pony.

Towards trial

The whole region was now agog to find out more about the astonishing arrest. In Cannock, on 19 August, large crowds swirled around the railway station and police court to watch George arrive for the first hearing.[3] The local magistrates in court that day included John Hatton, squire to Shapurji's parson for twenty-seven years, who actually shook hands with Charlotte and Shapurji before proceedings started. Once the charge of wounding a pony had been read, Inspector Campbell rehearsed the police evidence which was to become very familiar over the next two months – the evidence of the razors, the house coat (despite the fact that George was wearing the blue serge coat at the time in the evening when the police claimed he was out attacking the pony), the waistcoat, the muddy boots, and the trousers, along with George's words on his arrest. Neither the fact that the police surgeon had found hairs on George's clothes nor the police claim that the attack had taken place on the evening of 17 August was mentioned at this stage. The defence pointed out that Shapurji insisted that George had been in his bedroom all night, the only time when it

---

[1] Shapurji Edalji, *The Case of George Edalji*, p. 36.
[2] Ibid, p. 35.
[3] *Express & Star*, 20 August 1903.

seemed possible that George could have committed the crime. Once the proceedings were over Shapurji shook his son's hand and Charlotte kissed him in front of the whole court. Then George was whisked off to Stafford Prison.[1]

When proceedings resumed a few days later it was clear that George had created a new spectator sport. The quiet little town of Cannock was thrilled to be associated with his sensational case: to avoid the large crowd waiting at every vantage-point to meet the train from Stafford, Sergeant Parsons had to hustle his prisoner across the track in front of the engine and leap into a cab. The streets were lined with crowds too, and when the cab arrived at the court there was an anxious moment as the turbulent tide surged forward and managed to tear the cab's door from its hinges. When the court doors opened there was then a fight to get into the building, with men cursing and women shrieking in frustration.[2]

Inside, things were calmer, though two clear camps opposed each other. George Anson, Staffordshire Chief Constable was present himself to add the weight of his authority to his subordinates' claims, whilst the Edalji family turned out in force too. Even Horace was there; whatever bitterness the family was to feel towards him later, he was at least prepared at this point to travel all the way from Ludlow to support his brother. Whilst the Englishman George Edalji faced the bench, an effusive reporter from the *Express & Star* weighed him up in terms of all the prejudices of the time: 'His Eastern origin is shown in the olive complexion, dark hair, slight dark moustache, and piercing black eyes. He would look more at home in the flowing robes of the Parsee than in the light check suit and turn-down collar which he wore.'[3] The court was no more sympathetic: bail was set at a massive £500, with £200 to come from George, £100 from Charlotte, £100 from Shapurji and £100 from a friend. The incensed Shapurji, against all his instinct for correct procedure, got to his feet to declare that his son's practice would be ruined.[4] George was eventually remanded in custody and Shapurji left the court expostulating: 'You might as well live in Turkey.'[5]

Next it was the turn of the pretty village of Penkridge, north-west of Cannock, to have its peace disturbed. At the magistrates' court held there on 31 August the police sought to

---

[1] *Cannock Advertiser*, 22 August 1903.
[2] *Express & Star*, 24 August 1903.
[3] *Express & Star*, 24 August 1903.
[4] *Express & Star*, 24 August 1903.
[5] *Cannock Advertiser*, 29 August 1903.

spread their tentacles more firmly round their prey when prosecuting solicitor A. W. Barnes asked for a remand in order to present a new charge against George, that of threatening to kill Sergeant Charles Robinson; the charge derived from the threat contained in the letter of 10 July. George did not want bail, hoping that it might help his case; as he told one policeman, 'when the next horse is killed it won't be me'.[1]

Charlotte, Shapurji and Horace were back in court in Cannock on 3 and 4 September to hear the prosecution give an account of the evidence which was to be the basis of the prosecution at George's trial. The police, Barnes declared, were confident that the attack on the pony happened between 9.00 and 10.00 on the evening of 17 August; he was clearly tied down by Campbell's need to establish that the crime was done at the time that George was known to have been outside. The police and prosecution case was however fatally flawed, as it was the view of the colliery vet that the wound had been caused within six hours of his examination of the pony at 8.30 a.m. on 18 August. The garbled efforts of police witnesses so far as the question of surveillance of the vicarage was concerned left their tactics even more open to suspicion – Sergeant Robinson said that officers had watched the vicarage all night, Inspector Campbell said that just one man had carried out the watch, and Sergeant Parsons said there had been no watch.

When Inspector Campbell claimed that Shapurji had tried to wipe the razor clean after the police found it, Shapurji, in the colourful phrase of one journalist, 'ejaculated a denial', and Charlotte had to calm him down. Campbell, seemingly desperate to establish that the attack had taken place in the evening and not during the night, suggested that the pony must already have been cut when it was seen by Sergeant Parsons at 11.00 p.m., but that it was too dark for this to be noticed. The nationally famous handwriting expert, Thomas Gurrin, claimed that with certain exceptions all the anonymous letters were written by George. Dr Butter said that there were hairs on the coat of similar length to those on the piece of horse-skin, and that two of the red stains on the cuffs were blood, but that the grey stains were starch. Thomas Gurrin was called again, and claimed that George was the author of the letter threatening to kill Sergeant Robinson.[2] On the basis of this evidence, George was committed for trial at Stafford Quarter Sessions to answer the charges of wounding a pony and threatening to kill

---

[1] *Lichfield Mercury*, 23 October 1903.
[2] *Express & Star*, 5 September 1903.

Sergeant Robinson.[1] A great crowd gathered outside, eagerly trying to catch a glimpse of the accused man, but, as the local paper noted, this time 'there was no demonstration of any kind'.[2]

****

From the moment of the arrest the lives of the Edaljis were transformed. One of the first consequences of their trials was a sudden influx of 'worshippers' at St Mark's, some of whom travelled great distances to be there. Each Sunday from late August onwards the church was packed with people wanting to get close to the Edaljis' suffering and to hear Shapurji's response to each dramatic development.

Shapurji's audiences soon had another sensational twist in the story to excite them. During the night of 21/22 September, with George in prison, the Greens of High House farm were victims of yet another outrage. The Greens, the Edaljis' nearest neighbours to the east, had lived at High House farm for generations (their former home was still there during my teaching days in Great Wyrley). Elizabeth and Thomas, married in 1859, were active and respected members of the community.

Their son Harry, baptised by Shapurji in 1884, had been known to George for practically the whole of his life. Already during the outrages of 1903 the Greens had lost a sheep to the killer's blade. Then, on 22 September, John Jayes, a miner on his way to work at the Leacroft Colliery in Cannock, was walking past the Hattons' farm and near to the Greens' farm, five minutes' walk from the vicarage.[3] He came across the horrific sight of portions of an animal's entrails, and found a horse, a charger, suggested by the press to be worth £40, lying dead with a horrible slash across its abdomen. The horse belonged to Harry Green. According to one national paper the wounded animal had evidently galloped about a great deal, scattering its entrails about the field, before it lay down to die.[4] By early morning the usual crowd had turned out to drool over the view, including well-dressed women in carriages, a horde of cyclists of both sexes, and a posse of workers from Gilpin's ironworks taking advantage of their breakfast break.[5]

---

[1] *Cannock Advertiser*, 5 September 1903.
[2] *Staffordshire Advertiser*, 5 September 1903.
[3] *Express & Star*, 22 September 1903.
[4] *Illustrated Mail*, 16 October, 1903.
[5] *Express & Star*, 22 September 1903.

Paradoxically, Charlotte and Shapurji could take some kind of comfort from this new outrage, believing as they did that it seemed to support George's case. When Charlotte sent George a telegram with the news he replied that he was now 'overjoyed' that he had adopted the strategy of refusing bail.[1] Early developments seemed to justify this excitement, for unknown to the Edaljis there was another dramatic turn of events when on 29 September Harry Green himself confessed to this killing – of his own horse. His confession, written by a police officer but signed by himself, stated:

> *I the undersigned Harry Green of High House Farm do sign this on condition that no prosecution shall follow, and that I have nothing to do with any of the outrages that have been committed but the last.*[2]

On 5 October he was asked to make a second statement, supposedly to test his handwriting:

> *I had an aged horse in my Father's field which had been injured in the Yeomanry training thinking that it would never recover I killed it... The horse was killed to keep the Game rolling.*[3]

At first he refused to sign, but eventually he gave in. The papers announced that a confession had been made, but Green was not named; the police claimed that in return for immunity from prosecution the unnamed attacker had given them the names of three more men who had been involved. On 14 October, however, Green, who in the meantime had booked to sail off to a new life in South Africa, retracted his confession in front of a Birmingham solicitor, claiming that the police had forced it out of him. The police's response was to impound his ticket and tell him that he must be available for George's trial. Though he always maintained his innocence his life was now thoroughly entangled with George's.

National stage

On Tuesday 20 October the burgeoning Edalji road-show moved to Stafford, which is now my home town. Crowds swarmed into the Market Square that morning, some of them from the Great Wyrley community itself, to gape and to gossip about the stream of people entering the court building. C.F.

---

[1] *Express & Star*, 25 September 1903.
[2] Cited in Shapurji Edalji, *The Case of George Edalji*, p. 51.
[3] Cited in R. D. Yelverton, 'In the Matter of George Ernest Thompson Edalji', p. 31.

Vachell, counsel for the defence, arrived early, and was soon followed by W. J. Disturnal, counsel for the prosecution. The gathering clutch of witnesses included Harry Green, subpoenaed by the police to appear in court. Amongst others who got into the building was a huddle of well-off women with luncheon baskets and reading matter, excitedly prepared for the ups and downs of the trial.[1] Journalists from local and national newspapers buoyed themselves for days of avid reporting to a fascinated public throughout the land.

The tension affected the Edalji family in different ways. Charlotte and Shapurji arrived looking haggard and ill, bowed down by anxiety, but supported faithfully by their daughter. George was apparently in a different frame of mind, intent on making a good impression. It was the rule that he had to appear in court still wearing the check suit he had had on when arrested,[2] but he made every effort to groom himself, and his smartness was to be an early topic of conversation for his waiting audience.[3] It was in a Black Maria that he was taken the few hundred yards from Stafford Prison to the court buildings in the Market Square, and on arrival he was ushered through a labyrinth of dim passages below ground level (the holding cell under Court Number 1 is now a Stafford tourist attraction) before emerging blinking into the daylight to the excited stares of the crowd in the public gallery.[4] From their position behind him they eyed his every move as he sat in the dock, with his defence counsel, C. F. Vachell and W. J. Gandy, in the well below him.[5]

The Edaljis' feelings of grief and shame at this dark moment for the family were mingled with surges of anger. One focus of their indignation was the status of the court in which George was tried: Shapurji was bitterly critical of the fact that his son was not tried before a judge at the Assizes,[6] but at the Quarter Sessions. George himself was later to report his astonishment that his case was not even heard by Lord Hatherton, Chairman of the Quarter Sessions, in Court Number 1; instead it came before Court Number 2, described by Shapurji as 'the most inferior court with a jury in the county'.[7] The case was heard before Sir Reginald Hardy, a Staffordshire landowning baronet who had no legal training, just a desperate

[1] *Staffordshire Chronicle*, 24 October 1903.
[2] *The Umpire*, 18 November 1906.
[3] *Staffordshire Chronicle*, 24 October 1903.
[4] *Pearson's Weekly*, 7 March 1907.
[5] *Express & Star*, 21 October 1903.
[6] Shapurji Edalji, *The Case of George Edalji*, p. 8.
[7] Ibid, p. 8

urge to remove the cloud of notoriety which the outrages had left over his county. He did arrange to have a practising barrister in court with him, but as this barrister was on at least one occasion away in Court No 1 on other business the management of George's case remained amateurish.[1]

Ill-prepared muddle or something even worse, I would tell my students, also left a grubby blot on the performance of the prosecution at the trial. The colliery vet had already testified during the magistrates' court hearings that the outrage at the Plant colliery had taken place within six hours of the time he examined the pony, 8.30 a.m. on 18 August. Why then did counsel for the prosecution, W. J. Disturnal and H. A. Harrison, spend two days promoting Inspector Campbell's impossible story, namely that the pony had been attacked between 9.00 and 10.00 p.m. on the previous day? If the tactic was not based on utter incompetence or self-delusion on the part of the police and ill-preparedness on the part of the prosecution then we must believe there was a deliberate attempt to deceive the court.

It took Disturnal an hour to outline the prosecution case. Then he turned to his witnesses. Inspector Campbell, who spent four hours in the box on the first day, was given multiple opportunities to put the best possible sheen on the threadbare police evidence. Once he had stood down early on the second day, a series of prosecution witnesses flitted through the court, though not all those the defence camp had expected. One such missing witness was Walter Whitehouse, who had seen George enter the vicarage at 9.25 a.m. on 17 August: when Vachell cross-examined P. C. Cooper, he seized the chance to suggest that Walter Whitehouse had not been called because his evidence would not fit the police claim that the pony had been attacked between 9.00 and 10.00 p.m.

Whatever the jury made of this fleeting question-mark, its attention was soon consumed by something much more thrilling. This, the crucial phase in the presentation of the prosecution case, was the examination of the anonymous letters. Proceedings started with the reading of twelve of them in all their bloodthirsty detail. Then it was left to Thomas Gurrin, national authority on handwriting, to seal George's fate in the space of just two hours and earn himself the label 'trump card of the prosecution'.[2]

[1] Ibid, p. 8.
[2] *Express & Star*, 14 January 1907.

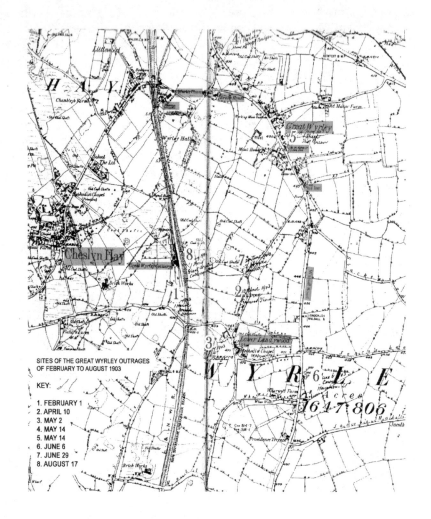

SITES OF THE GREAT WYRLEY OUTRAGES
OF FEBRUARY TO AUGUST 1903

KEY:

1. FEBRUARY 1
2. APRIL 10
3. MAY 2
4. MAY 14
5. MAY 14
6. JUNE 6
7. JUNE 29
8. AUGUST 17

**Sites of the Great Wyrley outrages
of February to August 1903**

Courtesy of the National Archives

It is hard to comprehend how the prosecution got away with this. Clearly Disturnal did need to prove that George wrote the letter containing the threat to kill Sergeant Robinson as this was one of the two crimes he was charged with. This charge was however dropped at the end of the trial, and so no jury ever had to give a verdict on whether or not George had written an anonymous letter. The other charge against him, on the other hand – that of maliciously wounding a pony – had no direct connection with the letters, all of which were written before the pony was attacked. All that the letters did was to claim that George was involved in the earlier outrages and, according to Disturnal, to predict another one. Despite this, Thomas Gurrin carried all before him with his repeated assertion that in his opinion most of the letters were in George's disguised handwriting. Somehow the prosecution managed to create the impression in the jury's mind that as George evidently wrote the letters implicating himself in the early outrages he must have been guilty of the one which took place on August 17/18.

When Disturnal sat down at the end of the second day, his case supposedly complete, there was much else over which the Edalji camp could mutter. There was particularly suspicious surprise over the fact that Harry Green had not been called, even though he had been subpoenaed to appear in court. The prosecution clearly did not trust him to say what the police originally expected – that he had killed his own horse on 21 September to try to help his imprisoned life-long neighbour out of his plight. His retraction of his confession made it dangerous to leave him open to cross-examination.

On the third day of the trial Vachell opened the case for the defence. He not only made no bones about assuming that Green was guilty of the outrage of 21 September: he also went much further. It was unlikely, he told the jury, that there were two 'fiendish minds' living in Great Wyrley. As Green had admitted to killing one horse there was no reason to believe that George could commit such atrocities as well. Again, the footprints leading away from the scene of the outrage of August 17/18, claimed by the police to lead towards the vicarage, could equally well be said to lead in the direction of the Greens' house nearby. Harry Green had no way of challenging this unscheduled prosecution.

The witnesses for the defence created a variety of impressions. George himself stepped purposefully out of the dock when called, and eager onlookers in the crowded court noted how utterly composed he appeared to be; he confirmed the details of his walk to Bridgetown on the evening of 17 August, and denied writing any of the letters. Apparently more conclusive evidence came from Robert Lewis, the vet who had examined the mutilated pony at 8.30 a.m. on 18 August. He confirmed that in his opinion the pony had been attacked in the six hours before he saw it. He also repeated the claim he had made at the magistrates' hearings that the weapon used for the outrage must have been stiff-handled, as the gruesome gash could only have been caused by an instrument with a strong grip; this made the razor a non-starter as the suspect weapon. Shapurji and Charlotte were both called, and each rehearsed evidence given previously. Shapurji, looking ill and speaking in a low voice, added for the first time that the reason he had not slept well on the night in question was that he suffered from lumbago.

On Friday, the fourth day, there was renewed licking of lips in court as the final dénouement approached. Vachell's summing up lasted two hours, and again the doings of Harry Green were emphasised in order to divert suspicion from George. Green had already admitted to killing a horse. Why, then, should George be suspected? Then it was Disturnal's turn to address the jury, and it was at this point that the prosecution produced an astonishing volte-face. Forced by the previous evidence of Walter Whitehouse and Robert Lewis to abandon the theory that George had attacked the pony between 9.00 p.m. and 10.00 p.m. on 17 August, Disturnal abruptly informed the jury that the attack had taken place during the small hours of the next day. George's clothes had been wet, not just damp, and as the rain only began around midnight that was when he must have been out. This desperate acknowledgement by the prosecution that the original police case was woefully inconsistent with the evidence was an admission at best of incompetence and at worst of a ruthless determination to secure a conviction at all costs. The theory also assumed that Shapurji had been lying throughout.

The prosecution's garbled efforts were nevertheless perfectly timed. Believing the police case would not survive close examination, counsel for the defence had been overconfident about this trial. Now it was too late to force the prosecution to answer one very obvious question. If George really did creep unseen through the dark, police-strewn countryside on a rain-sodden night, and slit open a pony with only two spots of blood on his coat to show for it, how did he see to do it? This was a man whose eyesight was so appalling that he had had to have his desk pointed out to him in exam rooms. There may have been an answer to the question, but the prosecution never had to find one. Edalji supporters grieved for years at this missing link in the defence case.

Sir Reginald Hardy, theoretically, had the duty of guiding members of the jury out of the morass, but during his final remarks he only succeeded in leading them further in. He made great play of the significance of the letters,[1] and when the jury retired at 2 o'clock it dutifully carried them off in order to seek proof that George attacked a pony after they were written. It did not take long to reach a decision: the jury was back in court by 2.50.

As George leant over the dock, the sunlight streaming down upon him, the foreman pronounced him guilty. A tremour appeared to some observers to pass through the Edalji family. George 'quivered like an aspen,'[2] according to one reporter, but otherwise appeared calm. Charlotte, Maud, and Shapurji, however, could not hide their shock.[3] 'I saw his mother faint,' wrote the colourful journalist from the *Express & Star*, 'and his father behave like one abstracted.'[4]

The bench retired to consider sentence, and Sir Reginald Hardy returned to make his views explicit, views which had been obvious even before the verdict: George had been 'very properly' found guilty. When sentence was passed – an awesome seven years' penal servitude – George seemed to pass into a hypnotic trance. It was almost a minute later that a warder tapped him on the shoulder, and then his being appeared to relax into resignation. It was 'the Oriental's acceptance of fate' commented the *Lichfield Mercury*, nonsensically. Other papers were even more unrestrained in their parade of the well-honed racial prejudices of early 20th century England. The *Birmingham Daily Gazette* believed that George had a genius for creation and a love of mystery, and used his talents in such perverted ways because of his 'Eastern extraction'.[5] The *Birmingham Daily Mail* saw George's behaviour as a 'throwback to prehistoric bestiality', with an admixture of some of the cunning Kipling used to attribute to the characters he set in the jungle.[6] The *Daily Mail*, which unhesitatingly informed the nation that George was undoubtedly guilty of all eight outrages of 1903, was clearly steeped in the absurdities of the 'science' of phrenology: 'Those who closely studied this extraordinary criminal in the dock,' it declared, 'would have no doubt that he is a degenerate of the worst type.

---

[1] *Express & Star*, 14 January 1907.
[2] *Lichfield Mercury*, 30 October 1903.
[3] *Express & Star*, 23 October 1903.
[4] *Express & Star*, 14 January 1907.
[5] *Birmingham Daily Gazette*, 24 October 1903.
[6] *The Birmingham Daily Mail*, 24 October 1903.

His jaw and mouth are those of a man of very debased life.'[1] Shapurji's view was very different: God 'looked for judgement, but, behold, oppression,' he wrote later, quoting Isaiah, 'for righteousness, but, behold, a cry'.[2]

No end

Shortly after the trial, Harry Green finally set sail for South Africa. The hope that this event and George's sentence would mean the end of the reign of terror in Great Wyrley was however soon shattered. Just three days after the verdict another threatening letter was posted to the offices of the *Express & Star* in Wolverhampton. It boasted that the 'Wyrley Gang' was still at large and thirsting for more blood:

> *SIR – I am very sorry that young Edalji who was convicted at the stafford quarter sessions on Friday last is an innocent man the man who killed them cattle at wryley is me and my name is G. h. darby the captain of the wryley gang... I will tell you how these cattle have been killed at wryley there are 15 men in the gang and 9 men used to be on the watch every night while I killed them and we used to do the police down with their eyes wide open... we shall kill all the horses what we find out in the fields at night and do the police down...*
>
> *Yours truley*
> *G. h. darby*
> *the captain of the wyrley gang*[3]

In my classroom we would stare at slide copies of these letters and try to decide what sort of lunatic could write them. The threats from the captain of the gang certainly seemed to become real on 3 November, when Great Wyrley shuddered over yet another gory overnight attack, this time on two horses. Early that morning, as work started on Herbert Stanley's lonely 100-acre farm at Landywood, a stable-boy found one of the horses, a ten-year-old roan mare, lying dead near the gate of a field in Street's Lane; its eyes were still staring open.[4]

[1] *Daily Mail*, 24 October 1924.
[2] Shapurji Edalji, *The Case of George Edalji*, p. 55.
[3] *Express & Star*, 26 October 1903.
[4] *Lichfield Mercury*, 6 November 1903; *Birmingham Gazette*, 3 November 1903.

**Harry Green, who confessed to the outrage of
September 1903 but then withdrew his confession**

Thomas Green, father of Harry Green and close neighbour of the Edalji family

Prison photograph of George Edalji showing him in the check suit he was wearing when arrested

headquarters market place wyrley
warning notice
that man who was seen early on
thursday morning in a field is the same
man who done the maiming outrage
it walsall early on friday morning
I paid him well to do the outrage
but if that man gave him up to
the police on thursday morning he
would have been a dead man before
long, signed g h darby captain of
the wyrley gang.

Postcard from the 'G. H. Darby' series

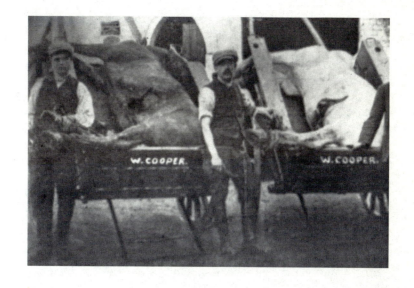

Outrage of November 1903

The animal had a great open eighteen-inch wound in its lower abdomen, and there were signs that it had travelled 140 yards after it had been cut – some of its intestines lay in a heap 50 yards away from the body, and bloodstains speckled the field.[1] An unborn foal, cut from the mare, was lying on the ground.[2] Another youth working for Stanley later went to harness the second horse, a dark-brown thirteen-year-old, but noticed that blood was dropping from the animal as he worked. It had a six-inch wound across the abdomen.[3]

The familiar figures of Superintendents Barrett and Bishop, and of Inspector Campbell, were soon at the scene, but the case now had such a high profile that Chief Constable Anson could not leave it to subordinates. He arrived from Stafford himself, bringing a camera with him – Patrick Lord Lichfield was not the first in the Anson family to use a camera for professional purposes.

****

Week on week, now, Sunday services at St Mark's were filled to overflowing. On the Sunday after the trial Shapurji caused a sensation at both Sunday services when he read out a letter from Roger Dawson Yelverton, Chancellor and Chief Justice of the Bahamas in the early 1890s and now a barrister in London.[4] The letter had been written on the very day of the trial verdict and declared that he, Yelverton, believed there had been a miscarriage of justice. That evening, in a crowded church, some of the congregation broke all protocol by bursting into applause when they heard this news.[5] During the week Yelverton, who was already preparing his case, travelled from London to meet the Edaljis at the vicarage, where letters of support were beginning to arrive.[6]

On 14 November St Mark's was again full to overflowing when Shapurji preached on the text 'That when you are in affliction Jesus knows'. Still deeply shocked and outraged at the treatment of his son he again used the power of the pulpit to make it clear to his parishioners that he would not be campaigning on George's behalf if he were not totally convinced

[1] *Cannock Advertiser*, 7 November, 1903.
[2] *Express & Star*, 2 November 1903.
[3] *Wellington Journal and Shrewsbury News*, 7 November 1903.
[4] Richard Lancelyn Green, *The Uncollected Sherlock Holmes*, Penguin Books, 1983, p. 118.
[5] *Lichfield Mercury*, 30 October 1903.
[6] *Cannock Advertiser*, 31 October 1903.

of his innocence. The sermon quickly turned into a defence counsel's final impassioned review of the evidence to a jury, and concluded with the ringing appeal: 'Let justice prevail though the heavens fall.'[1] Members of the congregation were invited to sign a petition on George's behalf as they left, and 200 did so.[2]

The following Sunday saw the church once more totally packed, with many standing in the aisles and others unable to get in at all. Shapurji chose another New Testament text reflecting his family's agony, one in which a nobleman says to Jesus: 'Sir, come down ere my child die.' Again members of the congregation trooped into the schoolroom after the service in order to sign the petition.[3] It took until December for the excitement to fade and attendances to dwindle.[4]

Confined to his prison cell, George could do little more than pray for the success of the campaign on his behalf. 'I hope Mr. Y will be able to do something,' he wrote in a letter to his mother, but then Charlotte received a letter from the governor of Stafford Prison with some more painful news: George had been moved from Stafford Prison, twelve miles away, to Lewes Prison, near Brighton, which was one hundred and forty miles further.

Outside prison the uproar about the trial verdict continued. George's aunt, Mary Sancta Stoneham, conducted her own campaign from Much Wenlock in Shropshire. She wrote to the press to declare that the accusation against George was 'utterly untrue and false',[5] but she was set back by the death of her friend Jasper More, M.P. for South Shropshire, whom she had hoped to enlist in Yelverton's support. Many others who had followed the trial in the national press were also shocked by the poverty of the evidence presented. The great criminal lawyer Sir George Lewis decided that George was probably innocent simply on the basis of *The Times* report. He himself was Jewish, and may have been able to identify more readily with George's situation than could other members of the establishment.[6] So far as he was concerned, the only points needing clearing up were the hairs on the coat and the blood on the razor.[7]

---

[1] *Cannock Advertiser*, 14 November 1903.
[2] *The Birmingham Daily Mail*, 9 November 1903.
[3] *Cannock Advertiser*, 21 November 1903.
[4] *Staffordshire Advertiser*, 5 December 1903.
[5] *Wellington Journal and Shrewsbury News*, 14 November 1903.
[6] John Juxon, *Lewis and Lewis*, Collins, 1983, pp. 297-300.
[7] B.R.L., 370795 (copy of letter from Sir George Lewis to R. D. Yelverton, 17 November 1903, in 'A Collection of MSS Formed by Sir J. B. Stone').

It was R. D. Yelverton, however, who played the leading role in the campaign, assembling evidence in George's support and marshalling his supporters. A petition was taken round Great Wyrley and other parts of the Midlands – on one day it was signed by dozens of people in Victoria Square in Birmingham.[1] By 21 November Yelverton was able to send a huge dossier to the Home Secretary, including a weighty and closely-argued statement on George's behalf, and a petition signed by 10,000 people, including 250 solicitors. He had worked with the Edalji family to collect dozens of letters in George's support; many were addressed to Charlotte, who was directing the postal campaign from the vicarage headquarters. The authors of these letters included a wide range of people: some of George's contemporaries at Rugeley Grammar School such as Macgregor Grier, son of the Vicar of Hednesford, who spoke of George's quiet, good-natured personality; local clergy; Mary Sancta Stoneham, Charlotte's sister; colleagues from the legal world; and Albert Holmes, son of the Joseph Holmes whose horse had been the first victim of 1903, who declared that George was exceptionally courteous and gentle. Yelverton's demand of the Home Secretary was that he should review the proceedings at George's trial, particularly the prosecution case.

The Great Wyrley community was also still seething with responses to the events of the year. There was continuing uncertainty about Harry Green's role in events, and there were angry exchanges of letters in the press between his brother-in-law and F. Arrowsmith of the Star Tea Company in Cannock; it was Arrowsmith who after the 21 September killing had put the police on Harry Green's trail by reporting a conversation at his shop in which Green intimated that he knew about the letters and the last outrage.[2] On 28 November parishioners met to discuss the question of a compensation committee, but some spoke darkly of the rumour that one person (they meant Harry Green) had killed his own animal in order to get the money.

Today, on Station Street in Cheslyn Hay, there still stands a late Victorian terraced house whose most recent use was as a Balti takeaway named 'The Raj'; in the brickwork are the initials 'J. E.' This house was one of three in a row built by John Edmunds between 1901 and 1904, and the one he and his family lived in – it was George Edalji who had done the conveyancing. John Edmunds had been sidesman at St Mark's church for years, and later members of the Edmunds family have played a leading part in the life of St Mark's church too. On 14 December 1903 he

---

[1] *Express & Star*, 18 November 1903.
[2] *Cannock Advertiser*, 21 and 28 November, 1903.

and his family showed their support for George by holding a meeting at the house attended by 35 people. Presided over by Albert Holmes, the meeting made plans for a George Edalji benefit fund.[1] Sympathies were running in the prisoner's direction.

There was nevertheless still a great deal of tension in the village, and it was exacerbated by the continuing flow of letters from 'G. H. Darby, Captain of the Wyrley Gang'. These frightening letters continued to threaten bloodshed not only in Great Wyrley, but also further afield. In the fifth in the series, signed as the Captain's writer and accomplice, the 'Gang' was said to have been behind a murder in Kidderminster, where a woman was killed because she allegedly overheard the 'Captain' planning to kill a horse with another member of the 'gang'.[2] Another letter threatened: '...we shall start killing the bluebottles and inspector Campbell who will be the first on the list because he is a day light robber...'[3]

****

Christmas 1903 was a sad time for two neighbouring families, the Greens and the Edaljis. In the weeks between Harry's confession and George's trial the Greens had suffered another trauma; Harry's three-year-old niece had died when her night-dress caught fire.[4] As for Harry, it was only after he sailed to South Africa at the end of October that the police had made his confession public. His father, Thomas, was furious that Harry had been given no chance to defend himself and took up the cudgels himself on his son's behalf. He wrote to the *Birmingham Daily Mail* to say that his son's confession was worthless and that if he had been called at the trial Harry would have said that he had no knowledge of the slaying of the horse. R. D. Yelverton travelled to Great Wyrley shortly before Christmas, specifically to see the Greens, and Harry's parents and sister all signed statements in his support.[5] Harry himself protested his innocence from distant South Africa, complaining in his letters to his mother about the 'false tales that have been put afloat concerning me'.[6]

---

[1] *Cannock Advertiser*, 19 December 1903.
[2] 'G. H. Darby' to *Express & Star*, 1903 (copy in S.C.P.M.).
[3] 'G. H. Darby' to *Express & Star*, 1903 (copy in S.C.P.M.).
[4] *Cannock Advertiser*, 10 October 1903.
[5] *Lichfield Mercury*, 18 December 1903.
[6] S.R.O., D3632/3/11 (Harry Green to Elizabeth Green, 4 April 1904, in correspondence of Sarah Elizabeth Green, 1859-1926).

So far as the Edaljis were concerned, their *annus horribilis* ended that Christmas with one son in prison and the other, for reasons which will become clear later, increasingly isolated from the rest of the family.

Sheep

All was not over for Great Wyrley, for with more killings in March 1904 the terror of the previous year was rekindled. The victims this time were two ewes and a lamb belonging to Henry Badger, tenant farmer and landlord at the Star Inn, who had already lost a horse during the outrages of 1903. This time a 45-year-old miner, Thomas Farrington, was quickly arrested and convicted of the crime. The case against him was that after a drink at the Royal Exchange Inn one evening he had been seen going into the yard where Henry Badger's sheep were kept. This yard lay next to the Walsall Road. After he came out of the yard he actually had the nerve (if guilty) to go to the Star Inn, where Maud and Henry Badger served. The next day, after the arrest, the police noticed that a button discovered at the scene of the crime matched the buttons on a pair of Farrington's trousers, from which a button was missing, and that the clothes he had worn the previous night also had sheep's wool on them. This, however, was the sum total of the evidence. 'Roderic Random', the lively *Express & Star* journalist who was at this trial as well as at George's, felt that the conviction, based largely on one button of a type commonly used, was even less satisfactory than George's.[1] Farrington was nevertheless sentenced to three years' penal servitude.[2] Three sheep obviously counted for less than half as much as one pony.

Whether or not this was a one-off copycat crime, reactions to the case are revealing. The *Daily Telegraph* asked scornfully whether it was possible that George would 'consort with a beer-swilling collier'.[3] As for the legal profession, it did not in this case react to newspaper accounts of a conviction on the basis of thin evidence which it did when one of its own, George Edalji, had the same experience.

Farrington's case was not the only reminder in these years that even if George was guilty animal-maimers were still on the prowl. In 1906 a horse was found maimed in Darlaston, and in a field nearby the police found a letter from the 'Captain of the

---

[1] *Express & Star*, 14 January 1907.
[2] *Staffordshire Advertiser*, 9 April 1904.
[3] *Daily Telegraph*, 23 February 1907.

Wyrley Gang' himself. 'Darby' again said he was responsible for the attack.[1]

The brick walls of Whitehall

Despite their suffering the three Edaljis left in Great Wyrley proved in the months and years after George's conviction to be campaigners of distinction. With conviction and with passion Charlotte and Shapurji worked alongside Yelverton to batter relentlessly at the gates of one of the citadels of empire, the establishment in Whitehall. Others picked up the gauntlet too – in 1905 the campaigning weekly *Truth* ran a series of articles in George's support – but what was going on behind the fortress walls of the Home Office nobody knew. All I could tell my 1970s classes was that the response to all the pleadings was negative.

Shapurji, in particular, was relentless in his attempts to break down the citadel's defences. The Home Secretary he had to deal with at first was A. Akers-Douglas, member of A. J. Balfour's cabinet. Balfour, successor to Lord Salisbury as leader of the Conservative Party, had been in Lord Salisbury's cabinet at the time of the latter's assertion that Britain was not ready for a black man to enter the House of Commons. Indeed it was Balfour's government which surrendered to contemporary pressures to scapegoat immigrants in general and Russian Poles, many of them Jewish, in particular, through the introduction of the Aliens' Act of 1905, which restricted immigration for the first time since 1826. In December 1905 the Liberals formed a new government under Campbell-Bannerman, with Herbert Gladstone as Home Secretary. Gladstone's grandfather had made a fortune out of slave-owning in the West Indies, and his father, the great Liberal Prime Minister, had in his younger days made speeches in defence of slave ownership; now Herbert was left to make decisions about another child of empire, the man who had been sent to prison by Sir Reginald Hardy, husband of Herbert Gladstone's own cousin.

Shapurji's battery of letters met with a brick wall of silence from successive Home Secretaries. His efforts culminated in January 1905 in a painstaking and comprehensive demolition of the prosecution case against his son, written in a lucid and polished style which compared well with that of his foe Chief Constable Anson.[2] The booklet started with the angry assertion that there was a conspiracy afoot in Great Wyrley from 2 July

---

[1] *Express & Star*, 26 October 1934.
[2] Shapurji Edalji, *The Case of George Edalji*, The United Press Association, 1905.

1903 onwards, with the promulgation of the false rumour that George had been arrested. The letters of 8 July and 16 July, written on the notepaper of a Birmingham stationer, seemed to Shapurji to be part of the conspiracy to frame his son. He then went on to pour contempt on the original efforts of the police and the prosecution to suggest that the pony at the Plant colliery had been attacked by George between 9.00 and 10.00 on the evening of 17 August – as Sergeant Parsons had seen the pony standing quietly at 11.00 p.m. these efforts seemed to constitute another conspiracy against George. The prosecution's desperate about-turn on the last day of the trial, when it was claimed that the pony had been attacked during the early hours of 18 August, confirmed all Shapurji's suspicions: 'It is not justice which they [the police] desire, but rather success in a case they undertake.'[1]

Any lingering faith which he might have had in the British establishment leached away in face of the wall of silence erected by the Home Office. He suspected that Anson was feeding the Home Secretary with secret 'evidence', but there was no way in which the Edalji family could find out what it was. 'I cannot but feel,' he concluded, in characteristically challenging language, 'that to keep my son in prison on the ground of such secret information... is nothing less than an act of oppression.'

****

Although I, too, could throw no light for my classes on what went on inside the Home Office in the months and years which followed George's trial, I could at least report a famous moment in 1906: in October of that year George was released, having served only three years of his term. The Home Secretary, it transpired, had decided not that George was innocent, merely that the original seven-year sentence had been too harsh. He was moved to Pentonville Prison, and when he emerged from there he was on licence, still a guilty man, a criminal who had to report regularly to the police.

It was a time of mixed emotions for him and his family: relief at his release was mixed with bitter anger over the fact that the humiliating court verdict of 1903 still stood. Quiet, unassuming George seethed. Immediately he took over the lead from his parents in the battle to prove his innocence.

[1] Ibid, pp. 10-18.

2. The story-teller

Innocence

November 2004. Next to me on Freda Shimmin's sofa, Maud, is a file with a collection of letters she retrieved from your Welwyn Garden City house in 1962. We have talked about the china teapot, the samplers, the picture of your great-uncle the Reverend Edward Bate Compson, Freda's memories of her first visit to your house in Welwyn Garden City whilst George was still alive, and of her second in her role as executor of your will after your death. She tells me of the huge chest bursting with cuttings relating to George's case which you still had in your archive five decades after his trial. Now at last I have a chance to look at the letters beside me, and yes, as expected, here is the now familiar handwriting of the great man himself ... Sir Arthur Conan Doyle. It's a letter he wrote to your mother in 1913. There was sure to be something from him. He was, after all, apart from your family the most important person in your life. Sir Arthur Conan Doyle, the man who eventually took control of George's story. The man who opened the next chapter I gave to my students.

December 1972. It's just over a year since I moved to Great Wyrley. Watching TV. Sir Arthur Conan Doyle is the subject of an episode in BBC2's *The Edwardians* series. The theme: his campaign on George's behalf. The film is a success, even shown later on American television with an introduction by Alistair Cooke. It's time for me to start reading the writings on which it is based.

****

Conan Doyle's autobiographical account of the way he first learnt of George's case was suitably dramatic. He happened to be reading a copy of the Manchester magazine The Umpire, he wrote in his Memories and Adventures in 1924. 'As I read,' he recalled with seeming vividness, 'the unmistakeable accent of truth fixed itself upon my attention and I realised that I was in the presence of an appalling tragedy and that I was called upon to do what I could to set it right.'[1]

---

[1] Arthur Conan Doyle, *Memories and Adventures*, Hodder & Stoughton, 1924, p. 216.

Arthur Conan Doyle

Sherlock Holmes, the creation who had made Conan
Doyle into Britain's most famous living writer
by the 1890s

George Edalji without glasses – he was said to have a vacant look due to his myopia

Kind permission of Grey House Books

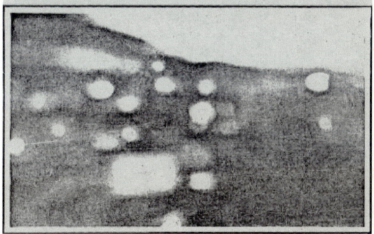

The 'London Sphere' claimed that the bottom
photograph showed the shop above as George Edalji
would have seen it without glasses

**George Edalji's direct gaze once he
started wearing glasses**

Kind permission of Grey House Books

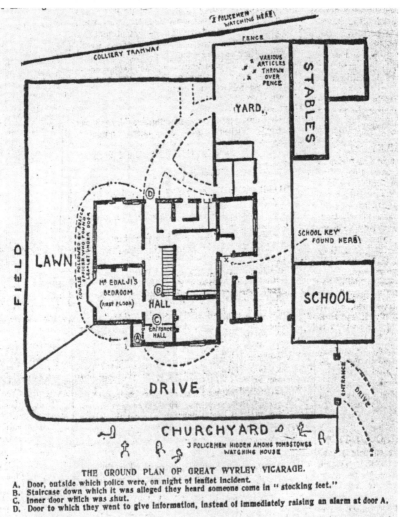

The following text labels appear within the plan:

2 POLICEMEN WATCHING HERE

COLLIERY TRAMWAY

FENCE

VARIOUS ARTICLES THROWN OVER FENCE

STABLES

YARD

FIELD

LAWN

POLICE FOLLOWED BY POLICE OFFICER WHO FOUND LEAFLET UNDER DOOR

Mr EDALJI'S BEDROOM (FIRST FLOOR)

HALL

SCHOOL KEY FOUND HERE

SCHOOL

Entrance HALL

DRIVE

ENTRANCE

DRIVE

CHURCHYARD

3 POLICEMEN HIDDEN AMONG TOMBSTONES WATCHING HOUSE

THE GROUND PLAN OF GREAT WYRLEY VICARAGE.

A. Door, outside which police were, on night of leaflet incident.
B. Staircase down which it was alleged they heard someone come in "stocking feet."
C. Inner door which was shut.
D. Door to which they went to give information, instead of immediately raising an alarm at door A.

**St Mark's vicarage on the night of the 'stocking feet'
incident, 18 December 1892**

There is a problem with this account: Conan Doyle had not really learnt of the affair by chance, for after his release from prison George had written to him personally with copies of a series of articles he had written for *The Umpire* in his first attempt to try to prove his innocence.[1] One Conan Doyle biographer suggests that the explanation of the difference lies with Dr Watson's real-life counterpart, Alfred Woods.[2] As Conan Doyle's secretary, Major Woods was in control of Conan Doyle's correspondence and withheld George's letter because Conan Doyle was still in mourning for his first wife Louise, who had died in July 1906 after a long illness.[3] The truth is that by 1924 Conan Doyle had simply forgotten that the copies of *The Umpire* articles had been sent by George himself. He actually told the true story in an interview less than a month after the event, but the story had been retold and reshaped so many times since then that he had come to believe another version.[4]

Still, Conan Doyle, who had been ill with anxiety during the final stages of Louise's illness, was now released after a suitable interval to marry Jean Leckie, with whom he had maintained an honourably platonic relationship for several years. Beset as he was by the emotional turmoil caused by Louise's death, by his passionate desire to marry Jean Leckie, and by the need to get the proprieties right in doing so, the Edalji affair was the spur which brought him out of lethargy into a hurricane of action. Once he had got his teeth into George's campaign, he spent 12 hours a day on it, through December 1906 and into January 1907.[5] His friend John Churton Collins, Professor of Literature at Birmingham University, got a whiff of his new mood when he visited him at his home at Hindhead on Boxing Day: 'Conan Doyle,' he noted in his diary, 'is on fire with the Edalji case.'[6] The eight months Conan Doyle eventually gave to the affair consumed his extraordinary energies and distracted him from his emotional stress.

His *Daily Telegraph* articles of January 1907 setting out his case became standard reading in my classroom. These articles, reporting his investigations to the nation, started with Holmesian certainties:

---

[1] *Daily Express*, 7 November 1934.
[2] Martin Booth, *The Doctor, the Detective and Arthur Conan Doyle: A Biography of Arthur Conan Doyle*, Hodder & Stoughton, 1997, p. 114.
[3] Ibid, p. 263.
[4] *Express & Star*, 14 January 1907.
[5] *Express & Star*, 14 January 1907.
[6] L. C. Collins, *Life and Memoirs of John Churton Collins*, The Bodley Head, 1911, p. 246.

The first sight I ever had of Mr. George Edalji was enough in itself to convince me both of the extreme improbability of his being guilty of the crime for which he was condemned, and to suggest some at least of the reasons which had led to his being suspected.[1]

He described how George came to meet him at his hotel, the Grand Hotel in Charing Cross. Conan Doyle was late, and found George reading the paper. Conan Doyle recognised him by his 'dark face', and noticed that George 'held the paper close to his eyes and rather sideways'. To Conan Doyle, a trained opthalmist, this proved not only a high degree of myopia, but marked astigmatism, and Kenneth Scott, an eye specialist, later confirmed that George had myopia of eight dioptres. When Conan Doyle asked George why his poor eyesight had not been mentioned at the trial, George told him the defence had been so confident that the prosecution case could not be sustained that they thought it not worth mentioning.

The very sight of George – mild-mannered, myopic, and middle class – thus convinced Conan Doyle of his innocence. He had already sifted through the papers on the case, including legal depositions and press cuttings. His next move, on 3 January 1907, was to travel to Great Wyrley itself. First he met Shapurji and Charlotte at the vicarage. Then he tramped off through the fields to the scene of the famous crime of 17/18 August 1903, following the most direct of three possible routes.[2] Afterwards he returned to the vicarage for breakfast, and then walked the other two routes. His walks have become part of the folk-memory; Tony Read, television script-writer, historian, and one of Cheslyn Hay's most famous sons, used to hear his grandmother tell of meeting Conan Doyle during his explorations, and the grandson of Louise Edmunds also still tells the story of his grandmother's conversation with Britain's great celebrity as he passed the garden behind the Edmunds' Station Street home.[3] Armed with impressions from these walks Conan Doyle was to report to his *Daily Telegraph* readers his astonishment that anyone could imagine that George, with his severe eyesight problems, could have followed the supposed route in the middle of a dark, wet night. When he got back to the vicarage he set about interviewing several local residents, and became so wrapped up in his cross-examinations that the Edaljis had no chance to see

---

[1] *Daily Telegraph*, 11 January 1907.
[2] Charles Higham, *The Adventures of Conan Doyle*, Hamish Hamilton, 1976, p. 202.
[3] Private communication, 10 April 2006.

him on their own – tea had to be taken in to him while he carried on with his work.[1]

Once back in London he had his findings published in the two articles in the *Daily Telegraph*.[2] Making the most of its coup, the paper ran an editorial, under the headline 'SHERLOCK HOLMES AT WORK', which was to set the tone for the public response which followed; Sherlock Holmes had come thrillingly to life. The articles, by the author's wish, were free of copyright and soon appeared in all sorts of journals, including the cheapest papers sold on the streets. In 18,000 words he tore apart the scanty police and prosecution case against his new-found protégé.

A previous history

'Let me now tell the strange story from the beginning,' he wrote, and picking up on a theme raised by Yelverton in his submission to the Home Secretary in December 1903 he embarked on the first detailed public account of some of the earlier events in Great Wyrley which did much to explain police attitudes to George Edalji in 1903. In doing so he suggested a sizzling new ingredient for my classroom repertoire.

The Edalji family, he reported, had by 1907 suffered not just from four years of anguish but from two decades of it. Their troubles began in 1888 – with a maid. Since arriving in Great Wyrley in 1875 they had always employed a maid-servant, and one of them, Susannah Lunt, had stayed for several years. The maid in 1888, however, may not have been so loyal or submissive. Certainly the 17-year-old Elizabeth Foster was not to survive twelve months in the Edaljis' employment.

It was in September 1888 that Shapurji received the first of the hundreds of anonymous letters which were to torture the family and the Great Wyrley community for decades.[3] It seemed harmless enough:

Sir, Evening Star, every evening; 3d. a week. – Will be very pleased with an order. Publisher 50 and 51 Queen-street, Wolverhampton.'

---

[1] *Cannock Chase Courier*, 11 January 1952.
[2] *Daily Telegraph*, 11 and 12 January 1907.
[3] *Cannock Advertiser*, 12 January 1889.

Dozens of letters in the same vein followed, however, and it was immediately obvious that Wolverhampton's evening paper, the *Express & Star*, had nothing to do with them. The situation became even more distressing when Elizabeth Foster herself received a letter, signed 'Thomas Hitchings', announcing that the author had written to her 'black master' asking him to buy the *Star*. Then the hatred spread further: scurrilous abuse started to appear on outhouses at the vicarage, including the view that 'Most of the Edaljis are wicked', and the writer's hostility was even expressed on the seat of the vicarage water closet. The letter-writing itself continued for four months; one letter received in December contained the bizarre threat that Shapurji would be shot if he did not order regular copies of the *Star*, and as a result he became afraid to leave the house. When Elizabeth Foster was threatened as well the family was so concerned that Shapurji arranged for her to sleep with Charlotte.

Finally Shapurji called in the police. What they found was that some of the envelopes used for the letters were similar to those in use in the vicarage and that some of the paper was from leaves torn from the children's school books. The letters were clearly being written by someone in the vicarage, and the maid became prime suspect. Sergeant Upton asked her to give a sample of her handwriting, and when it was compared with that of the letters the police found it to be very similar. This was enough; she was arrested, and charged with sending threatening letters.

When she appeared before Cannock Police Court in January 1889 there were three Edaljis present to act as witnesses: Shapurji suggested that the explanation for the fact that Elizabeth Foster received letters herself was that she wrote them to try to distract attention; Charlotte described a number of other incidents inside the vicarage which suggested the maid's involvement; and 12-year-old George reported that after he once saw a shadow like that of a man outside the glass door his father went out and found a letter on the doorstep.[1]

Elizabeth Foster was bound over to keep the peace, and ordered to pay costs. She and her family always angrily denied her guilt, however, and almost her last words on her deathbed were a demand that her husband should promise to campaign to clear her name.[2] Conan Doyle believed that the seeds of later troubles between 1892 and 1895, and of the troubles of 1903

---

[1] *Cannock Advertiser*, 12 January 1889.
[2] *Cannock Advertiser*, 11 March 1905.

themselves, might have lain in the desire for revenge on the part of Elizabeth Foster and her friends.[1] For the time being, though, the Edaljis were simply relieved: Shapurji congratulated Sergeant Upton on his success.

****

Having left school, George, in January 1892, went to study at Mason College (now Birmingham University), and thus began his fateful years of travel up and down the railway line between Great Wyrley and Birmingham. This route was used by boys from the locality travelling to Walsall Grammar School: Royden Sharp from Hednesford; Fred Brookes, son of William Brookes, the grocer and postmaster who lived on the Walsall Road in Great Wyrley; and Fred Wynn, son of William Wynn, a Great Wyrley painter and decorator.

Everything still seemed fine that Easter when the only surviving photograph of the Edalji family was taken, posing calmly if not comfortably around the vicarage door, mother, father and all three children. According to the family's later accounts as reported by Conan Doyle it was in July 1892 that their new troubles began, and it was as a result of the election campaign which was to end with W. E. Gladstone having his fourth and final innings as Prime Minister. Shapurji was a Liberal, and caused indignation in some quarters when he lent the St Mark's National Schoolroom for a Liberal party meeting, which he himself chaired.[2] Two days later a new anonymous letter appeared. Others followed, each one filled with abuse or threats: some demanded, without explanation, that George should not go to school with Fred Brookes, and others threatened to expose George Edalji and Fred Brookes if they did not admit to writing the letters of 1888 and to being responsible for an incident earlier in 1892 in which the Hattons' hay-ricks had been set on fire. Soon anonymous missives were pouring into the vicarage; at first many were sent through the post, but then for week after week they were either pushed under the doors or just left outside. Much of the abuse was focused on the Edalji family, but others in the locality were victims of the torrent of hatred too, particularly members of the Brookes family.

In the end Shapurji reported the matter to the police, and Sergeant Upton, the officer responsible for the Great Wyrley

---

[1] *Daily Telegraph*, 11 January 1907.
[2] George Edalji, *The Umpire*, 11 November 1906.

district though based in Cannock, returned to the scene of his investigations of 1888. His involvement did not stem the flow.

Then, in December 1892, came another mystery. A few minutes after George returned home from college one day a large key appeared on the doorstep of the vicarage. A few days later it was found to have been taken from Walsall Grammar School. Sergeant Upton thought he already knew who was behind all these activities, for on the evening of 18 December he and other officers were to be found watching the vicarage itself. At bed-time that night George went upstairs, blew out the candle on the drawers in his room, and got into bed. About the same time the police officers thought they heard someone coming downstairs 'in stocking feet' and breathing near the door. They looked into the hall, where they found a pamphlet which, disgustingly, was laced with excrement; the police assumed that George was responsible. Shortly afterwards a rumour circulated in the area that the police had caught George with a letter in the house. Shapurji reacted furiously, with the first of the dozens of letters he was to write in his son's defence over the next 15 years. He suspected Upton of circulating the story, and wrote to the *Cannock Advertiser* to pour scorn on the police claim to have heard stockinged feet and breathing through a thick outer door, when the Edalji household had heard nothing from inside.[1]

The episode of the key turned out to be a crucial turning-point in the Edaljis' lives. It was at this point that the Chief Constable for Staffordshire, George Anson, became personally involved in the affair, and it is at this point that direct accusations against George started, accusations which, as Conan Doyle stressed, created the atmosphere in which suspicion was to home in again on George so quickly once the letter-writing started in 1903. In January 1893 Anson wrote to Shapurji:

> *Will you please ask your son George from whom the key was obtained which you found on your doorstep on December 12?... I shall not pretend to believe any protestations of innocence which your son may make about the key. My information on the subject does not come from the police.*[2]

It is not clear what Anson's sources of information were apart from Sergeant Upton's reports, but as no action was taken

[1] *Cannock Advertiser*, 31 December 1892.
[2] Cited by Arthur Conan Doyle, *Daily Telegraph*, 11 January 1907.

Conan Doyle was convinced that there was no real evidence. Anson's declaration that he would not believe any protestations of innocence gave notice, however, that the pursuit of George and his family was not to be confined to the blustering of one or two wild letter-writers. Now the Staffordshire police force had been given a cue by its Chief Constable. This was the starting-point for Conan Doyle's account of what went wrong in 1903.

George Anson (1857-1947) was to play a central role in the lives of the Edalji family for 15 years, though his world was very different from theirs. Born at Shugborough Hall near Stafford, he was a member of Staffordshire's leading resident family, a family which belonged to the higher reaches of Britain's traditional ruling élite: in 1883 the Ansons had the third largest gross income in Staffordshire. The fact that his father was the third Earl of Lichfield was no doubt a decisive factor in the career of the man who became Staffordshire's Chief Constable in 1888 without any police experience. His appointment was not, however, entirely as an aristocratic figurehead. He was a man of some competence and intellect, and his professional experience equipped him in some degree for the post, which he secured in 1888 against competition from 67 other candidates. He had held a commission in the Royal Artillery, retiring with the rank of captain and a battery of testimonials to his leadership qualities and popularity.[1] Now he joined a force which by the beginning of the 20th century served a population of over a million people, and which was composed of 40 superintendents and inspectors, 92 sergeants, and 624 constables.[2] He was to remain in post for a remarkable 41 years.

****

From December 1892 George was clearly under suspicion. The incident of the Grammar School key was however just the start of the Edaljis' new troubles. The wave of anonymous letter-writing continued unabated, and the family was also assaulted with a whole series of hoaxes which put the events of 1888 in the shade. As Conan Doyle commented, 'it is really wonderful that they [the letters] did not accomplish their proclaimed purpose, which was to drive their victim off his head'.[3]

---

[1] S.R.O., Q/Acp/11/1-3, Court of Quarter Sessions – Constabulary.
[2] George Rickwood and William Gaskell, *Staffordshire Leaders*, E.R. Alexander and Sons, 1907, p. 52.
[3] *Daily Telegraph*, 11 January 1907.

Many of the letters which appeared at the vicarage from December 1892 to 1895 were seemingly the work of a religious maniac:

> *I have written to Fred Wootton (curly head) and told him that if he holds any communication whatsoever with Fred Brookes (grocers kid) and George Edalji we shall treat him and his father and mother in the same way as we treated you and Mr. Brookes. We are going to order a truck load of coal to be sent to Wyrley station for you, it would have been ordered before, only my mate was a fool, for one night when your kid was returning from Birmingham he got into the same compartment as my mate, and he (fool that he was) was so excited that he lost the letter... Do you think I am afraid of anybody, whether in heaven or in hell or on earth or on the moon? I fear nobody. I hate most people. I love Sergeant Upton, my mate, my brother, and the memory of my poor dead kinsman and a few others. And I tell you I swear by God that I will murder George Edalji and Fred Brookes soon, the only thing I care about in the world is revenge, revenge, revenge, revenge, sweet revenge, I long for, then I will be happy, yes happy, yes happy in hell, in hell, in hell...*

> *Do you think that when we want we cannot copy your kid's and that grocer's kid's writing. Our only reason for not forging their signatures and yours is that you all write such a vulgar hand that no manager of newspapers would suppose it was written by a parson. I am God, God, I am God, I am God, I am God, I am Christ, I am Christ, I am Christ. I am Holy Ghost, I am Holy Ghost. I am not the Devil, but you are like him, but I am god Almighty, God, God, God, I am God. Hurrah for Upton, Hurrah for Upton, hurrah for Upton. I am, Dear Pharisee, yours faithfully*
> > *God Almighty*
> > *I am God, I am God.*[1]

The obsession with sin and the dread of hell which fill the God-Satan letters was not an unusual disease. Charles Kingsley's character Alton Locke in the novel of the same name says at one point: 'I was a child of hell, and a lost and miserable sinner, I used to have accesses of terror and that I should surely wake next morning in everlasting flames.' These were the kinds of fears which exposure to the more extreme forms of

---

[1] Cited by Shapurji Fdalji in letter to *Cannock Advertiser*, 25 March 1893.

Evangelicalism and other strands of Christian thinking might produce.

The question 'Do you think that when we want we cannot copy your kid's and that grocer's kid's writing' held burning significance for future attempts to ascertain the authorship of the letters of 1892-5 and 1903. The letters in this series, sometimes signed 'God-Satan', were written in a flowing hand. The writer showed an intimate knowledge not just of 'that grocer's kid' Fred Brookes but also of a host of people living in the immediate neighbourhood of the vicarage; as Conan Doyle said, 'as many as twenty names will be given, most of them with opprobrious epithets attached.'[1]

It was the Edaljis, however, who came in for the central torrent of virulent abuse. On one occasion Shapurji was asked: 'Do you think, you Pharisee, that because you are a parson God will absolve you from your iniquities... ' Charlotte was 'your damned wife'. Maud was a 'horrid little girl'. George seemed to be the target of particularly diabolical hatred: the threat to murder George in the letter cited above, along with the promise of 'revenge, revenge, revenge, revenge sweet revenge', did not make for happy reading. Curiously, the writer appeared to have a frantic admiration for members of the local police force: 'The following in this district we love truly – the police of Cannock in general.' Sergeant Upton was praised to the skies: 'Ha, ha, hurrah for Upton! Good old Upton! Blessed Upton! Good old Upton! Upton is blessed! Dear old Upton!'[2]

A particularly cruel moment came in October 1893, when Shapurji was told: 'Hurrah we know now where your wife's relations live.'[3] This was Much Wenlock, home of Mary Sancta Stoneham, Charlotte 's sister. Mary Stoneham, the mother of Mary Sancta and Charlotte, had also lived there but had died the previous month and been buried next to her husband, Thompson Stoneham, in St Mary's churchyard in Ketley. There was a repeat of this particular kind of cruelty on Christmas Day a year later, when a letter informed Mary Ann Whitehouse, servant at the vicarage, that her sister had died. This was untrue.[4]

The cruder handwriting of other letters which appeared in the same period suggested that they might have been written by

---

[1] Conan Doyle, *Daily Telegraph*, 11 January 1907.
[2] From letters of March & April 1893, cited by Conan Doyle, *Daily Telegraph*, 11 January 1907.
[3] R. D. Yelverton, 'In the Matter of George Ernest Thompson Edalji', p. 12.
[4] R. D. Yelverton, 'In the Matter of George Ernest Thompson Edalji', pp. 12-13.

another person. Some of these letters attacked James Aldis, Head of Walsall Grammar School from 1881 to 1897:

> *Sir you headmaster me and George Edalja are going to leave and join the army because we wrote the letters and so we are going to set the blasted school on fire if you toutch us we will kick you black and blue...*

Although he had in fact made the school more liberal than it had been during the reign of terror of the previous head Aldis was certainly seen by some pupils as 'strong' and 'austere'.[1] This letter, however, revealed a personal fury which went beyond traditional classroom resistance to authority.

A third ingredient in the letter-writing outburst of 1892-5 was the sending of hoax communications to victims outside the Edalji household. Postcards 'signed' by Charlotte or Shapurji were received by all sorts of people. Within the space of a few days in early 1893 three clergymen, two doctors, and a Hednesford builder came to the vicarage believing that their invitations were genuine.[2] The wants or offers of the Reverend Shapurji Edalji were announced in all sorts of papers – at one point he even became a marriage broker, cataloguing the charms and fortunes of a number of women he was ready to dispose of to eligible bachelors:

> *YOUNG LADY (25) handsome, agreeable and thoroughly domesticated, who has just been left £7,000... wishes to correspond with kind hearted gentleman, view early matrimony, address in the first instance... to S. Edalji, Great Wyrley...*[3]

More hoaxes were played on individuals. In 1895, a vicar in Lincolnshire travelled all the way to Great Wyrley on the strength of the following plea:

> *Great Wyrley Vicarage*
> *Nr. Walsall, Staffs*

DEAR SIR,

> *A woman who refuses to give her name was found in my garden yesterday week in a dying condition, she has only*

---

[1] D. J. P. Fink, *Queen Mary's Grammar School*, Queen Mary's Club, Walsall, 1954, pp. 328-329.
[2] *Lichfield Mercury*, 27 January 1893.
[3] Cited by R. D. Yelverton, 'In the Matter of George Ernest Thompson Edalji', p. 13.

this morning recovered consciousness and she keeps on asking for you by name... She is tall, aged about 62, has black hair, the front teeth projecting, doctor says the only thing is to get you over. I promised I would write and you would come on Tuesday... Could you manage to get here on Monday evening about 6...

. . *Believe me, yours sincerely,*

SHAPURJI EDALJI. [1]

An Essex clergyman received a card from 'S. Edalji' informing him that:

Unless you apologise at once and by telegram for the outrageous hints you give in your sermons concerning my Chastity, I shall expose your adultry and rape.

On other occasions tradespeople delivered goods to the vicarage which the Edaljis had not ordered. Details were given by Shapurji in 1895 when he tried to alert the nation to the family's plight by writing to *The Times*, saying that amongst the goods ordered, some of which were actually delivered, were house wines, spirits, medicines, books, furniture, clothes, and musical instruments.[2] Sometimes rubbish was strewn all over the vicarage lawn, and objects were left on window-sills or pushed under the door – in 1894, in particular, there was a torrent of deposited articles.[3]

Chief Constable Anson, who had never been to the vicarage and depended largely on Sergeant Upton for his information, was convinced that he knew who was behind the letters and hoaxes. In April 1895 he sent his Deputy Chief Constable to tell Shapurji that either he or his son was at the bottom of the letter-writing, and in July he himself wrote to Shapurji to say:

I know the name of the offender... I prefer to keep my suspicions to myself until I am able to prove them, and I trust to be able to obtain a dose of penal servitude for the offender.

This bullying letter was targeted at George. Conan Doyle's conclusion in his *Daily Telegraph* articles was stark: '... if the Staffordshire police took this attitude towards young Edalji in

---

[1] Letter to Rev. George Ward of Holy Trinity, Rathbury, Lincolnshire, July 1895, cited by R. D. Yelverton, 'In the Matter of George Ernest Thompson Edalji', pp. 14-15.
[2] *The Times*, 16 August, 1895.
[3] George Edalji, *Pearson's Weekly*, 14 February 1907.

1895, what chance of impartiality had he in 1903, when a culprit was wanted for an entirely new set of crimes? It is evident that their minds were steeped in prejudice against him...'[1]

The God-Satan stream of letters continued into 1895. In May came: 'Revenge, revenge on you and your perjured damn son... S. Edalji the black.' In October it was: 'Vengeance on you now for certain, you bastard... God-Satan.' Then, in December, came a letter which had the Stafford station postmark, as if the writer were on his way north: 'I have great pleasure in informing you that it is now our intention to renew the persecution of the Vicar!!!... Wishing you a Merry Christmas and New Year... God Satan.' Suddenly, however, the stream dried up – apart from one last bogus advertisement in the *Blackpool Times* on Christmas Eve:

> WANTED *immediately lady or gentleman to adopt an Orphan Girl aged 7, handsome and remarkably intelligent... £100 paid down to suitable person – For full particulars and explanation, Rev. S. Edalji, Great Wyrley, Walsall.*[2]

After this, silence. No more letters. No more hoaxes. No more police threats to expose George. Gradually the gathered clouds seemed to pass away. Shapurji destroyed many of the letters. Eight years of calm suggested that the torment was over.

Evidence

Having established why the police were already against George before the Wyrley outrages occurred, Conan Doyle turned to the outrages and letters of 1903.

So far as the letters were concerned he saw a connection with those in the 1892–5 series. There were similarities in phrasing, in the level of audacity, in the violence of language, and in the focus on the Edalji family, which seemed to point to a common origin. Admittedly the handwriting styles varied, but as one of the original persecutors boasted that he could imitate George's handwriting, the variance, Conan Doyle suggested, need not be taken too seriously. It seemed absurd for the police to claim that George could have been responsible both for producing the earlier series and for writing letters

[1] Conan Doyle, *Daily Telegraph*, 11 January 1907.
[2] *Blackpool Times*, 24 December 1895.

incriminating himself during the outrages of 1903. Why should a successful young lawyer do this? There was also new evidence to report: the professional credibility of handwriting expert Thomas Gurrin, so crucial for George's conviction, had recently been destroyed by the discovery that his evidence in the case of Adolf Beck had been responsible for the incarceration of an innocent man.

As for the outrage of 17/18 August, Conan Doyle was utterly contemptuous of the evidence produced. If the coat seized by the police had been worn to go out during the wild night of August 17/18 'it would not have been damp but sopping wet'. The blood stains on the coat could have been from a splash from the gravy of underdone meat. In any case, the most adept operator could hardly rip open a horse and 'have only two threepenny-bit spots of blood to show for it'. Although the police were adamant that the coat and pony-hide had been packaged separately, Conan Doyle was cynical and suggested that through negligence hairs might have been transferred from one to the other when they were sent off to the police doctor. The trousers were said by the police to be stained with dark mud around the bottom, but the mud at the place of the outrage was quite different, a yellow-red mixture of clay and sand. The footprints were said to have been made with George's boot, but any clear footprints must have been left after the rain stopped, whilst any made before the rain would be blurred beyond identification. George's own remark when arrested, that 'I have been expecting it for some time', was quite understandable in view of his belief that the police had a down on him and the fact that he was being accused in anonymous letters.

Conan Doyle lambasted the way in which the trial was conducted. Sir Reginald Hardy's lack of legal training was a crucial factor, particularly as he was dealing with a jury of Staffordshire people whose emotional response to animal outrages on their doorsteps needed cool legal guidance. Conan Doyle put great stress on the honesty of the Edalji family: 'An experienced barrister who knew them well remarked to me that they were the most precisely truthful people he had ever met.'

When he began to point the finger of blame at those responsible for the blighted lives of the honest Edaljis he was very conscious of the parallels with the Dreyfus affair in France. Alfred Dreyfus, a Jewish army officer, had been accused in 1894 of selling military secrets to Germany. He was convicted of treason, with 'experts' claiming that a *bordereau*, or memo, found at the German Embassy was in his handwriting. He was then imprisoned on Devil's Island, off the coast of French Guinea. The real culprit was however later found to be a Major Esterhazy, and the French establishment, buoyed by an orchestrated outburst of anti-semitic feeling, went to extraordinary lengths to cover up the mistake. Then, in 1898, Emile Zola, the leading French writer, published an open letter to the French President entitled 'J'accuse', which became one of the most famous front pages in the history of journalism. In it he delivered a fiercesome onslaught on the antics of the French establishment in the Dreyfus case, and in the following year Dreyfus was given a pardon. Conan Doyle was aware that he was the Emile Zola of the Edalji affair in England, and the British public saw him as their champion, their Emile Zola, too: 'Who could deny,' one of Conan Doyle's most respected biographers has written, 'that Conan Doyle was the incarnation of the English conscience?'[1] Now, in 1907, Conan Doyle used the British press to appeal to the British public to denounce an injustice perpetrated and covered up by members of the British establishment. Indeed, he made a specific comparison with events in France:

> ...in all its details this seems to me to form a kind of squalid Dreyfus case. The parallel is extraordinarily close. You have a Parsee, instead of a Jew, with a young and promising career blighted, in each case the degradation from a profession and the campaign for redress and restoration, in each case questions of forgery and handwriting arise, with Esterhazy in the one, and the anonymous writer in the other. Finally, I regret to say that in the one case you have a clique of French officials going from excess to excess in order to cover an initial mistake, and that in the other you have the Staffordshire police acting in the way I have described.

He then put the full spotlight on the racial prejudice which he believed to be at the core of George's unjust persecution from 1892 onwards:

> Now, I have no doubt Captain Anson was quite honest in his dislike, and unconscious of his own prejudice... As I trace the course of events this dislike of their chief's filtered down until it came to imbue the whole force...

His conclusion was that the Staffordshire police force should be completely reorganised, that there should be an enquiry into any irregularities in procedure at Stafford Quarter Sessions,

[1] Pierre Nordon, *Conan Doyle*, John Murray, 1966, p. 122.

and that the culprit at the Home Office should be sought out and punished. As events developed during 1907 he was to take an even more cynical and wide-ranging view of the British establishment, but for the moment he signed off with a flourish, knowing the weight his name carried:

> *Now we turn to the last tribunal of all, a tribunal which never errs when the facts are fairly laid before them, and we ask the public of Great Britain whether this thing is to go on.*

Responses

Conan Doyle's intervention stirred a huge reaction. Newspapers all over Britain reported his doings, and for days the pages of the *Daily Telegraph* bulged with letters about his findings. As with Emile Zola in France, the literary world responded immediately. George Meredith, the novelist, wrote to congratulate him: Sherlock Holmes, he said, had shown 'what can be done in the life of breath'.[1] Conan Doyle's friend, James Barrie, author of *Peter Pan*, also wrote to compliment him on his work, declaring that he thought the worst aspect of the affair was the behaviour of the police.[2] Conan Doyle contacted his friend and fellow member of the Crimes Club, John Churton Collins, Professor of Literature at Birmingham University; in March Collins wrote a passionate demand for justice for George in the *English Review*, and roused Birmingham University in support (Birmingham University was originally Mason College, at which George studied).[3] Other universities, particularly Dublin University, followed Birmingham's lead. R. D. Yelverton, who had toiled hard for four years to achieve the same objects as Conan Doyle, worked willingly with the great publicist, and his Temple chambers became the headquarters of an Edalji committee, which was formed when the Home Secretary did not immediately respond to Conan Doyle's demands. Yelverton was chair, and Churton Collins was a leading force. Other supporters included the leading solicitor Sir George Lewis, chair of the Law Society, along with another of Conan Doyle's friends, Walsall-born Jerome K. Jerome, author of *Three Men in a Boat*. George's supporters and sections of the press became ever more insistent that this case, coming so soon after Adolf Beck's,

---

[1] 14 January 1907, cited in Pierre Nordon, *Conan Doyle*, p. 122.
[2] Cited in Pierre Nordon, *Conan Doyle*, p. 122.
[3] L. C. Collins, *Life and Memoirs of John Churton Collins*, p. 203.

made the establishment of a Court of Criminal Appeal an urgent necessity.[1]

The campaign was not the preserve of indignant writers and friends of Conan Doyle. The mainstream publication *The Police Review and Parade Gossip* was just as passionate, and George's case was the main talking-point in the journal for months. The Home Office was savaged regularly – 'the iniquitous use of the secret dossier', 'Star Chamber traditions of secrecy', the 'gross stupidity of a notoriously effete department'.[2] Understandably, the *Review* did appeal for Anson to be allowed to explain himself in the face of Conan Doyle's attacks in the *Daily Telegraph*, but it suggested too that the police and Home Office might have colluded to maintain a wrongful conviction; by May it was openly accusing the Staffordshire Chief Constable of prejudice.[3]

****

All these developments drew anonymous letter-writers out of the cupboard yet again. The first letter, sent to George in January, was signed 'Martin Molton', and Conan Doyle came to term the whole 1907 series the 'Martin Molton' letters. Anson was also a recipient; one letter in January promised that 'I guarantee to crush Edalji'. At about the same time letters were sent to the man who was soon to emerge as Conan Doyle's suspect. Even Conan Doyle himself became a victim. In April he was sent a letter informing him that 'we are the narks of the detectives', and this was followed in May with a blood-curdling warning to him to stop his crusade:

> *I know from a detective of Scotland Yard that if you write to Gladstone and say you find Edalji is guilty after all... they will make you a lord next year. Is it not better to be a lord than to run the risk of losing kidneys and liver. Think of all the ghoolish murders that are committed why then should you escape...*
> *A Nark London*[4]

Another returned to the theme of Walsall Grammar School in the 1890s, when James Aldis was head:

---

[1] *The Times*, 11 February 1907.
[2] *The Police Review and Parade Gossip*, 18 January, 15 March, 31 May 1907.
[3] *The Police Review and Parade Gossip*, 18 January, 31 May 1907.
[4] Cited by Anson in a note on his 1910-11 correspondence with Conan Doyle, May 1920, S.C.P.M.

There was not education to be had in Walsall when that bloody swine Aldis was high school boss. He got the bloody bullet after the governors were sent letters about him. Ha, ha.

A fourth repeated the virulent racist hatred of the Edaljis, with echoes of the Europe-wide anti-semitism which had blighted the career of Dreyfus in France:

The proof of what I tell you is in the writing he put in the papers when they loosed him out of prison where he ought to have been kept along with his dad and all black and yellow faced Jews... Nobody could copy his writing like that, you blasted fool.[1]

Enquiry

In February, meanwhile, Herbert Gladstone had relented in the face of the onslaught orchestrated by Conan Doyle. As there was no Court of Criminal Appeal which could order a re-trial, a Committee of Enquiry was established. Three men were invited to join – Sir Arthur Wilson, a high court judge, the Rt. Hon. John Lloyd Wharton, a Conservative M.P. and legal expert, and Sir Robert Romer, a recently retired judge. There was a hitch when Romer refused to serve, partly because the committee would not be able to call witnesses and, in his view, could not decide on George's guilt without them.[2] This troublesome man was replaced with someone likely to be far more compliant, Sir Albert de Rutzen, London's chief magistrate.[3] The significance of his appointment was most aggressively described years later by the novelist Compton Mackenzie, who had known Conan Doyle at the time of the affair. In a blistering attack on the injustice he believed was done to George Edalji he was quite blunt as to the purpose of the Committee of Enquiry: 'the white face of Captain the Hon George Augustus Anson,' he said, 'must be saved at the expense of George Edalji's brown face'. De Rutzen and Anson were in fact both descended from the same slave-owner in the West Indies, and de Rutzen's aunt was the first Countess of Lichfield, Anson's grandmother. De Rutzen was now aged 76, but Compton Mackenzie had no doubt that it was not old age but kinship which was responsible for 'betraying the law' when the

---

[1] Cited in Peter Costello, *The Real World of Sherlock Holmes*, Robinson Publishing, 1991, p. 84.
[2] *The Times*, 2 March 1907.
[3] *Staffordshire Advertiser*, 2 March 1907.

Committee of Enquiry reported.[1] He might also have suggested that the white face of Sir Reginald Hardy, trial chairman in George's case, needed saving: Hardy's wife was the niece of W. E. Gladstone and therefore the Home Secretary's cousin.

Whilst the Committee of Enquiry was getting under way, *Daily Telegraph* readers, including members of the Parsi community, responded to an appeal from the paper for contributions to a fund in George's support. The fund was administered by three of George's most powerful allies, Sir Horace Voules (editor of *Truth*), Sir George Lewis (who had long been active on George's behalf), and Sir Arthur Conan Doyle himself.[2]

The Committee of Enquiry's report, dated 23 April, was in fact utterly infuriating for George's growing army of supporters. The Committee did decide that George was innocent of the attack on the pony, but the sting of the report came at the end. In a desperate face-saving device, the Committee insisted that George was nevertheless guilty of writing the letters: 'Assuming him to be an innocent man,' it concluded, 'he has to some extent brought his troubles on himself.' It therefore recommended that George be given a free pardon, but no compensation for his three years in gaol. Gladstone responded on 16 May: 'I have decided to advise his majesty, as an act of royal clemency, to grant Mr. Edalji a free pardon. But I have also come to the conclusion that the case is not one in which any grant of compensation can be made.'

The Committee's report was totally unsatisfactory. George was never convicted of writing the letters, and yet the refusal to pay compensation assumed he had been. The cynical verdict of one of my 1970s sources, Conan Doyle biographer Pierre Nordon, was that the practical result of the report was to shield Anson.[3] As to George himself, he was at least no longer under police supervision, but still described the Home Secretary's decision as 'the grossest insult'.[4] In Great Wyrley, Shapurji hotly denied that George had written the letters.

The Committee of Enquiry's irrational recommendation became the subject of furious parliamentary questions. Most of the flood of questions between May and August were directed at Gladstone – six on one day in May: 'May I ask if a free

---

[1] Compton Mackenzie, *On Moral Courage*, Collins, 1962, p. 178.
[2] *Daily Telegraph*, February 1907, passim.
[3] Pierre Nordon, *Conan Doyle*, p. 127.
[4] *Pearson's Weekly*, 6 June 1907.

pardon means a free pardon,' demanded Pike Pease, the M.P. for Darlington, 'and, whether, in the opinion of the home office, this gentleman is innocent or guilty.'[1] In June another M.P. asked bluntly if inaccurately: 'Is Edalji being thus treated because he is not an Englishman?'[2] The most persistent of George's supporters in parliament was the ambitious and flamboyant newly-elected M.P. for Walton in Liverpool, F. E. Smith, later to become Lord Birkenhead and one of the most famous advocates of his day. In one of his lengthy questions about George, he pointed out to Herbert Gladstone that the Committee of Enquiry had based its conclusions on the assumption that George had written the anonymous letters, and yet the jury had not convicted him of this. Like Conan Doyle, he drew parallels with events in France: 'What has become,' he demanded to know, 'of the indignation aroused in this country by the Dreyfus case?' He quoted the Committee of Enquiry's damning assertion that 'The police carried out their investigations, not for the purpose of finding out who was the guilty party, but for finding out evidence against Edalji.' [3] Gladstone, left with only five minutes on this occasion to reply to Smith's 'question', responded with some heat. He was applauded as he left the House – some Liberals still felt the need to stand by their government[4] – but the *Police Review* commented acidly that the lateness of the hour had precluded any response to Gladstone's 'hysterical reply'.[5] On a further occasion Viscount Castlereagh tried to shake the government by addressing his question to the Prime Minister himself, demanding to know if Campbell-Bannerman realised how dependent George now was on family and friends, and whether the government would hold an inquiry on the question of the letters; the Prime Minister side-stepped this and asked Gladstone to answer on his behalf.[6]

The suspect

Despite the parliamentary onslaught on the Home Secretary's decision, as well as the outrage of Conan Doyle and the rest of George's supporters, the Home Office refused to take any further action. This merely spurred Conan Doyle into new efforts. Already, in May, he was writing more articles for the

[1] 30 May 1907, *The Parliamentary Debates*, 4th Series, clxxv, Wyman & Sons, 1907, pp. 77-9.
[2] 27 June 1907, *The Parliamentary Debates*, 4th Series, clxxvii, p. 98.
[3] *The Times*, 19 July 1907.
[4] *Staffordshire Advertiser*, 20 July 1907.
[5] Cited in *Express & Star*, 3 August 1907.
[6] 17 June 1907, *The Parliamentary Debates*, 4th Series, clxxviii, pp. 160-161.

Daily Telegraph, entitled 'Who Wrote the Letters?', again with the confidence of the Sherlock Holmes whose brilliantly perceptive analysis of handwriting had helped to unravel a bewildering mystery in 'The Reigate Squires'.[1]

In the first of the three articles he poured scorn on the claim of the now discredited handwriting expert Thomas Gurrin that George wrote some of the anonymous letters of 1903. He began to build the hypothesis that the person who did write the letters was actually an enemy both of George and of Greatorex, the boy whose 'signature' appeared on some of the letters. Some of the names in the letters, he pointed out, were of people who lived near Greatorex in Hednesford, two stations up the line from Great Wyrley and well away from the neighbourhood familiar to George. He also set great store by the fact that the writer seemed to have the sea on his mind, as if he had just returned from a life on board ship.

In the second article in the series he put Sherlock Holmes to work on the clues provided by the letters of 1892-5. He came to the conclusion that the letters were written by conspirators – two adults (or perhaps one) and a boy. These conspirators, he thought, must have lived under one roof, as they used the same sort of paper and the same sort of envelopes. In some cases writing in the hand he believed to be that of the boy appeared on the same paper as writing in the hand he believed to be that of one of the adults. The writers seemed to pride themselves on their powers of forgery: 'Do you think we could not imitate your kid's writing?' they asked the Edaljis exultantly in 1892. Conan Doyle's hypothesis now gathered its own momentum. The boy (whom he nicknamed 'foulmouth') must, he suggested, have attended Walsall Grammar School. One reason was that apart from the Edaljis two other families in Great Wyrley, the Brookes and the Wynns, had received anonymous letters, and they had sons at Walsall Grammar School. In addition, the Headteacher himself had received letters in the same boyish hand, including the one which informed him that 'me and George Edalja are going to leave and join the army... and we are going to set the blastd school on fire if you toutch us we will kick you black and blue'. One of the adult writers, Conan Doyle claimed, must have been to the school as well, though he would have been in one of the older classes if he was still there in 1892. The script and contents of this writer's letters (the 'God-Satan' letters) showed a much more alert and ingenious mind.

---

[1] Arthur Conan Doyle, 'The Reigate Squires', published in *The Strand Magazine*, 1893, reprinted in William S. Baring-Gould (ed.), *The Annotated Sherlock Holmes*, 2 vols, John Murray, 1968.

The connection of two such brothers with Walsall Grammar School would also explain the appearance of that school's key on the vicarage doorstep in December 1892.

One of the adult writers Conan Doyle identified with the 'God-Satan' letters, with their extraordinary mixture of grim humour, hysterical religion, and outrageous blasphemy. He quoted from one letter in the series, which ran:

> I must live in Heaven and partly in hell, so if that ever-accursed monster Satan tries to detain me in hell I will fight with him and throw myself into the gulf which is fixed between hell and Heaven, and then I shall be able to climb out of the gulf into Heaven. And moreover, if God tries to push me back into hell I will defy God and struggle with Him, and if I cannot prevail I will hold on to God and fall with Him over the precipice of hell.

> If you wish to escape having your house blown up by dynamite you are to do this thus, namely, order the postman to take Mrs M.'s body out of her grave and bring it to your house. You are then to break open her head, take out her brains, and boil them in a cauldron of red wine for three hours. Next you are to order Mr._____ to come to your house, make him open his mouth and drink the contents of the cauldron whilst boiling. If you do this to my satisfaction I will ask God not to give you such a hot place in hell.

The handwriting in the countless pages of this manic material flowed easily, as if by an educated hand. These letters ceased in 1895. Now, in 1907, Conan Doyle claimed that he had tracked the author down – God-Satan was living in Long Beach, California.

The second batch of letters and postcards of 1892-5 were the hoaxes, sent to tradesmen asking them to bring goods to the vicarage, or to clergymen begging them to come on some urgent errand. These were written in a smaller, closer hand, and were free of the mania of the 'God-Satan' letters. The handwriting was not entirely dissimilar from that of 'God-Satan', and Conan Doyle suspected that both might have been written by the same person.

The third article addressed the question of the 'Martin Molton' letters of 1907. Conan Doyle tried to demonstrate that the boyish 'foulmouth' hand of 1892-5 had become the hand which wrote the series of threatening letters of 1907. He rounded off his case triumphantly by identifying this writing with that in the Greatorex letters of 1903 as well.

****

Conan Doyle continued to search for evidence which would clearly establish that George had not written the letters, and in May/June he consulted another specialist. This was Lindsay Johnson, a handwriting expert who billed himself as having helped Maître Labori, counsel for Albert Dreyfus in France, to establish that the famous *bordereau* had actually been written by Major Esterhazy; Johnson declared that George could not have written the letters.[1] Conan Doyle was also almost ready to deliver his next bombshell to the Home Office, his case against the man he believed to be the real criminal. He had been on the trail of his own suspect since January, when he wrote to his mother: 'All my energies have gone towards the capture of the real offenders. These are three youths (one already dead), brothers by the name of Sharp. The case I have against them is already very strong but I have five separate lines of enquiry on foot, by which I hope to make it overwhelming. They are decently educated men as is evident from the letters.'[2]

When he produced his 'Who Wrote the Letters?' articles in May, therefore, Conan Doyle was not really hypothesising about the character of unknown letter-writers but rather building a case against an actual family which he could not name. Louise and Peter Sharp of The Mount, Hednesford, had had seven children, six of whom were living at home in the 1890s. In his articles Conan Doyle clearly thought that the author of the 'God-Satan' letters of 1892-5 was one of the sons, Frank; this was the man he claimed was living in California. Wallie Sharp, another son, may also have been involved, according to Conan Doyle; he may have been the author of the hoax letters. A third son, Royden, was in his targets as the boy-author ('foulmouth') of 1892-5, the Greatorex of 1903, and the Martin Molton of 1907, as well as one of the perpetrators of the animal outrages. From January to July Conan Doyle was preparing his case against Royden. As his local sleuths he used two men to feed him with information, the F. Arrowsmith of the Star Tea Company in Cannock who had informed on Harry Green in September 1903, and a man named Beaumont, of Wolverhampton Road in Cannock. By July he was prepared to present his allegations to the Home Secretary.[3]

---

[1] J. D. Carr, *The Life of Sir Arthur Conan Doyle*, John Murray, 1949, p. 234.
[2] Arthur Conan Doyle to Mary Conan Doyle, 27 January, 1907.
[3] Arthur Conan Doyle, 'Statement of the Case against Royden Sharp', 1907.

His statement built up such a damning picture of Royden Sharp that I soon made it a key part of my 1970s teaching about the case. Born in 1879, Royden Sharp went to Walsall Grammar School, where his brother Wallie was an elder scholar at the time. Conan Doyle obtained Royden's school records, which showed him not only to be a poor scholar, always bottom of his class, but also a behaviour problem – his Easter 1892 report said that he had been caned daily and had falsified fellow students' marks. In the summer of 1892, significantly, he was reported to have forged letters. Fred Wynn, by 1907 a painter in Cheslyn Hay in his father's footsteps, had been at school with Sharp, and he told Conan Doyle that he had known Sharp to slit open cushions in railway carriages. On one occasion Wynn and Fred Brookes got on the train and were followed by Royden, who ran in and put his head through the window, smashing it to bits. Royden reported to the authorities that the other boys had done it, but later he was made to pay himself. In the summer of 1892 Royden left the school, either because his father withdrew him or because he was expelled. It was at this point that the 1892-5 letters started. Members of the Brookes family were often victims, and Wynn received two letters too.

Royden went to school in Wisbech for a time, and then was apprenticed to a butcher. When his father died in 1893, his uncle, W. A. Greatorex, became his trustee. After a great deal of trouble with him, Greatorex sent Royden to sea. Royden sailed from Liverpool in December 1895 – the time that the hoaxes and anonymous letters to the Edalji family ceased. Conan Doyle suggested that it was significant that the last of the anonymous communications of 1892-5 was sent from Liverpool's pleasure-resort, Blackpool, shortly before Royden sailed away. Royden came home in 1901, but then went to work for ten months on a cattle ship between Liverpool and America. By the time of the outrages in 1903, significantly, he was back living with his mother, sister, and brother Wallie on Hednesford Road in Cannock.

To support his contention that Royden wrote the 'Greatorex' letters of 1903, Conan Doyle claimed that Royden's attempts to implicate Wilfred Greatorex in the outrages were an act of revenge against the Greatorex family – this was because the Sharps' trustee, W. A. Greatorex, had regulated their financial affairs too tightly. As for the letters' naming of George Edalji as an accomplice to the outrages, Conan Doyle believed that racial prejudice was the reason. He pointed to the internal clues in the letters, particularly the allusions to the sea, as evidence that Royden wrote them. The 1903 'Lover of Justice' letter was ascribed by Conan Doyle to Wallie Sharp. He went on to claim that Royden was also the 'G. H. Darby' who had poured out letters in the weeks after George's trial.

When he moved from his parade of evidence suggesting that the Sharp brothers wrote the letters to his attempt to prove Royden was linked with the outrages, Conan Doyle was making a huge leap. He made much of a conversation which Royden had in July 1903 with his aunt, Mrs Greatorex, the wife of W. A. Greatorex, when she visited the Sharps. After referring to the outrages, Royden went to the cupboard and dramatically produced a large horse-lancet, saying: 'This is what they kill the cattle with.' Conan Doyle assumed that Royden had taken the lancet from the cattle ship he had worked on during the previous year, and claimed that only an instrument of this kind, not an ordinary knife, could have been responsible for the peculiar nature of the wounds suffered by the animals attacked in 1903. Somehow Conan Doyle even managed to get hold of the horse-lancet.[1] How his local sleuths Beaumont and Arrowsmith managed this is a matter for speculation, but the BBC television play of 1972 offered sheer fantasy: Conan Doyle was shown standing on watch whilst Wilfred Greatorex went into the Sharps' shed, and Conan Doyle was then to be seen using his boxing skills when Royden Sharp suddenly appeared on the scene.[2]

Conan Doyle's evidence with respect to the letters was certainly stronger than that with respect to the outrages. He nevertheless assumed that he had done enough to show that there was a case for Royden to answer, and he suggested to the Home Secretary that two men could supply further important evidence – Harry Green, who had left for South Africa after the trial, and Jack Hart, a butcher of Bridgetown near Great Wyrley, who was a friend of the Sharps. He also suspected that Fred Brookes and two others knew something about the affair. The outrage of November 1903 had in his view been carried out by Jack Hart, acting in collusion with Royden Sharp.

When Conan Doyle's allegations against Royden Sharp reached the Home Secretary he was horrified to be told: 'I see no more evidence against these two brothers than against myself and my brother.'[3] In August the Home Office presented the House of Commons with an official legal opinion that there was not a prima facie case against Conan Doyle's chief suspect.[4]

---

[1] Arthur Conan Doyle, *Memories and Adventures*, p. 220.
[2] Jeremy Paul, *The Edwardians*: Conan Doyle (copy in C.L.)
[3] Arthur Conan Doyle, *Memories and Adventures*, p. 221.
[4] 12 August 1907, *The Parliamentary Debates*, 4th Series, clxxviii, p. 784.

Bruised by his failure to achieve what Sherlock Holmes would have accomplished in the space of a few pages, Conan Doyle continued with his crusade in fits and starts for a number of years. He had however already lost.

An outrage

In August of that year, 1907, George took a break from London and the last ten months of tension, and travelled to Yarmouth by pleasure steamer. Unfortunately there was nowhere he could put his past behind him. Whilst he was there the press pounced on him to comment on yet more horrifying events in Great Wyrley. Two mares belonging to Harrison's Colliery, one brown and one grey, had been attacked during the night of August 27/28. The brown mare was found dead with a 19-inch wound across its stomach and its entrails lying beside it.[1] It had plunged about the field in agony before it died. As for the grey mare, this was an even more agonising sight, especially as it was in foal: it had a gaping 21-inch wound and its entrails were hanging from its stomach, but it was still alive. The vet could not allow it to suffer any longer, asked for a gun, and shot the mare without ado. As in the dark days of 1903, Inspector Campbell was soon on the scene directing investigations. The site was also visited by Chief Constable Anson himself, along with Chief Superintendent Bishop, who had been promoted since his hunt by dog-cart for the killers of 1903. As if George's free pardon counted for nothing, he had to assure the press that he had not been in Great Wyrley since October, and Shapurji, faced with the equally hurtful suspicions of Staffordshire journalists, pointed out that as his son was in Yarmouth he could hardly have had anything to do with events in Great Wyrley. Conan Doyle, interviewed by *Tribune*, suggested that the problem was that the real culprit (in other words Royden Sharp) was feeling confident enough to resume his work now that the Home Secretary had refused to investigate Conan Doyle's case against him.

With the Great Wyrley and Cannock area again in a feverish state, the police this time made a quick arrest – of Hollis Morgan, a 22-year-old pork butcher's assistant who was working in a slaughter-house in Wolverhampton when Chief Superintendent Bishop came for him. Satisfaction at the speedy discovery of a suspected culprit soon dissipated, however, for

---

[1] *Wellington Journal and Shrewsbury News*, 7 September 1907.

after Morgan had already been remanded by magistrates under the chairmanship of Lord Hatherton the police abruptly dropped the case against him. Perhaps a pork butcher's assistant born in Shapurji's parish seemed a likely candidate for mutilating horses. The only thing he had actually done, however, was to have been involved in a pub argument eighteen months earlier; in it he had said he thought that George was innocent and that he would not mind committing an outrage himself in order to prove it.[1] The fact that he lived in Wolverhampton, eight or nine miles from the scene of the crime, makes it difficult to understand how it could be assumed that he had turned his talk into action, though the police pointed out that he did have a bike. His delighted family and friends organised a welcome tea on his return home, with Shapurji and Charlotte as guests[2]

In the meantime the latest outrage sparked some of the responses only too familiar in the area, including a new burst of anonymous letter-writing. One victim was Shapurji himself, who was told: 'You get indoors at night or you will know about it.'[3] Then, when Morgan appeared in court, his landlady and others connected with the case became new victims of the pen of 'G. H. Darby'; one police inspector was even threatened with a bomb, which 'Darby' said would come from Great Wyrley.[4] Fascination with the case also once again turned services at St Mark's into magnets for people from all over the Black Country; on one Sunday Shapurji could only offer the gossip-seekers the information that Hollis Morgan had once been a quiet member of his Sunday school class, whilst a week later his listeners heard a sermon on Christian endurance which a local paper described as excellent, but which could not satisfy the lust for titbits.[5]

One other response to the outrage attracted outrage of its own. Five thousand postcard photographs of one of the disembowelled mares began to circulate in the area, much to the disgust of Alfred Sambrook and other parish councillors who discussed developments at a special meeting; one suggestion was that the Postmaster-General should be asked to destroy any of these morbid cards which might be sent through the post.[6] Newspapers such as the *Daily Telegraph* were also upset, particularly as the photographs were getting into the

[1] *Express & Star*, 16 September 1907.
[2] *Cannock Courier*, 19 September 1952.
[3] *Staffordshire Advertiser*, 7 September 1907.
[4] *Express & Star*, 18 September 1907.
[5] *Express & Star*, 9 and 16 September 1907.
[6] *Staffordshire Advertiser*, 7 September 1907; *Cannock Advertiser*, 7 September 1907.

hands of children.[1] Times have changed since then: some of the five thousand postcards were still part of family inheritances in Great Wyrley in the 1970s, when students brought them to show me at school.

Weddings

One truly happy event took place on 18 September: in a private ceremony at St Margaret's church, Westminster, Sir Arthur Conan Doyle and Jean Leckie were finally married. Afterwards the small wedding party retired to the Hotel Metropole, where 250 invited guests were waiting in the Grand Reception Room to enjoy their champagne, caviar, and smoked salmon.[2] As the newly-weds entered the hotel, Jean was so badly hampered by the long train of her gown that Conan Doyle simply swept her off her feet and carried her in one powerful movement up the red-carpeted stairs. Among the assembled guests who witnessed this dramatic entry were many famous names, including J. M. Barrie, Jerome K. Jerome, Bram Stoker, and E. W. Hornung (Conan Doyle's brother-in-law and author of the 'Raffles' stories). There was also one surprise guest hidden in the crowd – the unassuming figure of George Edalji. The new national figure had brought with him one-volume editions of the works of Shakespeare and Tennyson as a gift,[3] and when his turn came he stammered out his thanks and congratulations to the newly-weds: later, as the couple were preparing to leave, he tried to congratulate them again.[4] 'He came to my wedding reception,' Conan Doyle recorded later, 'and there was no guest whom I was prouder to see.'[5]

This was the satisfying ending to Conan Doyle's story of the Edalji case and the one used by most of his biographers. My 1970s classroom account ended here too. I myself married in 1974, 100 years after the extraordinary wedding of Charlotte Stoneham and Shapurji Edalji in Ketley. Being married to a German gave me my first inklings of what the experience of others in marrying across cultures and histories might be. With my new German perspective and a growing realisation, in particular, of the triumphalist attitudes towards war in these islands I became much more aware that others do not always see the English as we see ourselves.

---

[1] Cited in *Express & Star*, 7 September 1907.
[2] Charles Higham, *The Adventures of Conan Doyle*, p. 208.
[3] J. D. Carr, *The Life of Sir Arthur Conan Doyle*, p. 236.
[4] Ibid, p. 236.
[5] Sir Arthur Conan Doyle, *Memories and Adventures*, p. 219.

We had two daughters. When in 1977 I mentioned the birth of the second to one of my classes, one student, who was learning German, exclaimed 'Oh, yow'm a Vater then, sir, ain't you?' I was by now well enough advanced in south Staffordshire dialect to be able to understand her English. The continuing strength of this dialect was a link with the past, the world of the isolated mining community into which the Edalji children had been born. Although it was now in mushrooming commuter-belt territory on the south side of Cannock Chase, the life of Great Wyrley was still distant from the world of the inner city in Walsall, Wolverhampton and beyond, and post-war immigration from the lands of the former empire seemed to be an issue for others. Four years later the eruptions on the streets of Handsworth, Toxteth and Brixton made me realise that Britain was changing in ways I had not grasped.

George Anson, Chief Constable of Staffordshire

the public press.
You vindictive wretch ...
you to do ... whatever your
vengeance prompts you
but spare Oh spare the
honest public

Believe me
Yours very sincerely
God Satan
I am Satan

'God Satan' letter from the 1892-5 series

Kind permission of Grey House Books

sir
you   head master me and
George Edalja are going to
leave and jin the army.
teacrs wro wrote the
letters and so we
are going to set the
Cardd school on fire
if you touch. us we will
kick you black and
blue your

fool. we dont care
what you say.

**Letter from the 1892-5 series attributed by Conan
Doyle to 'foulmouth'**

Kind permission of Grey House Books

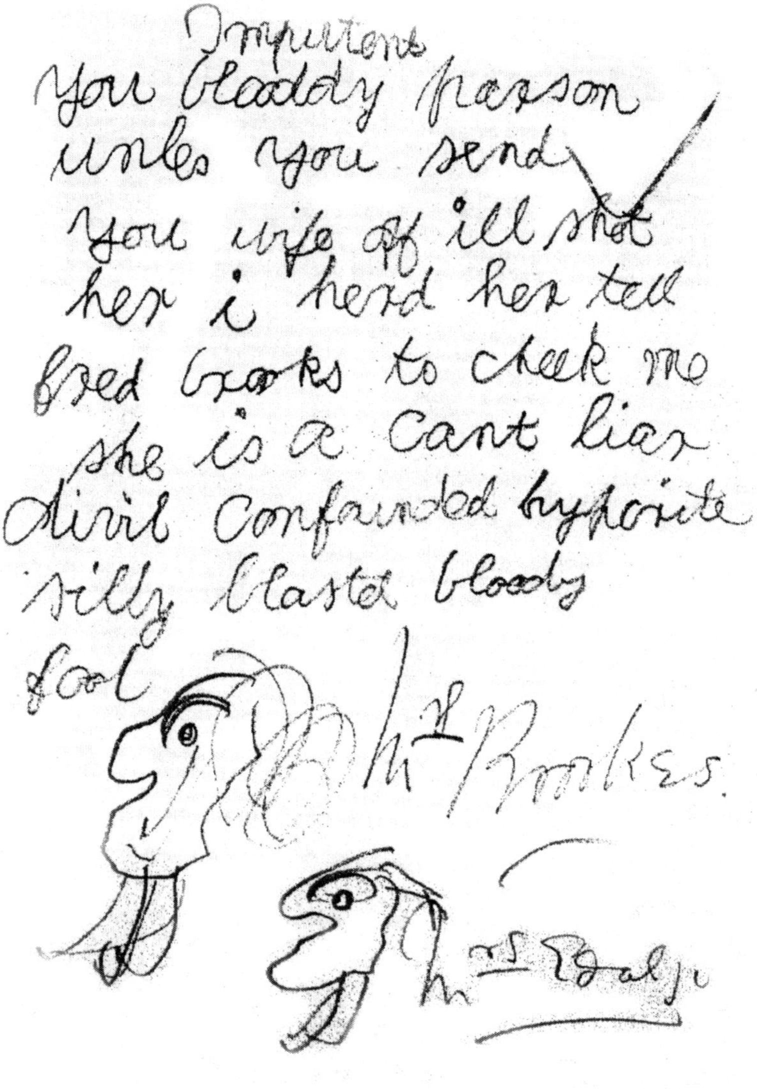

Impurtent
You bloddy parson
unles you send
you wife of ill shot
her i herd her tell
fred brooks to cheek me
she is a cant liar
divil confounded hypocrite
silly blaster bloody
fool
Mr Brookes.
Mrs Edalji

Letter from the 1892-5 series
Courtesy of the National Archives

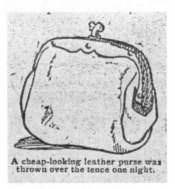

A cheap-looking leather purse was thrown over the fence one night.

One morning an empty phial was found.

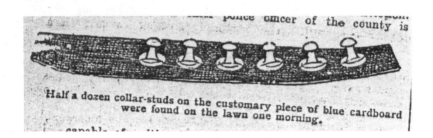

Half a dozen collar-studs on the customary piece of blue cardboard were found on the lawn one morning.

Objects left outside St Mark's vicarage in the 1893-1895 period

run the risk of losing kidneys and liver Think of all the ghoolish murders that are committed why then should you escape

No. 5

Letter to Conan Doyle from the 1907 'Martin Molton' series

Courtesy of the National Archives

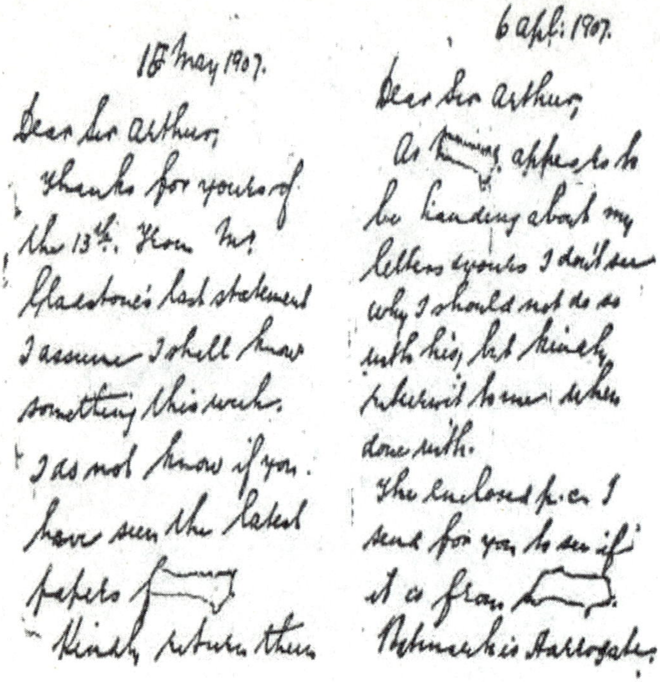

15th May 1907.

Dear Sir Arthur,

Thanks for yours of the 13th. From Mr Gladstone's last statement I assume I shall know something this week.

I do not know if you have seen the latest papers from [redacted]

Kindly return them

6 Apl: 1907.

Dear Sir Arthur,

As [redacted] appears to be handing about my letters to yours I don't see why I should not do so with his, but kindly return it to me when done with.

The enclosed piece I send for you to see if it is from [redacted]

Between his Autographs.

Specimens of George Edalji's handwriting, 1907

**Conan Doyle claimed Royden Sharp showed his aunt a
knife used by the animal - slashers**

Kind permission of the Black Country Bugle

The photograph of the outrage of August 1907 used for
a run of 5000 postcards

Conan Doyle's second wedding, 1907, at which George Edalji was a guest

3. Other eyes

Questions

1983. I am called to the school phone. At the other end is a stranger, Michael Harley. He is researching a book on the Edalji case which John Murray has agreed to publish. Can he come into school and compare notes? He does come, though his visit has to be packed into the usual hectic school day. I am asked to rush off to take a cover lesson, so I hand over my pile of Edalji material; at least he can spend the time picking out any treasures he might need. On my return, though, his face shows no look of excited new discovery. There is nothing in the collection he does not know already. I have met an Edalji expert.

For the next half hour an earthquake rumbles through all my assumptions about Conan Doyle and his Edalji campaign. Michael Harley simply does not accept Conan Doyle's view of the case. George, he believes, was a far more devious person than the helpless victim we have known through Conan Doyle and his many biographers for over 70 years. The chivalrous but gullible Conan Doyle was completely taken in by the mild-mannered, middle-class myopic.

****

The key to the Harley challenge to the Conan Doyle orthodoxy lay in the once-secret Home Office files on the case; he was the first person to make a comprehensive study of the mounds of documents, eight boxes of them, which had become available for inspection at the Public Record Office (now the National Archive). In one of a number of articles outlining his early findings he reported on the sources which had set his imagination on fire. Most striking was a letter sent to Chief Constable Anson in January 1907 containing the startling suggestion that in 1902 George had had a 50 guineas bet with other solicitors that he would kill six cows, six sheep and six horses in his father's parish by the end of 1903; the letter claimed that this was to help pay for his losses in a lawyers' fraud the previous year.[1] The letter, received by Chief Constable Anson just before Conan Doyle went public in the *Daily Telegraph*, was anonymous, proving nothing. It did however

---

[1] *Cannock Advertiser*, 19 August 1983.

offer a tantalising new line of enquiry, and now a modern sleuth was on the trail; here was an Inspector Rebus[1] rather than a Sherlock Holmes, unmoved by middle class protestations of innocence delivered in educated tones, unimpressed by clever writers or their world-wide reputations. Michael Harley believed that George had written this letter himself, in a hand which attempted to disguise its authorship, just as he had written some of the abusive letters of 1892-5 and the Greatorex letters of 1903.[2]

Was George desperate for money in 1902? Was there a fraud? A further clue is contained in a letter now held in Birmingham Central Library which George wrote in December 1902, two months before the first outrage in Great Wyrley. The man who wrote to Sir J. B. Stone, M.P. for Birmingham, did not match up with the shy, harmless George who in Conan Doyle's imagination only left home to go to work. It was an out-and-out begging letter:

> I am reduced... to absolute poverty... through having had to pay a large sum of money (nearly £220) for a friend for whom I was surety. I borrowed from three money-lenders... but their exorbitant interest only made matters worse, and two of them have now presented a bankruptcy petition against me but are willing to withdraw it if I can raise £115 at once.

Michael Harley did not reveal all his evidence, but his study of the Home Office files certainly made him believe that George's financial problems were the result of dealings more shady than he would admit. George was in serious financial straits in early 1903 and in danger of being struck off the Roll of Solicitors. Harley knew full well that he needed much more than this if he was to make a case against George, but if there were any truth at all in the claim that George made a sensationally daring bet in 1902 his financial desperation at least offered an explanation for it.

It was one thing to believe that George was guilty of anonymous letter-writing and unsavoury financial dealings, but could Harley also produce any new evidence that George was connected with the outrages? Here the starting-point was 29 June 1903. The scene at Blewitt's Quinton Colliery. The

---

[1] Ian Rankin's Inspector Rebus stories are set in and around Edinburgh. Conan Doyle's Sherlock Holmes figure was based on Dr Joseph Bell, who taught Conan Doyle when he studied medicine in Edinburgh.
[2] *Cannock Advertiser*, 4 November 1983.

turning-point for George. One horse still standing but dripping its entrails, the other disembowelled and dead. Michael Harley revealed two pieces of information on this key event which completely contradicted the story George's supporters had chosen to believe. First there was a report in the Home Office files that George was spotted at the scene of this crime, and second the police began to concentrate on George after this incident because he was incriminated by someone close to his own family.

Here, in these snippets of evidence, was the launch-pad for a new investigation. For Michael Harley the Edalji case was a cold case, so many questions unasked, a whole new explanation possible. The anonymous letter to Anson claiming that George had laid a bet that he would kill 6 horses, 6 cows and 6 sheep in Great Wyrley parish by the end of 1903 was, he believed, written by George himself. George was 'Martin Molton', just as he had been 'Greatorex' in 1903 and one of the letter-writers of 1892-5.

Reputations

There was another dimension to Michael Harley's challenge to the familiar version of events. He in the role of Rebus thought much more of Chief Constable Anson than he did of Sir Arthur Conan Doyle in the role of Sherlock Holmes.[1] Anson, he believed, had been much maligned since Conan Doyle's merciless identification of him as chief culprit in 'the British Dreyfus case'. He, on the other hand, described Anson as 'the epitome of an English country gentleman but with a clever incisive brain', and believed that Anson's handling of the evidence was far more rigorous and professional than that of Conan Doyle, the campaigner who only wanted evidence which would support his preconceived view. He pointed out, moreover, that Anson had once described Horace Edalji as 'the epitome of an English gentleman', and that this suggests that Anson's view of the Edalji family was not shaped by racial prejudice.

Conan Doyle, on the other hand, he saw as naïve, with a world-picture shaped by romantic ideas about chivalry from the tales he had read with his mother as a child. This was also the man who became so obsessed with spiritualism that at one point during the Great War he claimed to be in touch with

---

[1] Michael Harley, 'An infamous Anson?', in *Staffordshire History*, 2, Spring 1985.

thirteen mothers who were corresponding with their dead sons; in the 1920s he was still packing lecture halls all over the country with his talks about 'the psychic quest'. Even more telling was the matter of the fake 'fairy' photographs. When he heard in 1920 that two young girls in Cottingley in Yorkshire had three years earlier claimed to have found fairies at the bottom of their garden, Conan Doyle accepted the authenticity of photographs purporting to record the event although there were clear signs that they had been fabricated. Indeed, in 1922 he wrote a whole book on the subject, *The Coming of the Fairies*, in which he declared that 'other well-authenticated cases will come along'.[1] Michael Harley was convinced that Conan Doyle's trusting nature made him easy game for George Edalji's schemes.[2]

In his printed articles Michael Harley never claimed explicitly that George was responsible for slashing open the bellies of Great Wyrley's animals, but the last time I saw him he was hot on the trail of new evidence, including reports of a footprint found on the window-sill of St Mark's vicarage after the night of one of the attacks. He also suggested that George's eyesight problems were such that he might actually have been able to see more clearly in the dark; George was able to get around the village quite easily, as his evening walks demonstrated. Like Conan Doyle, though with a completely different starting-point, Harley had become a man with a mission. He went on to scour the land for conclusive evidence, buoyed up by a meeting with Richard Lancelyn Green, the doyen amongst Conan Doyle experts, who was sympathetic towards his case.

Sadly he moved away from the area and was in the end unable through illness to push a book into publication which would have seized the Edalji story from the grasp of Conan Doyle and turned it on its head. Other writers did follow his lead, though, and by the 1990s the Conan Doyle version of the Edalji story was no longer so easily accepted: Paul Lester in his book *Sherlock Holmes in the Midlands* (1992) also used the Home Office evidence to challenge the orthodox Conan Doyle view and leave the question of George's responsibility for the animal outrage open;[3] Jennifer Ward, who had access to further material made available by the Staffordshire police, told the Police History Society in 1994 that George had indeed written some of the letters which implicated him in the cattle-

---

[1] Arthur Conan Doyle, *The Coming of the Fairies*, Hodder & Stoughton, 1922.
[2] Michael Harley, *Cannock Advertiser*, 11 November 1983.
[3] Paul Lester, *Sherlock Holmes in the Midlands*, Brewin Books, Studley, 1992, p. 48.

maiming;[1] and in 1996, a BBC radio play, which was partly a factual drama-documentary and partly a piece of creative speculation, left the listener with the impression that George might have been guilty both of the anonymous letter-writing and of the horse mutilation.[2] Ex-Police Sergeant Alan Walker, Curator of the Staffordshire Police Museum, conducted much research of his own from the 1980s, and continues to argue for George's guilt; as an experienced police officer he knows how convincing families can be in denying one of their member's guilt.

Immersed as I was in the suffocating twenty-four-hours-a-day world of a teacher I could not follow Michael Harley's path to the Public Record Office. I was grateful however to be able to introduce his ideas into my lessons and by 1987 had produced a work-pack for Staffordshire schools which took advantage of his research to present the whole case as an investigation, leaving it to pupils to act as detectives and draw their own conclusions from the evidence presented. Rebus versus Holmes.[3] I could no longer make a certain judgement myself

[1] W.S.L., CB (FAM) EDAJI/S (Jennifer Ward, 'The Letter Writers of Wyrley', unpublished text of talk to Police History Society, 1994).
[2] Tony Mulholland, *Conan Doyle's Strangest Case*, broadcast on BBC Radio 4, 1996.
[3] Roger Oldfield, *The Case of George Edalji*, Staffordshire County Council, 1987.

BOOK II: A LIVING FAMILY

1. Challengers

Late 1986. Another son of Bombay stares through our TV screen, seemingly just at me. It's a Channel 4 recording. For half an hour he tells me what it's like watching my world from his. As a fledgling Advisory Teacher for Multicultural Education I am getting used to grappling daily with the ugly evil of racism, but this is still tough. He tells me:

> *If you want to understand British racism... it is impossible even to begin to grasp the nature of the beast unless you accept its historical roots; unless you see that 400 years of conquest and looting, centuries of being told that you are superior to the fuzzy-wuzzies and the wogs... leave their stain on you all; that such a stain seeps into every part of your culture, your language and your daily life; and that nothing much has been done to wash it out...*[1]

Salman Rushdie, born in 1947, migrated from Bombay to England, just as Shapurji Edalji once did. His views on the British and their empire are however poles apart from Shapurji's.

****

White Britain's view of itself had already received one huge jolt in the 1980s. The inner city troubles of 1981, from Toxteth in Liverpool, where Shapurji Edalji once served as curate, to Handsworth in Birmingham and to Brixton in London, had spurred a new awareness of the consequences of Britain's imperial past. The post-war migrants from the former lands of empire had faced prejudice and discrimination from the start, and nothing had changed for their children born and brought up in the Motherland itself. The events of 1981 were a shocking symptom of the fact that British society was scarred by deep-rooted inequalities.

One token response by the government was to offer grants to local education authorities to allow them to appoint advisory teachers who would promote 'multicultural education' in schools with few or no black or minority ethnic pupils. It was via this route that I left Great Wyrley High School in 1986 to work in a team of three advisory teachers charged with the task of bringing a new understanding of the issues facing

---

[1] Salman Rushdie, 'The new empire within Britain', broadcast on Channel 4, December 1982; text given in *New Society*, 9 December, 1982, pp. 417-20.

multicultural Britain to Staffordshire's hundreds of 'all-white' schools. Whatever we did for the schools, the experience certainly changed me; my ideas about myself, about Britain, and about what was important in the Edalji story, were transformed.

****

One challenge came from multiculturalists and antiracists around me who were bursting to expose the 'stain' of colonialist racism in the literature of the past which had helped to shape the 'stain' of racism of the present. Writers under the spotlight included a long list from the Edaljis' time – G.A. Henty, R.M. Ballantyne, H. Rider Haggard, John Buchan. Such lists made me think particularly of my last year at primary school. Although our inspiring teacher was absent for long periods because of a malarial condition contracted whilst on service in India, he nevertheless spent enough time with us to leave many memories of richly varied classroom inputs. I still have a beautiful hand-produced certificate awarded for winning an art and craft competition; the award was for a clay model entitled 'My Impression of Allan Quatermain'. The idea came from the teacher's readings from Rider Haggard's *King Solomon's Mines* (1887), whose hero Allan Quatermain became mine too; I was enthused into reading the rest of Rider Haggard 's main novels in the months which followed. In the 1980s, however, I had to reconsider what effect these first forays into adult literature might have had on me. Analysts all around me were now pointing to the ways in which Rider Haggard's belief in British cultural superiority was reflected in his novels. In *King Solomon's Mines*, for example, all the British characters, especially Allan Quatermain, are good, whilst the three evil characters – Gagool, Twala, and Scragga – are all African. The black characters are also expendable – Khiva the Zulu sacrifices himself to save the white Captain Good from a gruesome end. These were the images of Africa I was brought up on.

Our teacher then read to us from John Buchan's *The Thirty-Nine Steps* (1915), and soon I was working my way through all of Buchan's most famous novels as well. His stories were thrilling, but they too, I became acutely aware in the 1980s, were filled with a belief in empire and underlying notions of racial superiority: 'I haven't the privilege of your name, sir,' one character tells the hero of *The Thirty-Nine Steps* in gratitude for his help, ' but let me tell you that you're a white man.' The task of considering how my mind might have been stained by such messages was painful.

The greatest writer in English which Bombay has produced apart from Salman Rushdie was born in 1865. Indeed it is possible that Shapurji, who by that time was a Church of England man, attended his christening in St Thomas's Cathedral. It was this son of Bombay, Rudyard Kipling, who at the end of the 19th century produced the most famous expression of the feeling which had developed in Britain that the superior Anglo-Saxon peoples had a world mission:

Take up the White Man's burden -
Send forth the best ye breed -
Go, bind your sons to exile
To serve your captives' need;
To wait, in heavy harness,
On fluttered folk and wild -
Your new-caught, sullen peoples,
Half devil and half child. [1]

Here the perspectives which seeped through the writings of Rider Haggard, John Buchan and others were given their most memorable form.

As for Conan Doyle, sometime guest of Rudyard Kipling whilst the latter lived in Vermont, here was another author I read in boyhood. He, certainly, liked to think that he was not prejudiced. His whole account of George Edalji's case was based on the premise that it was Chief Constable Anson's racial prejudices which had infected the Staffordshire police force and created the climate which led to George's conviction. The evidence of his writings, however, undermined his credibility as a campaigner against racial prejudice. The Sherlock Holmes stories, after all, did little to promote positive images of South Asia and its peoples. The tone is set in *A Study in Scarlet* in which Dr Watson is portrayed as a doctor who once served with the British army in India, 'deep in the enemy's country...', against the 'murderous Ghazis', from whom he was rescued by his dutiful orderly; he is therefore on the side of the heroic British in their struggle to control a primitive colonised people. In 'The Speckled Band', Sherlock Holmes deals with Dr Grimsby Roylott, who having been turned mad by his immersion in 'alien' Asian culture returns to England and uses an Indian 'swamp adder' to poison one step-daughter and try to poison another. As for the few Asian characters in the Sherlock Holmes stories, they tend to be treated negatively: an Indian

[1] 'The White Man's Burden', 1899, *The Works of Rudyard Kipling*, The Wordsworth Poetry Library, 1995, pp. 323-324.

student in 'The Three Students' is described as 'a quiet inscrutable fellow as most Indians are'.

As an Advisory Teacher for Multicultural Education, daily engagement with these issues was distressing. Salman Rushdie's analysis, I realised, was just the tip of an antiracist iceberg, and it did as much as Michael Harley's work to dent my image of Conan Doyle as the noble campaigner for justice. Conan Doyle's attitudes on race suggested that he was no hero, just a man of his time. It was time to throw away Sherlock Holmes's magnifying glass and try to re-examine the Edalji story through Salman Rushdie's glasses.

****

A similar challenge was embodied in the words of an African proverb to be seen on an Oxfam poster on the walls of our multicultural education resource centre: 'Until the lions have their historians, tales of the hunt shall always glorify the hunter.' Where did this leave the history I had been taught, from schoolday accounts of the exploits of Clive of India, Horatio Nelson and the Duke of Wellington to university lectures by Hugh Trevor-Roper? A television remark by Trevor-Roper in 1963 was still notorious among antiracists in the 1980s: '... there is only the history of the Europeans in Africa. The rest is darkness.' At this time one song by Bob Marley seemed to have more meaningful things to say about the '400 years of looting and conquest' than did many of the writings of the historians from the tiny tribe of white looters and conquerors to which I belonged:

> Old pirates, yes, they rob i
> Sold I to the merchant ships,
> Minutes after they took i
> From the bottomless pit.
> But my hand was made strong
> By the 'and of the almighty.
> We forward in this generation
> Triumphantly.

Everywhere multiculturalists and antiracists were striving first to expose the historical roots of the 'stain' and the distorted view of history which it produced, and second to give due weight to the perspectives, experiences and achievements of the looted and the conquered – one fifth of the world's peoples so far as the British empire was concerned. It was in 1986 that Rozina Visram published her *Ayahs, Lascars and Princes,* a pioneer study of the lives of those who have come to

Britain from South Asia, lives which had had little or no mention in traditional accounts of British history.[1] She celebrated the achievements of dozens of people, including the three Parsis from Bombay who were the first South Asians to be elected to the British House of Commons: Dadhabai Naoroji, a Liberal, elected in 1892; Mancherjee Bhownaggree, a Conservative, elected in 1895; and Shapurji Saklatvala, a Communist elected on a Labour Party ticket in 1922. The significance of their success is underlined by the fact that no other South Asian was elected until Keith Vaz was returned in 1987. Whilst celebrating South Asian achievement Visram also addressed the other side of the coin, the 'stain', and traced its development through time: she reported, for example, Prime Minister Lord Salisbury's notorious comment after Naoroji was defeated in his first attempt to get into Parliament in 1886: 'I doubt if we have yet got to the point of view where a British constituency would elect a black man.'

Above all, so far as I was concerned, Rozina Visram mentioned Shapurji Edalji. She was the first to point out that Shapurji was much more than the father of a victim of the 'stain'. He was a pioneer, a South Asian who made a career not just in the Church of England but in its homeland. Unfortunately that was almost all she could say, for historians had never done anything to add to Conan Doyle's brief references.[2] It now seemed to be my role in life to plug the gap.

---

[1] Rozina Visram, *Ayahs, Lascars and Princes: Indians in Britain 1700-1947*, Pluto Press, 1986.

[2] See also Rozina Visram, *Asians in Britain: 400 Years of History*, Pluto Press, 2002, pp. 79-82.

Towers of Silence, Bombay, in the 19th century

Kind permission of Temple Smith

Bombay, 1831, with Parsis in the foreground

Kind permission of Temple Smith

An image of British colonial rule – the Watson Hotel, Bombay

Kind permission of Temple Smith

2. Pioneer

Sacred to the memory of Rev. Shapurji Edalji, 42 years vicar of this parish, born in Bombay, died 23 May 1918 aged 76 years.

By the time I left Great Wyrley High School I had stood dozens of times at Shapurji's graveside in St Mark's churchyard to stare with teenage groups at this bald description of a life. What else was there to say about it? We glanced, and then turned to the vicarage and the more exciting story of that famous night in August 1903. The year 1986 was a big turning-point: in my new job in multicultural education I was driven by the desire to retrieve Shapurji from his lonely grave under the trees.

But where to start? The chances of tracing his Bombay origins seemed remote. All there was to go on was the staccato entry in Crockford's Clerical List:

EDALJI, Shapurji, Great Wyrley Vicarage, Walsall. – Free Kirk Coll Bomb 1864. St Aug Coll Cant 1866. (Ordained deacon) 1869. (Ordained priest) 1870 Ox. Vic. of Gt. Wyrley... 1876... C. of St. Clem. Toxt. Pk. Liv. 1872; St. Jas. Farnworth, 1870-72; Burford, Oxon. 1869: H. Trin. Ox. 1869-70; St. Levan, Cornwall, 1873-74; St. Thos. Toxt. Pk. Liv. 1874-5; Bromley St. Leonard, 1875-76.[1]

Research breakthroughs can however be exhilarating. At the end of a day in Oxford investigating other aspects of the story I called into the Indian Institute to glance hopefully through a biography of John Wilson, the missionary who founded the Free Kirk College in Bombay mentioned in the entry in Crockford's. I was astonished to find that the book actually referred to Shapurji's baptism in 1857.[2] From here one source led to another, and I entered into a world which I had imagined I would never find. By the 1990s Shapurji had become part of my life.

Conversion

I think often of a day in Bombay in 1856, the day that young Shápurjí Edaljí travelled stubbornly through the streets

---

[1] *Crockford's Clerical Directory*, 1902.
[2] George Smith, *Life of John Wilson*, John Murray, 1878, p. 459.

of his home city, the day that he opted for worms rather than vultures.

This is not to say that worms were at the forefront of his mind when he started his nerve-wracking ride to John Wilson's mission house that day. No, his thoughts were almost certainly focused on the Christian life to come and the everlasting life which would follow. He was entering a world shaped by three Johns: John Calvin, the Reformation leader; John Knox, founder of the Church of Scotland; and John Wilson, the Free Church of Scotland missionary who was waiting for him. He was committing himself to a future devoted to eliminating the wicked idolatry which he now believed corrupted the hearts and minds of his fellow peoples of South Asia.

His decision would make a difference to the worms, though. If he had remained a Parsi, as he was brought up to be, his body on death would have been offered up to the vultures hovering over the Towers of Silence in his native city. Now, by choosing Christianity, his passing would mean a hole in the ground and eternity with the worms. Indeed, that is where he now is, in his shy grave under the trees in St Mark's churchyard, and I sometimes wonder how well Great Wyrley's worms have done their job these last ninety years.

He was perhaps fourteen on that day in 1856, little more than a child, and yet he had already endured three stormy years with his family since he first became interested in Christianity.[1] At one point his parents took away a Bible he had acquired, so he decided to leave religious books with friends and tear out a few pages at a time to keep in his pocket and read secretly. On another occasion he was thrown out by his father, who was furious at the Christian company he was keeping. Then, in 1856, he joined a classmate at Elphinstone College, Syed Hussain, in a first attempt to enter Wilson's mission house in preparation for conversion. There was however a barrage of begging and emotional pressure from his brother and the rest of the family. He relented and returned home for a month's trial to see if they could learn to tolerate his abominable Christian beliefs.[2]

---

[1] Shapurji was hazy on the year of his birth. The information on the gravestone presumably came from his own records, and yet in 1893 he had said he was born in 1840 or 1841: W.S.L., 190/3/96, Shapurji Edalji to Rupert Sims, 25.2.1893, 'Letters to Rupert Sims', p. 21.

[2] John Wilson, *The Star of Bethlehem and the Magi from the East: A Sermon Preached on the Occasion of the Baptism of a Parsi Youth 31st August, MDCCCLVI*, Smith Taylor & Co, Bombay, 2nd ed., 1857, p. 123.

It was no good. He made his plans, escaped from the family home, and rode through the streets of Bombay. He knew the dangers. Sixteen years earlier John Wilson had made his first converts, three more Parsi youths from Elphinstone College, and the baptism of one had taken place under police protection. Later, in 1856 itself, four more Parsi youths at the Elphinstone College (all aged between seventeen and nineteen) announced that they wanted to become Christians. Three eventually gave up under relentless pressure from the Parsi community which included the ruthless tactic of telling them that their mothers were dying under the strain. The fourth went through with baptism but needed police protection afterwards on his way to and from school. As for Syed, Shápurjí's classmate, when he first told Wilson that he wanted to convert to Christianity Wilson suggested to Bombay's Deputy Commissioner of Police that Syed might be poisoned once his plan became public.[1]

Despite all this, Shápurjí, by far the youngest Parsi to offer himself for baptism, travelled on. And when he reached the mission house he was received with open arms by John Wilson and his Free Church of Scotland colleagues. Shápurjí's obstinacy, and the worms, had won.

Roots

The Zoroastrianism which Shápurjí had renounced had a far longer history than that of the Christianity he aimed to embrace. Its creator was Zoroaster, the son of a priest in Persia, who may have lived around 1500 BC, two hundred years before Moses. Many of his beliefs are familiar to Jews, Christians, and Muslims: he was the first person to have taught a belief in one Creator, and central to his ideas were the existence of the devil, heaven, hell, the resurrection of the dead, final judgement, and heavenly bliss.[2]

Two of the faiths of the Middle East which Zoroastrianism helped to shape – Christianity and Islam – had by Shápurjí's time contributed towards its dangerous decline. A key turning-point was the spread of Islam to Persia in the 7th century, which led to the persecution of Zoroastrians. One group migrated to India, and according to Parsi tradition eventually landed on the coast of the Gujerat in 936.[3] When many later settled in the

---

[1] Charles Forjett, *Our Real Danger in India*, Cassell, 1888, p. 26.
[2] John Hinnells, 1981, *Zoroastrianism and the Parsis*, Ward Lock, 1987, p. 7.
[3] Mary Boyce, *Zoroastrians: Their Religious Practices and Beliefs*, Routledge & Kegan Paul, 1979, p. 166.

seaport of Surat these exiles came to be known as the 'Parsis' (the 'Persians'), and to this day many still prefer not to be described as Indian. Though they made Gujerati their first language, the emigrant community maintained their religious traditions for century after century. Then, towards the end of the 17th century, the Parsis found a new destiny. In 1662 the British acquired an undeveloped swamp, infested with malaria and cholera, to the south of the Gujerat; Bombay was part of the dowry of Catherine of Braganza on her marriage to Charles II. Parsis were soon attracted south to the infant settlement.

In 1668 Bombay was handed over to the East India Company to administer. At first the Company saw Bombay mainly as a stepping-stone to the riches of the rest of India and the Far East – cotton goods from the Gujerat, spices from the East Indies, and, by the 18th century, tea from China. This perch on the west Indian coast was however from the start no mere staging-post; the granting of a charter to the Company was the first step in a process which was to transform the British presence in India into what Gandhi referred to as 'the most powerful secret operation the world has ever known'.[1] The settlement soon mushroomed beyond the original fort, land was reclaimed from the flats which separated the islands, and by the 19th century Bombay was a fast-expanding city, attracting thousands of Indians from its hinterland, as well as fortune-hunters and servants of empire from Britain. As Shápurjí grew up in the 1840s and 1850s, Bombay was on the verge of challenging the status of Calcutta as India's greatest city.

By the 19th century the Parsi community included many of Bombay's leading families. Among them were dynasties of shipbuilders such as the Wadias, one of whose ships sailed the world for years with his personal side-swipe at British racism on the kelson: 'The ship was built by a d--d Black Fellow AD 1800'.[2] Bombay-built 'China clippers' were the backbone of the lucrative opium trade, and it was on board a Wadia ship that the treaty ceding Hong Kong to Britain was signed in 1842. The Parsis of Bombay were the English-speaking middlemen who oiled the wheels of trade – as well as shipbuilders there were merchants (Shápurjí's father was one), shopkeepers, brokers, and bankers. After the British, the Parsis were the richest and most powerful group in the city. By the 1850s they owned more than half of Bombay Island.

---

[1] Gillian Tindall, *City of Gold*, Temple Smith, 1982, p. 60.
[2] Gillian Tindall, *City of Gold*, p. 92 and p. 99.

****

Sometime after the age of seven, Shápurjí would have been through his initiation ceremony. Beforehand, he would have to learn the two most important Parsi prayers, one of which, the Ahura Vairya, was probably composed by Zoroaster himself, making it the equivalent of the Lord's prayer in the Christian tradition:

> *He (Ahura Mazda) is as much the desired Master as the judge according to Asha (Righteousness). He is the doer of acts of good purpose of life. To Mazda Ahura is the kingdom...* [1]

On the day of the ceremony, Shápurjí would be expected to have a bath, and then put on white trousers and a shawl. Meanwhile the family and members of the Parsi community would gather. The guests no doubt included some of those Parsi men of enterprise who were at the heart of Bombay's economic life. The Parsi women, though left in the background on occasions like this, had more freedom than women belonging to other faith groups in the city – they were not in purdah, and could remarry if they were widowed. It was not until the 1860s, however, that they were to play a significant part in the social interactions with the British which helped to make economic co-operation between the two communities even more smooth. [2]

The ceremony would proceed with the lighting of a ritual fire, and then prayers would be said. Shápurjí would have to recite a prayer on his own, probably the Ahura Vairya. The priest would invest him with a sacred shirt and cord (the 'kusti'). Shápurjí, under the guidance of the priest, would recite prayers, and then declare his faith in the worship of Mazda:

> *O Almighty, come: come to my help. I am a worshipper of God (Mazda). I am a Zoroastrian worshipper of God. I agree to praise the Zoroastrian religion, and to believe in that religion.* [3]

Next the priest would bless him and sprinkle rice. Presents would be given, and guests would share in a meal. The initiation ceremony was the first occasion on which a child could put on the kusti, the sacred cord which was seen as the

---

[1] John Hinnells, *Zoroastrianism and the Parsis*, p. 40.
[2] Gillian Tindall, *City of Gold*, p. 185.
[3] John Hinnells, *Zoroastrianism and the Parsis*, p. 43.

armour of God against evil. Parsis believe that once a child has been initiated, his or her thoughts words and deeds are stored and will determine the soul's fate at judgement. For Shápurjí, as for any child, this was a solemn moment.

Stains

Britain's relationship with South Asia was changing rapidly at this time. Indeed, the more I read about Shapurji's life the more apparent it became that the growth of the empire in general and of Bombay in particular did indeed leave a 'stain' upon their builders. Four hundred years ago, after all, the British knew almost nothing of India, and even when they acquired Bombay in 1662 it soon became just an East India Company trading-post on the fringe of a great sub-continent, much of which was still ruled by the Mughal emperors from Delhi. The Company's ships buzzed like flies around the coastline of this Goliath, trying to open up its markets. Then came two centuries of infiltration, looting and conquest, and by the time of Shapurji 's youth in the 1850s Britain ruled India. Bombay was no longer just a trading-post; it was rapidly becoming an imperial city, controlled by civil servants shipped out from Britain and shaped to the needs of empire.

It was this unequal power relationship which caused 'the stain' to seep ever more deeply into every aspect of British culture. There were still 'Orientalists' in the early 19th century who believed that India was already a 'moral and civilised' society, and that the British should not try to change it. As more and more of India fell under British rule, however, the idea took root that the reason for Britain's success was the superiority of Europe over Asia, and of British people over all others; Thomas Babington Macaulay proclaimed humbly that the British had become the greatest and most highly civilised people that the world had ever seen, the acknowledged leaders of the human race,[1] and that 'a single shelf of a good European library was worth the whole native literature of India and Arabia'.[2] People with such views held it as their moral duty to spread western enlightenment and reason throughout India. Macaulay, sent to India in 1835 to serve on the governor-general's council, declared that Indians should receive the

---

[1] Peter Fryer, *Staying Power: The History of Black People in Britain, Pluto Press, 1984*, p. 183.
[2] E. L. Woodward, *The Age of Reform 1815-1879*, Clarendon Press, 1938, p. 390.

education of a 'gentleman', to make them into faithful replicas of their rulers in all but blood.[1]

The first important British educational institution in Bombay had already been built: this was Elphinstone College, established to educate Indian boys on the British model – they were offered hefty doses of Shakespeare and had the certainties of Christianity dangled before their noses. Unsurprisingly in view of the role they played in the city, the Parsis provided one of the largest groups of students passing through the college for the rest of the century. One of the first was Dadabhai Naoroji, the man who later became the first Asian M.P. in the British House of Commons and whose achievements eventually earned him the nickname 'Grand Old Man of India'. It was at this college (or institute, as it became in 1840) that Shápurjí Edaljí received his induction into the British world-picture in the 1850s. He was followed in the 1860s by the Parsi Mancherjee Bhownagree who was to become the second Asian M.P. in the House of Commons;[2] unlike Naoroji he was a Conservative whose Indian nationalist critics would bluntly rename him 'bow-and-agree'.[3]

****

Religion was a key to the development of British attitudes. Many Evangelicals brooded heavily over their belief that the Hindu religion was one 'grand abomination', and that India was full of 'dark and bloody superstition'.[4] The East India Company had originally forbidden any Christian missionary activity in those parts of India which it controlled, but the ban was lifted in 1813, and the process of evangelisation began in earnest. John Wilson, a Church of Scotland missionary, settled in Bombay in 1829 and became a leading figure in the Christian life of the city. He was a learned and good-humoured man, but his task, as he saw it, was to spread the light of the gospel in a sea of heathen darkness.[5] Above all he targeted the Parsis, whose faith was more similar to Christianity than were Buddhism, Hinduism, Sikhism and other religions of South Asian origin. When in 1839 three young Parsi men at Elphinstone College announced that John Wilson had persuaded them to be baptised as Christians[6] the Parsis withdrew their sons from the college in angry protest. One of

---

[1] Hermann Kulke and Dietmar Rothermund, *A history of India*, Routledge, 1986, p. 251.
[2] Rozina Visram, *Ayahs, Lascars and Princes*, p. 92.
[3] Ibid., p. 95.
[4] Ibid., p. 6.
[5] Gillian Tindall, *City of Gold*, p. 187.
[6] Ibid., p. 102.

the boys, Dhanjibhai Nauroji, pushed on with his resistance and in 1843 travelled with Wilson to Edinburgh, where he became the first Asian to study Christian theology at a British university. He was ordained in Edinburgh, and returned to India to work in the Bombay mission and elsewhere. Here was Shápurjí's future role-model and mentor.

Wilson meanwhile pursued his onslaught on Zoroastrianism with the publication in 1843 of a tract entitled *The Parsi religion as contained in the Zend-Avesta, unfolded, refuted and contrasted with Christianity.*[1] Most of the Zend-Avestas, the sacred writing of the Zoroastrians, had been written down in the period after the death of Alexander the Great in 323 BC, when under the Parthians Zoroastrianism was for five hundred years the official religion of Persia. Some of the holy scriptures survived only in Pahlavi (a Middle Persian language) either as original works, or as translations from the Avestas. Wilson's linguistic skills completely wrong-footed the Parsi community, for knowledge of the ancient languages had been virtually lost, even amongst priests, and there was no way of refuting his arguments.

By the 1850s some Parsis were recovering the initiative. They turned back to their own sacred texts, studying them in their original languages and making them more accessible by translating them into Gujerati. Many sought to reinterpret the meaning of Zoroastrianism for a new age.

As the debate about the future of Zoroastrianism went on, the wellbeing of the Parsi community was threatened in 1856 by John Wilson's next conversions. First there was the furore when four older Parsi students at the Elphinstone Institute wrote to him saying that they were convinced that Zoroastrianism was a false religion, that they wanted to be baptised, and that they needed protection from the hands of their relatives.[2] Outraged members of the Parsi community tried to have one of the boys' teachers at the college, Ardshír Frámjí, charged with teaching them Christianity. Then the younger boys, Shápurjí Edaljí and Syed Hussain, also taught by Ardshír Frámjí, made their move.[3]

---

[1] John Wilson, *The Parsi religion as contained in the Zend-Avesta, unfolded, refuted and contrasted with Christianity*, Bombay, 1843.
[2] John Wilson, 'The Star of Bethlehem and the Magi from the East: A Sermon Preached on the Occasion of the Baptism of a Parsi Youth 31st August, MDCCCLVI', Smith Taylor & Co, Bombay, 1856, pp. 4-12.
[3] Rev. Robert Hunter, *History of the Missions of the Free Church of Scotland in India and Africa*, T. Nelson & Sons, 1873, p. 243.

Five months later, Shápurjí and Syed[1] were baptised, and the *Bombay Gazette* reported its relief that there were no disturbances by either Parsis or Muslims.[2] The two youths then settled to life at the mission, though in a city surging with tension as a result of events elsewhere: starting with uprisings among sepoy soldiers, violent resistance to the British spread during 1857 through huge swathes of northern India. The Deputy Commissioner of Police in Bombay, Charles Forjett, desperately wanted to avoid a similar scenario in his own city, and eyed the different faith communities with varying degrees of suspicion. The Parsis were alright; they had sent a message to the government pledging their loyalty, and Shápurjí no doubt agreed that the British were victims of an ignoble 'mutiny'. The danger so far as Forjett was concerned lay with the Muslims and Hindus. He focused his energies first on Moharram, which the 150,000 or so Muslims in the city were about to celebrate; this, he thought, could provide the flashpoint. 'Every scoundrel in the town,' he recorded later in his memoirs, 'was closely watched and kept in a state of terror. When, on my rounds at night in disguise, I found anybody speaking of the successes of the rebels in anything like a tone of exultation, I seized him on the spot. A whistle brought up three or four policemen who, too, followed in disguise, and the person or persons were at once bound and walked off to prison.'[3]

Faced with this kind of ruthlessness, the Muslims promised obedience. Next, Forjett believed he had found a plot amongst the Hindus to take over the town during Diwali. The alleged plot was 'discovered', in a casual conversation with a sepoy, by none other than Rev. Dhanjibhai Nauroji; indeed the latter later claimed that he had been the one who 'broke the backbone of the mutiny' by passing the information to Forjett via his patron Rev. John Wilson.[4] Though nothing actually happened, Forjett had two ring-leaders taken to the Esplanade, tied to the mouth of a cannon, and blown to pieces.[5]

During Diwali the following year the rule of the East India Company was brought to an end, and the British Crown took direct control of India: administration was now based in

---

[1] According to a classmate of the two boys, Syed died in London after retirement from the Judgeship of Karachi Small Cases Court: Sir D. E. Wacha, *Shells from the Sands of Bombay: My Recollections and Reminiscences 1860-75*, 1920, p. 651. Wacha was a founder member of the Indian National Congress.

[2] *Bombay Gazette*, 10 February 1857.

[3] Charles Forjett, *Our Real Danger in India*, p. 119.

[4] Dhanjibhai Nauroji, *From Zoroaster to Christ*, Oliphant, Anderson & Ferrer, 1909, p. 78.

[5] Charles Forjett, *Our Real Danger in India*, p. 142.

Whitehall. Perhaps Shápurjí heard Queen Victoria's sovereignty over much of India proclaimed from the steps of Bombay's town hall in 1858.

Impact

Shápurjí in the meantime started his studies at the Free Church General Assembly Institution, founded by Wilson on Christian principles, and by 1859 had made the decision to enter the ministry. Rev. Dhanjibhai Nauroji taught at the Institution for a time, but it was dominated by Scottish missionaries. Between them the staff provided students with an hour of Bible-reading each day and a stream of spiritual lectures, whilst Shápurjí himself was one of those given specialist training for a vocation in the church. Apart from their religious impact, the missionaries had another life-long influence on the future Vicar of Great Wyrley: in the early 1980s the Staffordshire researcher Michael Harley found older residents of the parish who remembered from their childhood that Shápurjí had a Scottish accent, 'not broad, but a definite "burr"'.[1]

Shápurjí was a great catch for the Free Church of Scotland. Talented speakers of native languages were desperately needed for the mighty project of winning South Asia for Christianity. Missionaries from Britain were often required to learn a language in order to continue with their work, but native speakers like Shápurjí were essential. In 1863 he published his first book, a Gujerati-English dictionary, a great tool for the cause.[2] He may also have been in the audience at some of the lectures given in the early 1860s by the German Martin Haug, who had come to Bombay to study the Parsi religion for its own sake, unlike John Wilson who wanted to undermine it. Certainly Haug and his colleague E.W. West gave Shapurji the opportunity to undertake translation work. When in 1864 Haug gave a lecture 'On an Original Speech of Zoroaster' the proceeds were used as prizes for the best translation by Parsis of two Pahlavi works. One of these translations, of the Pandnamah of Adarpad Maraspend, was published in 1869. Shápurjí followed by translating this Gujerati version into English in 1870.[3]

---

[1] Michael Harley, *The Blether*, February 1987 (copy in C.L.)
[2] Shápurjí Edaljí, *A Gujeráti and English Dictionary*, Trübner, 1863.
[3] Shápurjí Edaljí, *The Pand-Nameh, or a Book of Parsé Morality, translated into English from Gujarati*, Trübner, 1870.

The college had many famous visitors, including David Livingstone, a member of the Free Church himself, who stayed at the college during Shápurjí's first year.[1] The ferment of religious debate at the college was also stimulated by the visit of a leading figure from the Brahmo Samaj of Calcutta. It was this visit which inspired Shápurjí in 1864 to deliver a lecture on the Brahmo Samaj movement to the Bombay Dialectic Association, and in doing so to reveal a great deal about his world-picture at this stage in his life.[2] The Brahmo Samaj (the Society for the Transcendental Deity) had been founded in Calcutta in 1818 by a Hindu, Raja Ram Mohun Roy. Roy aimed to conduct Hindu worship using Christian forms, and his reform movement had a great impact in many parts of India. In his lecture Shápurjí told his listeners that he did not totally reject the efforts of the supporters of the Brahmo Samaj. To him, as an Evangelical Christian, nothing could be worse than the religious condition of India before the influence of Christianity. Thirty years earlier, he suggested, the whole of India had been 'sunk into the deepest pit of degradation, meanness and iniquity... the foulest and most cruel idolatry the world ever had swayed the hearts and homes of the vast multitude'. To Shápurjí, the Brahmo Samaj's attempts to abolish idolatry were to be admired. He insisted, however, that Roy had been mistaken in claiming that the ancient Hindu writings, the Vedas, taught monotheistic worship. He also took the opportunity to assert that those who claimed that the Zend-Avestas, the ancient Zoroastrian writings, taught monotheism were equally wrong. In addition he rejected the worship of the elements, which he said was taught in both the Vedas and the Zend-Avestas. For him, only the Bible, the inspired word of God, represented the supernatural revelation which provided the basis for religious belief, and only Christ had the true theory of atonement. What India needed was men like Wickliff, Luther, Calvin, and Knox.

****

Whilst he was developing his Evangelical world-picture at college, Shápurjí was working on a second publication. His fascination with English culture led him at this stage to produce a Gujerati translation of Samuel Johnson's *The History of Rasselas*,[3] a still widely-popular romance about the

---

[1] Elizabeth Hewat, *Christ and Western India*, published by the Rev. J. Kellock, Wilson College, Bombay, 1950, p. 195.
[2] Shápurjí Edaljí, *The Brahma Samája*, Free General Assembly's Institute, Bombay, 1864.
[3] Shápurjí Edaljí, *A Translation of Johnson's 'Rasselas'*, Trübner, 1866.

search for happiness of Rasselas, son of an Emperor of Abyssinia.[1]

In the same year, 1866, he was finally awarded his licence as a preacher, and John Wilson could launch his catch upon the world. Wilson had been planning for some time to involve Shápurjí in the realisation of an ambition he had cherished for nearly thirty years. The project stemmed from a journey Wilson had made in 1839, accompanied by his famous early convert, Dhanjibhai Nauroji. Their travels had taken them to the northern Konkan, where they had come into contact with the Waralis, a people living in the forested hills spreading eastward from the coast north of Bombay; according to the language of the magazine of the Free Church in Scotland, the Waralis lived in 'dense and gloomy jungle' and were just one of a number of different 'races' who exhibited 'almost every known type and variety of barbarism'.[2] It was always Wilson's ambition to prove the virtues of Christianity to the Waralis, and Shápurjí seemed ideal for the job; the oldest Parsi settlements in India lay in the same region and it was assumed that he would be well fitted for evangelism among his own birthright community. The Free Church in Scotland, whose magazine described Shápurjí proudly as 'one of the most active and enthusiastic of our converts',[3] was asked to send £300 to finance the first mission of Wilson's young protégé.[4]

He started his lonely mission in April 1866, and within a few months not only John Wilson but also the governor of Bombay himself, Sir Bartle Frere, as well as Scottish readers of the Free Church magazine, were rejoicing over his reports.[5] During his first few days, he noted, the Waralis kept running away from him, but gradually they accepted his presence. His learnt European horror at the 'ignorance' and 'degradation' of these 'savages' seemed confirmed when he gave a man some soap to wash a wound and the man smeared it on as an ointment; he was shocked that Warali people could not count to twenty without making mistakes; and he worked hard to develop in them an awareness of the horrors of hell. On no occasion did his reports seek to explain how the Waralis had survived in the rainforest for centuries without the benefits of soap, mathematics, or a fear of eternal damnation.

---

[1] Samuel Johnson, *The History of Rasselas, Prince of Abyssinia*, 1759, published in Donald Greene (ed.), *Samuel Johnson*, Oxford University Press, 1984.
[2] *The Free Church of Scotland Monthly Record*, 1 June 1867.
[3] *The Free Church of Scotland Monthly Record*, 1 June 1867.
[4] *The Free Church of Scotland Monthly Record*, 1 January 1866.
[5] *The Free Church of Scotland Monthly Record*, 1 September 1866.

Shápurjí's work was not confined to the Waralis. He sought also to convert Parsis, Hindus, and Muslims in the communities around Sanján, and even remonstrated with Roman Catholic converts whom he saw as 'poor and ignorant'. Indeed, he complained that the presence of Roman Catholics was undermining his Evangelical work with other groups: how could he 'denounce the idolatry of the heathens' when, as some Hindus pointed out to him, 'the Christians worship a painted god and a painted goddess'?[1]

The year or so away from Bombay did not help his health. He lived in spartan conditions, water supplies were poor, and he was afflicted at various times by fever, headache, nausea, and stomach and rheumatic pain. During one return visit to Bombay he suffered from fever 'of a malarious character' and eventually had to spend three months in bed. At this point he resigned his post.[2]

In his year of effort he had done no better and no worse than the thousands of other missionaries involved in the great Evangelical project: according to the 1981 census over 98% of Waralis were still Hindu, and in most areas the Christian population was less than 1% of the whole.[3] Indeed, the 19th century assumptions about pre-literate groups which Shápurjí demonstrated are now being turned on their heads. Yashohara Dalmia's introduction to *The Warlis: Tribal Paintings and Legends* (1982) starts with the sentence: 'In the mythic vision of the Waralis death came upon man because he humiliated mother earth.'[4] This view of the environment is one which many westerners now believe they can learn from. Perhaps it will be the one which prevails in the end.

Redirection

During his lonely twelve months in northern Konkan, Shápurjí was afflicted by another kind of fever. Between the nausea and the headaches his mind itself was humming from pressures of a more spiritual kind. His faith in Calvinism, as evidenced by his impassioned plea in his 1864 lecture for more men in India like Calvin and Knox, had crumbled in the

---

[1] *The Free Church of Scotland Monthly Record*, I June 1867.
[2] W.S.L., 190/3/96, Shapurji Edalji to Rupert Sims, 25.2.1893, 'Letters to Rupert Sims', p. 21.
[3] K. S. Singh, *The Scheduled Tribes*, OUP 1997, p. 1175.
[4] Jivya Soma Mashe, *The Warlis: Tribal Paintings and Legends*, Chemould Publications and Arts, Bombay, 1982, p. 3.

following years. Not only did he come to question Calvinist theology itself, it also struck him that a little ritual would be just the thing for bringing such people as the Waralis to the Christian faith. Gradually the attractions of the Church of England became more and more obvious. He read commentaries on the 39 Articles and found he could subscribe to them. He even decided that bishops were not such a bad thing after all.[1]

His change of direction, which grieved the Free Church community as much as his original conversion to Christianity had upset the Parsis in general and his own family in particular, had been stirred by a particular group of men. The Church of England had its own missionary networks in Bombay, and they were just as anxious as the Free Church of Scotland to get their hands on able young men such as Shápurjí. There were two main Anglican missionary bodies – the Society for the Propagation of the Gospel in Foreign Parts, formed in 1701 as an offshoot of the Society for the Propagation of Christian Knowledge, and the Christian Missionary Society, founded by William Wilberforce and the Evangelicals in 1797. It was the S.P.G. which managed to capture Shápurjí first – the C.M.S. came later, once he was in England.

The focal-point for the S.P.G. in Bombay, as for Anglican life in general, was St Thomas's, where in bygone ages looters and conquerors such as Robert Clive and the Duke of Wellington had knelt to pray. Even John Wilson encouraged students to visit it – if Shápurjí did witness the baptism of Rudyard Kipling there in 1865 this might be the reason. Certainly he became involved with three energetic S.P.G. missionaries who had come to join the Bombay establishment in the mid-1860s. The first was Charles Kirk, former curate in Stoke Newington, whose mission was to the labourers on the Great Indian Peninsular Railway; it was he who in 1866 took Shápurjí in hand by inviting his young protégé to live with him on the Esplanade – perhaps partly so that Shápurjí could help him with his Gujerati, where he was making so little progress that he would soon be in danger of being sent home.[2] The other two men, Rev. James Taylor and Rev. George Ledgard, were former students at St Augustine's College in Canterbury, a college whose sole aim was to prepare young men to serve as missionaries abroad. Between them these men gave Shápurjí a new ambition – to go to St Augustine's himself. The Governor

---

[1] C.C.A., U88 A2/7 C21A (Shápurjí Edaljí to Thomas Kirk, 2 April 1867).
[2] USPG, CLR 3 Copies of letters received from Bombay (1842-67), Letter from Colonel Tremenheere, 9 July 1867.

of Bombay may have helped – he knew of Shápurjí's work in northern Konkan and he knew that the bishops of India looked to St Augustine's College to supply them with more missionary material; he took a close interest in the work of the English college which Shápurjí now had in his sights.[1]

Whilst he was trying to convince the Waralis of the truth of Christianity and himself of the virtues of Anglicanism, Shápurjí had another task to complete – his third book. The S.P.G. was later to offer him a scholarship at St Augustine's, but for the moment his *A Grammar of the Gujaráti Language*[2] was his ticket to England. He would work late into the night to get it finished and raise money for his grand project. Written in English, the book was aimed at British people. Perhaps his books on Gujerati were part of the armoury of Dadabhai Naoroji, appointed Professor of Gujerati at University College in London in 1856, or his successors; the fact that another edition of the Gujerati-English dictionary was published in London in 1884 suggests that it was being well used.[3]

****

Shápurjí's plan delighted most of his S.P.G. friends, but not all. Rev. James Taylor wrote to his old mentor, the Warden at St Augustine's, to praise Shápurjí's firmness in the face of bitter persecution by his Parsi relatives and of harassment by Free Church missionaries anxious to bring him back into their fold.[4] Charles Kirk informed St Augustine's via his brother Thomas, who was Head of Wrexham Grammar School, that Shápurjí would bring honour to the college.[5] Only Rev. George Ledgard had doubts – he could see that Shápurjí would do well at college, but was not convinced that he would go back to India and work successfully as a missionary; here were the seeds of Shápurjí's next controversy.[6]

In the summer of 1867 he finally set sail for England and there is no evidence that he ever returned or even that he had any futher contact with his family. Certainly he published his translation of a Zoroastrian text in 1870, and his dictionary went to a new edition in 1884, but there is no sign that he ever spoke his first language, Gujerati, again. Nor is there any

[1] St Augustine's College, Canterbury, *Occasional papers 1858-1934*.
[2] Shápurji Edalji, *A Grammar of the Gujaráti Language,* Trübner, 1867.
[3] J. F. Kirk, *A Supplement to Allibone's Critical Dictionary of English Literature, and British and American Authors,* 2 vols, J. B. Lippincott & Co., 1891.
[4] C.C.A., U88 A2/7 C21A (Rev. James Taylor to Henry Bailey, 19 March 1867).
[5] C.C.A., U88 A2/7 C21A (Thomas Kirk to St Augustine's College, 1867).
[6] C.C.A., U88 A2/7 C21A (Rev. George Ledgard to St Augustine's College, 1867).

evidence that he had contact with Parsis in Britain, though he was certainly to become well known to Indian Christians.[1] Whether gradually and imperceptibly, or by conscious decision, he became English.

Training

It was presumably in one of the Bunder boats which took passengers out to the great steamships anchored at the Apollo Bunder that Shápurjí slipped away from his home city.[2] When he finally steamed across the Arabian Sea, away from his Parsi past, he had plenty of time to reflect on the fire which burned constantly below the ship's decks. No self-respecting Parsi priest would be prepared to lose his ritual purity by using a form of transport – steam train or steam ship – which depended on fire, and other more conservative Parsis felt the same way.[3] From the time that these forms of transport had arrived in South Asia, however, other Parsis had been more flexible about using them, whilst Shápurjí's own spiritual journey had led him not merely to reject non-Christian ideas but to see them as contemptibly heathen.

The Middle East route from Bombay to England had largely supplanted the Cape route, even before the Suez Canal opened in 1869. The first stop was Aden, where it is likely that he stepped ashore. That was advisable as the process of coaling the ship was so filthy, but fortunately some enterprising Parsis had set up a hotel in Aden to receive the weary travellers.[4] The next leg of the journey involved another voyage by steamship, up the Red Sea. At Suez Shápurjí could glimpse work in progress on the Suez Canal, with 25,000 Egyptians, forced into labour, on site.[5] Then came a journey by the new railway line from Suez via Cairo to Alexandria on the Mediterranean. Once in Alexandria he would probably have stepped on board another ocean-going steamer heading for Trieste, and then taken the overland route as far as the English Channel.[6]

For his first few days in England he was based in Charles Kirk's old parish in Stoke Newington. From here he not only visited the London office of his sponsoring body, the S.P.G., but also met the man who was to be the third German Orientalist in

---

[1] P.R.O., HO 144/985, no. 79 (correspondence from Indian Christian Association, sent by Yelverton to Home Office, 1 March 1904).
[2] Gillian Tindall, *City of Gold*, p. 23.
[3] Mary Boyce, *Zoroastrians: Their Religious Practices and Beliefs*, p. 199.
[4] Sarah Searight, *Steaming East*, Butler and Tanner, 1991, p. 88.
[5] Ibid., p. 112.
[6] Gillian Tindall, *City of Gold*, p. 175.

his life.[1] Dr Reinhold Rost was one of the most remarkable linguists of his time. He not only had expert knowledge of Sanskrit, but was also familiar with twenty or thirty other languages of the east, and taught several of them during once-a-week trips to St Augustine's. Two years later he was to become librarian at the India Office and lay the organisational foundations of its enormous collection, now in the British Library.

****

In view of his new commitment to Anglicanism, the journey by steam train from London to Canterbury was for Shápurjí like a homecoming. It was at Canterbury in 597 AD that St Augustine, as a missionary to the heathen tribes of Britain, had set about introducing England to the doctrines of the Roman Church. He became the first Archbishop of Canterbury, and beside Canterbury Cathedral there rose St Augustine's Abbey, for centuries a main centre of learning in England. When Henry VIII established the Church of England in the 1530s the abbey was dissolved. It was only three hundred years later, in the 1830s, that a number of local people decided that something must be done about the ruined state of the abbey buildings. In the spirit of the new imperial age, money was raised to convert part of the site into a missionary college (today a boys' school), to train young men for ministry in the colonial Church. The college was opened in 1848, and by the 1860s between five and seventeen students were matriculating each year at an institution with a staff of six.[2] The institution was closely tied to the Anglican establishment – its Warden, Henry Bailey, was an honorary canon of Canterbury Cathedral.

The most poignant testimony to the ethos at the college to which Shápurjí had committed his fate can still be seen on the walls of its dark, intimate, lower chapel. These walls are filled with dozens of inscriptions recalling the men who lived up to the college's expectations by sailing from their completed studies in England to convert the 'heathen' in the furthest reaches of the British Empire. Many did not last long in the climates of the lands they sought to win for Christianity. The college had had a total of just over one hundred students in the eighteen years before Shápurjí's arrival, and a fair number were already dead.

---

[1] C.C.A., U88 A2/7 C21A (Shápurjí Edaljí to Henry Bailey, 26 August 1867).
[2] C.C.A., A2/5/18 (matriculation book); *Kelly's Directory of Kent*, 1871. ·

St Augustine's College, Canterbury

The memorials in the chapel include the names of: J. B. Freer, admitted to St Augustine's in 1849, missionary to Newfoundland, died 1865; W. Hacketts, admitted in 1854, missionary to Sarawak, died 1865; and C. Roberts, admitted in 1858, missionary to Quebec, died 1864.

The college had the declared aim of attracting young foreigners who had been converted to Christianity in their own lands. The object was to train them and then send them home as missionaries. Shápurjí himself intended to return to India after his training and a period of service as a priest in England – at least that was what he told an audience in Burford in 1869.[1] Foreign students at St Augustine's did not however always find that their careers went to plan. One popular student in the 1850s was an Inuit who died of a chill on his return to Newfoundland.[2] Shápurjí might have taken particular note of another case, that of Johann Jerrom of Bombay, admitted in 1862, who had died at sea on his return home.[3] The college also attracted one or two sons of chiefs in southern Africa – ideal candidates for turning Christianity into an instrument of British control on their return. One such student, admitted in 1861, died of gastric fever in England in 1863. Cases like these sharpened Shápurjí's deliberations about the best course of action so far as his own health problems were concerned: did he have the best chance of a long life in England or in Bombay? The path he finally chose was to bring him into more bitter conflict, this time with his own college.

[1] *Jackson's Oxford Journal*, 5 June 1869.
[2] Rev. E. R. Orger, *The Life of Henry Bailey, DD*, Hugh Rees, 1912.
[3] Henry Bailey, *Twenty Five Years of St Augustine's*, *Letter to Late Students*, S. Hyde, 1873.

He was in fact one of three foreign students who were received into residence as probationers during 1867. Despite the college's keenness to broaden its intake, all three had lower status than their British counterparts in the college community. The other two were from southern Africa – Nathaniel Cyril Mhala and Jonas Ntsicho.[1] During 1867 Mhala joined with two more students from southern Africa to write to the college warden to plead for equal treatment with regard to the wearing of caps and gowns. They told the warden that they felt particularly self-conscious when they went to church with the other students, as they were not dressed like them. They were not entitled to wear cap and gown until they had taken the exam, which they could not do because they did not have a western education. 'Europeans,' they wrote as though they accepted the British view, 'are supposed to be more witty than the outward nations.'[2]

Shápurjí's feelings were rather different. At twenty-five or twenty-six he was older than many of the other students. He had received a western education, and had already published four books. His linguistic skills were moreover a great resource: the college was so committed to giving students destined for South Asia an awareness of the languages they would meet that Dr Rost's weekly sessions on Sanskrit, Tamil, and other languages went on for forty-five years.[3] Indeed, the college was anxious enough to recruit men such as Shápurjí to assist in the great project of the evangelisation of India that in the 1850s it had established special awards to try to attract them.[4]

Despite all this, Shápurjí had little status within the college. His qualifications from Wilson College carried less weight than those of men from Haileybury or Eton. His name was never formally entered in the admissions register. One possible if surprising explanation is that he failed the matriculation examination of 1867.[5] Perhaps he was also viewed as an ex-heathen from a heathen land. Certainly the extensive records leave virtually no trace of his time in Canterbury, nor did the college record his later achievements. The warden maintained an avid correspondence with ex-students overseas – Rev. James Taylor, the missionary who had gone from St Augustine's to Bombay in 1865 and been so positive about Shápurjí's missionary potential, was in 1868 still writing from his new

---

[1] St Augustine's College, *Occasional papers 1858-1934*.
[2] C.C.A., A3/1/2 (file c.1860-1960).
[3] C.C.A., A2/5/4 (clippings 1849-1982).
[4] C.C.A., A3/3/15 (scrapbook c.1840-1880).
[5] Inf. from Anne M. Oakley, Senior Research Archivist, C.C.A.

home in Bombay with detailed accounts of the difficulties of 'evangelising the heathen'.[1] The college did not show the same interest in students who stayed in England. One of Shápurjí's main failings was that he broke the cardinal rule of the college – he did not sail away when he had finished. The fact that he became probably the first South Asian to hold an English living, a missionary amongst the working classes of the Midlands, inspired no pride in those who helped to bring it about.

Life at the college itself was almost monastic.[2] From the time that the community was woken by the tolling of a bell at 6 a.m. and students prepared to cross the cloister to the 7 o'clock service in the chapel, until evensong and the curfew bell at 10.30 p.m., this close-knit community (a 'band of brothers' as one ex-student described it) moved steadily through its strictly ordered existence. Weekday mornings were taken up largely with four hours of lectures and classes, on such subjects as ecclesiastical history, the catechism, Holy Scripture in the original languages, and the practical aspects of the pastoral role. They also included Greek and Latin classics, taught by Reverend Orger, the Vice-warden – Shápurjí may have been at a disadvantage here, though European languages were taught at the Elphinstone Institute he had attended in Bombay and he knew some Greek. Dr Rost's weekly visits extended the range of languages taught. Once a week, students retired to the nearby hospital, where there was teaching on medical subjects by Dr Lochée; one missionary later wrote back that this teaching had helped him to save hundreds of lives.[3]

When Shápurjí's training was finished, in the summer of 1868, he plunged into another battle. The terms of his scholarship were that he should go to some post in India, where he would be ordained. The S.P.G. dashed his hopes by deciding that for the time being he should only be given lay work. As ever, he determined to stand against the establishment for what he thought was right, however few his allies. He refused the post and set about finding work in England, applying for curacies far and wide. To St Augustine's this was treachery – the college could not afford to lose out in its competition with other missionary enterprises, which vied with each other to supply men for ministry overseas. He was refused a testimonial, and despite the fact that his conduct had been 'regular and diligent' the Reverend Orger labelled him 'disputatious' to outside

[1] St Augustine's College, Canterbury, *Occasional papers 1858--1934.*
[2] Henry Bailey, *Twenty Five Years of St Augustine's, Letter to Late Students.*
[3] Henry Bailey, *Twenty Five Years of St Augustine's, Letter to Late Students.*

enquirers.[1] This hostility did nothing to disarm the usual prejudices of the world beyond Canterbury. A Guildford rector informed St Augustine's that he liked Shápurjí's application for a curacy but that 'his name makes me fear he is not an Englishman'; if Shápurjí did not have a 'pure English accent' he would not 'suit my people'. [2]

In the teeth of the 'stain' in general and of the college's hostility in particular, Shápurjí battled to get a position. Finally a temporary solution was found. He would travel not east, but west – to Oxford. There he would apply for ordination as a deacon and take up a curacy in nearby Burford – paid for by his great supporter in Bombay, Charles Kirk. After that, the college assumed, he would go out to India for his ordination as a priest.

[1] C.C.A., U88 A2/7 C21A (Rev. E. R. Orger to Rev. W. W. How, September 1868).
[2] C.C.A., U88 A2/7 C21A (Robert Trimmer to St Augustine's College, 15 August 1868).

Shapurji Edalji as a clergyman

Kind permission of St Mark's church

St Clement's church, Toxteth

Hotbed

Although Oxford was swimming with would-be clergymen, it was an unnerving place for an Asian after the cloisters of St Augustine's. The first undergraduates from India were not to matriculate until three years later, and there were as yet very few of Shápurjí's compatriots around. The city was nevertheless teeming with ideas about South Asia and Britain's relationship with it. One towering figure in university life was Benjamin Jowett, who became Master at Balliol two years after Shápurjí's arrival. Jowett did much to reinforce the paternalistic view of empire: in one conversation he informed Florence Nightingale that he would like to rule the world through his pupils. His influence encouraged recruits from the middle class to join with the aristocracy as imperial administrators who would govern the empire in a humanist spirit. John Ruskin, who became Professor of Fine Art a few months after Shápurjí moved to Oxford, went further: in his inaugural lecture in 1870 he suggested that England 'must found colonies as fast and as far as she is able, formed of her most energetic and worthiest men...' Among Oxford's specialists on India was Sidney Owen, who had served for two years as Professor of History at Shápurjí's old college in Bombay, Elphinstone; Owen, who in 1864 became the first Reader of Indian History at Oxford University, believed British rule would provide the framework for the evangelisation of India. Even the Professor of Sanskrit, M. Monier Williams, who was born in Bombay, placed his expertise in the service of Christian imperialism: his inaugural lecture in Oxford was a plea for missionary organisations to arrange for the missionaries to learn Sanskrit so that they could engage in intellectual discussions with the Hindu pandits.

There was on the other hand the influence of yet another German Orientalist in Shápurjí's life, Friedrich Max Müller, Fellow of All Souls and Lecturer in Modern Languages and Comparative Philology; he lost out to the more orthodox Monier Williams in competition for the professorship of Sanskrit. Max Müller was a brilliant populariser of the study of the origins of languages and religions, and was responsible for such monumental work as the translation of Oriental documents in the series *The Sacred Books of the East*; Martin Haug's collaborator in Bombay and Munich, E. W. West, contributed Pahlavi translations to this series, and Shápurjí himself was known to this academic network. Max Müller's liberal view was encapsulated in the title of his defence of

Indian character, *India – What Can It Teach Us?*[1] He was not enthusiastic about the increasing number of Indians who came to study in Oxford in the 1880s – he thought they often went home with inappropriate and anglicised values. Indians admired his view that Anglo-Saxons, Teutons and Indians were all the same race – Aryan – but imperialists used it to justify imperial rule in India as a 'family reunion' – a return of the more vigorous Aryan branch to govern the branch whose energies had been sapped by climate.

It was against the backdrop of this debate about India that Shápurjí became entangled both in the global missionary plans of Oxford's competing Church of England factions and in the work of those researching his birthright religion, Zoroastrianism. The missionary certainties of St Augustine's had given some relief from the white heat of Bombay's religious controversies. Oxford, however, was another matter. This city's religious storms had blown across the whole land for three decades, and Shápurjí's fate there was to find himself tossed between the clutching hands of three very different giants in the struggle for revival in the Church of England: Richard Meaux Benson, charismatic young priest and inspiration behind the newly formed Society of St John the Evangelist, who himself belonged to the camp created by the Oxford Movement in the 1830s; 'Soapy Sam' – Samuel Wilberforce, Bishop of Oxford – who was High Church rather than Evangelical (unlike his famous father, William), but no supporter of the Oxford Movement; and Alfred Christopher, Rector at St Aldate's in the heart of the city, whose rectory was the engine-room of the Evangelical enterprise in Oxford.

It was Benson, minister at St John's in Cowley on the edge of Oxford, who drew Shápurjí to Oxford in the first place. The urge to carry forward the Anglican revival inspired by the Oxford Movement coursed through the veins of this extraordinarily energetic man. The Movement's most prominent leaders – John Keble, John Henry Newman, and E. B. Pusey – were all Oxford dons who aimed to rejuvenate the Church of England in the face of threats to its privileged position in national life; supporters of this Anglo-Catholic movement came to be called 'Tractarians', after the ninety tract manifestoes published between 1833 and 1841. The movement stressed the fact that the Church of England remained part of a universal Catholic Church; indeed, Newman eventually converted to Catholicism. Keble and Pusey remained, however, and the Tractarians had a permanent influence not just on

[1] Max Müller, *India – What Can It Teach Us?* Longmans & Co, 1883.

priests such as Benson but on lay figures from W. E. Gladstone to Lord Salisbury. Benson was nevertheless not so impressed with a development which had occurred when Tractarian ideas passed out of Oxford colleges and into the parish churches. This was the stress on the importance of ritual, which led many priests to bring back surplices and other outward symbols, and sharpened the anger of those who saw the Tractarians – or ritualists – as Roman Catholic in all but name.

Benson's greatest inspiration was E. B. Pusey, who undertook missionary work in England's slums. Benson himself had wider missionary ambitions – he dreamt of bringing the revived Anglicanism to the east. Already in 1859 he had written enthusiastically to Dr Bailey, the Warden at St Augustine's, to ask for the names of men who might join him in a devotional college in the north-west provinces of India. By 1866, however, he had moved on to a much larger project. With two others he founded the Society of St John the Evangelist, a celibate community for men. The 'Cowley Fathers' described themselves as a congregation of mission priests, and became the first stable men's community within the Church of England since the Reformation; the aim was to establish mission houses in India. The opening of the St John's mission house in Cowley in October 1868 gave Oxford a new centre of religious energy, and Benson had a hypnotic effect on those involved with the fledgling community. Most people addressed him as 'Father', and his personality was described by some as 'ecstatic', whilst one undergraduate who attended a retreat at Cowley in 1870 wrote of 'an ineffaceable memory of a man belonging to another world'.[1] As a part of the mission house, Benson also opened Benson's Hall, under licence from Oxford University. The hall was for men who wanted to prepare for ordination but could not afford college expenses. W. Butterfield, the Oxford Movement's leading architect, who had restored and enlarged St Augustine's in Canterbury as a theological college, was already supervising the building of a new Oxford University college, Keble. This college also aimed to help men needing assistance in entering into the ministry. Benson's Hall would not be needed for long.

Though its life was short, Benson's Hall provided Shápurjí with a useful stepping-stone. Thanks to Benson's approaches to St Augustine's, Shápurjí moved to the hall in late 1868, a potential catch for the Cowley Fathers' missionary dreams.[2] It gave him somewhere to stay as he prepared for ordination,

---

[1] M. V. Woodgate, *Father Benson*, Geoffrey Bles, 1953.
[2] O.R.O. c.249 (ordination candidates' papers, 1869).

though the High Church atmosphere among the early Cowley Fathers displayed little of the tolerance towards Indian aspirations and culture shown by Oxfordians like Max Müller: Benson later compared the Taj Mahal unfavourably with Keble College. Within a few years the Cowley Fathers were ministering to Eurasians and poor Indian Christians in Bombay. They also established mission houses in South Africa. Today the mother house is in Westminster.

From his Cowley base, Shápurjí looked to the Bishop of Oxford, Samuel Wilberforce, for his next career move. 'Soapy Sam' was an institution. He had been Bishop of Oxford for twenty-three years, and was a leading figure among orthodox Anglicans; he once collected signatures from 11,000 clergy in support of a declaration of orthodoxy. He had never committed himself to the Oxford Movement which had caused such a cataclysm in Oxford's religious life in the 1830s and 1840s. He had however faced head-on the second cataclysm in religious life which hit Oxford in the years just before Shápurjí's arrival; this was when he publicly denounced Charles Darwin's evolution thesis in *The Origin of Species*.[1]

Wilberforce had nevertheless given a mighty impetus to religious reform in his diocese. He was determined to see a revival of faith during his term in office, and he wanted zealous, hardworking men: Shápurjí Edaljí fitted that bill. At the time of his appointment as Bishop of Oxford in 1845 Wilberforce had found ordination practices lax and unsatisfactory, and he gradually introduced a far more rigorous process for applicants for ordination.[2] These were the procedures Shápurjí had to follow when in 1868 he applied from Benson's Hall for ordination as a deacon. In January 1869 his *de quis* was read in St John's Church, and Benson was one of those who signed a testimonial to his good character in support of his application. In February Reverend John Burgess of Burford nominated Shápurjí with a view to taking him on as a curate. Finally Shápurjí stood with other ordinands before the bishop for their big day. An Oxfordshire paper gave him a special mention:

Among the Deacons ordained by the Bishop of Oxford on Sunday was Mr. Shapurji Edulji – a Parsee, it might be presumed. In India there are a good many native clergymen, but Mr Edulji has not been set apart for the evangelisation of his own countrymen. He takes his place

[1] Standish Meacham, *Lord Bishop: The Life of Samuel Wilberforce 1805-73*, Harvard University Press, 1970, pp. 212-217.
[2] Ibid., p. 105.

among the clergy of England, and is appointed curate of Burford and Fulford.[1]

The beautiful village of Burford lies just under twenty miles from Oxford, and the church of St John the Baptist was described by *Jackson's Oxford Journal* as 'one of the noblest in the Diocese'.[2] The incumbent of this agricultural parish, the Reverend John Burgess, was attracted to the Tractarian Movement.[3] He was horrified at the fact that his dynamic Evangelical predecessor had turned the church into a meeting house. By the time Shápurjí arrived Burgess had already introduced a surpliced choir, and was planning radical structural repairs which would restore the Church to the traditional pattern. Shápurjí might have moved twenty miles, but he was still in the orbit of the group which had introduced him to Oxford: his former patron, Richard Meaux Benson, was invited to preach in Burford in June. The Reverend Mr Burgess not only gave Shápurjí no stipend, he also left him with little to do: Shápurjí conducted no baptisms or burials during his curacy. In March 1869, however, he did give a talk in the National Schoolroom which attracted the admiration of the local press. The subject was missionary work, and he explained that his aim was to prepare himself for the evangelisation of his fellow-countrymen, after a period gaining experience in an English parish. According to an Oxfordshire paper he 'gave a very clear account of the various forms of heathenism in India'.[4] Shápurjí's Christian patrons since John Wilson, the Bombay missionary who had converted him to Christianity in the 1850s, had clearly made an effective job of transforming their protégé's world-picture into a British one.

****

Shápurjí had now spent two years in three High Church institutions – St Augustine's College, Benson's Hall, and St John the Baptist in Burford and Fulford. Despite this he never fully suppressed within himself the Evangelical influences of his Bombay days with John Wilson. Indeed, even whilst still resident at the Anglo-Catholic Benson's Hall he had been drawn into treacherous fraternisation with the opposition. The Evangelicals in Oxford were as passionate as Benson about their version of Anglican revival, and soon after his arrival Shápurjí made contact with Alfred Christopher, Rector at the

---

[1] *Jackson's Oxford Journal*, 27 February 1869.
[2] *Jackson's Oxford Journal*, 5 June 1869.
[3] Raymond and Joan Moody, *The Book of Burford*, Barracuda Books, 1983, p. 42.
[4] *Jackson's Oxford Journal*, March 1869.

hotbed of evangelicalism in the city, St Aldate's. Christopher was an inspiration to hundreds of people anxious to 'bring a saving knowledge of the Gospel home to unawakened souls'. [1] One of his main aims was to arouse interest in foreign missions, and he was secretary to the Oxford association of the Church Missionary Society for nearly fifty years. He keenly attended lectures by such models of missionary activity as George Selwyn, Bishop of New Zealand and later the Bishop of Lichfield who preferred Shápurjí to a Staffordshire living. His dynamic leadership had produced a Sunday School attendance of over three hundred per week by the time Shápurjí arrived. As for his undergraduate following, a rectory room had to be built behind his house to cope with the numbers attending Bible meetings. He also held 'missionary breakfasts' which sometimes attracted over one hundred enthusiasts; attenders heard such speakers as Sir Bartle Frere, the Governor of Bombay who was so keen to build the missionary project in India and had followed Shápurjí's career there. Whilst Shápurjí was still involved with the Society of St John the Evangelist in Cowley in early 1869 he was part of this world of Canon Christopher. Perhaps he heard Christopher preaching or even participated in Christopher's weekly seminars for students. Certainly Christopher knew him well enough to write a testimonial for him when he applied for ordination. [2]

A few months earlier the Evangelical empire in Oxford had won significant new territory. In the parish of St Ebbe's, one of the poorest parts of the city, the old incumbent finally died; he had been rector for sixty years and described as 'insane' for fifty of them, but only death could get rid of him. His replacement in 1868, Edward Hathaway, was a key figure in Evangelical circles and founder of the Oxford Evangelical Trust; the Evangelicals were delighted to see him installed in the parish which butted on to St Aldate's. In 1869 he needed a curate at Holy Trinity church, in the southern part of his parish. The man he chose was Shápurjí, a possible building-block in the Christian Missionary Society project to evangelise India. By November Shápurjí was back from Burford and at work in the heart of Oxford.

Holy Trinity had been built in 1845 because the mother church in St Ebbe's had been filled to overflowing by the efforts of enthusiastic Evangelical clergy; the project had been dear to the hearts of Oxford's Evangelical community as it sought to

---

[1] J. S. Reynolds, *Canon Christopher of St Aldate's Oxford*, The Abbey Press, Abingdon, 1967.
[2] O.R.O., c. 250 (ordination candidates' papers, 1870).

spread its influence from the university to the parishes. By 1868, with the arrival of Hathaway, the whole of St Ebbe's parish had become a new focal-point for Evangelicalism. He simplified the interior of the church buildings, preached the doctrines of the reformed church, and quickly attracted back many of those who had drifted away to Holy Trinity in previous years.

When Shápurjí came to Holy Trinity, so close to the pulse of Evangelicalism in Oxford, he was making a final decision about his niche within the Church of England. There is no extant evidence that he ever actually called himself an Evangelical, but his interests, writings, and connections for the rest of his life all show that that was where his heart lay. Whilst he was at Holy Trinity the incumbent Robert Guinness left and was eventually replaced by the third leading Evangelical clergyman in Oxford in this period, Sidney Linton. Christopher and Hathaway (as well as Linton) appointed some notable curates in their time. To this group Shápurjí was not just a man of talent with Evangelical leanings but a future missionary to India. Christopher and his entourage were driving-forces in the Church Missionary Society, which had such a fierce interest in the evangelisation of Shápurjí's homeland. The C.M.S. at that time maintained three hundred and three ordained missionaries overseas, many of them in India, and one hundred and five were native to the countries they worked in.[1]

Even before his official departure, Guinness had left most of the occasional offices – baptisms, marriages, burials – to be carried out by his three curates, and in the interregnum before Linton's arrival they took on even more responsibility. Shápurjí played a large part: the parish registers show him baptising the children of craftsmen, labourers, and a servant and a porter working in Oxford University colleges.[2] In the midst of his duties, however, he had to be thinking of the next stage in his life. First of all he had to work on the documentation for his ordination as priest. In May 1869, three months after his ordination as deacon, he had already written from the vicarage in Burford to ask for a copy of the bishop's instructions for candidates for ordination as priests the following Lent, and by early 1870 his application was being formally processed.[3] Next he had to find himself a new curacy, and in January 1870 he was in New Bury, a district of Farnworth in Lancashire,

---

[1] *Jackson's Oxford Journal*, 13 February 1869.
[2] O.R.O., PAR/193/1/R2/3 (Holy Trinity baptisms register, 1868-74) and PAR/193/1/R5/1 (Holy Trinity burials register, 1849-73).
[3] O.R.O. c. 250 (ordination candidates' papers, 1870).

conducting four burials as he prepared for a move to the parish of St James'.[1]

These steps provoked a final showdown with St Augustine's College. In February 1870 the new Bishop of Oxford told Shápurjí personally that Henry Bailey had objected to his application for ordination. Bailey claimed that Samuel Wilberforce had ordained Shápurjí as deacon on the understanding that after a year as curate in Burford he would go back to Bombay to be ordained and serve under Charles Kirk.[2] Shápurjí wrote to Bailey to tell him politely that this was not the case – the understanding was that he would be ordained as priest in England and then go out to India.[3]

Whoever was right, it became increasingly clear that the longer he stayed in England the more Shápurjí thought he would stay longer. Charlotte Edalji suggested over thirty years later that Shápurjí had been advised whilst in Oxford that he should stay in England because his health had been so poor during his later years in India. In the end Shápurjí won his battle with St Augustine's and the college washed its hands of its failure; no attempt was made to keep in touch with his pioneer career.

Samuel Wilberforce's successor as Bishop of Oxford was John Fielder Mackarness, but the rigorous procedure which Shápurjí had to follow as candidate for ordination was no doubt that introduced by Wilberforce. Candidates were summoned to Cuddesdon College (founded by Wilberforce in 1854) a month in advance of their ordination, and requested to submit credentials for the exam a week before their arrival – the testimonial letters, a certificate of baptism, and a certificate of attendance at required university lectures.[4] Despite Wilberforce's requirements, no evidence was produced of Shápurjí's date of birth, presumably because he did not have any. Curiously, he was one of only two ordinands who had not sent in all the other necessary documentation right up to the last minute.[5] Later, shortly after he became Vicar of Great Wyrley, he was criticised for failing to keep up with the churchwardens' accounts. These two instances suggest that this conscientious and highly competent man was not at first quite comfortable with the demands of British bureaucracy.

---

[1] St James' parish registers (held by churchwarden).
[2] C.C.A., U88 A2/7 C21A (Samuel Wilberforce to Henry Bailey, 1 March 1869).
[3] C.C.A., U88 A2/7 C21A (Shápurjí Edalji to Henry Bailey, 7 February 1870).
[4] Standish Meacham, *Life of Samuel Wilberforce*, p. 105.
[5] O.R.O., c. 250 (ordination candidates' papers, 1870).

If Wilberforce's approach did continue under Mackarness, candidates in Lent 1870 would have met for three days at Cuddesdon College, and been subjected to three demanding days of questioning and prayer, with twice-daily addresses from the Bishop himself. The ordination ceremony itself was conducted in the parish church of Cuddesdon in March 1870; again, it was Wilberforce who had introduced the practice of holding ordinations in parish churches throughout the diocese.[1]

Shápurjí later made the remarkable claim, one which has until now never been reported apart from in a contemporary newspaper, that he was the first 'ordained native Indian clergyman in England'.[2] This fact may have made his pioneering career even more special but in 1870 he still faced another nervous time as he tried to break his way into the British establishment. Bishops such as Mackarness had some patronage, but otherwise had to cajole patrons into accepting the priests they had ordained, and if they could not the individual priests had to find a way in for themselves. Private patrons controlled nearly half the benefices, and for the Crown, and for collegiate and cathedral bodies, connection was more important than past achievement; only a few hundred benefices were in the charge of trustees who wanted the best man for the living they controlled. Overall, there was a shortage of livings in relation to the number of ordained priests. Shápurjí's chances were not good.

Still, he had fulfilled the ambition for which he had struggled virtually alone for many years: he was now an Anglican priest, and as an ordained priest he preached his farewell sermon at Holy Trinity before his move to Farnworth – the Reverend Sidney Linton noted the event in his log book.[3]

****

During this crucial year Shápurjí found time to produce two publications which provide intriguing commentary on his past and his present. The first, a discussion on Judaeo-Christian ethics entitled *The Sixth Commandment (A Sermon)*,[4] was the work of the man he had become, a Christian in England. The second, a translation into English of the Pandnamah, an ancient Zoroastrian work on morality, was the

---

[1] Standish Meacham, *Life of Samuel Wilberforce*, p. 105.
[2] *Bolton Chronicle*, 12 March 1870.
[3] O.R.O., PAR/193/9/J1/1 (Holy Trinity log book, 1870-1953, started by Linton).
[4] *Crockford's Clerical Directory*, 1872.

work of the person he had once been, a Parsi in Bombay.[1] This translation was from the Gujerati version and is evidence of the contacts he had with the network of European academics engaged in opening Zoroastrianism and other religions to the west. The Gujerati version which he translated had itself been translated from the Pahlavi original in response to the offer of a prize by the German scholar Martin Haug in Bombay in 1864. Even more prestigious for Shápurjí was his contact with that major Oxford figure Friedrich Max Müller, the Fellow of All Souls and Lecturer in Modern Languages and Comparative Philology who believed that the west could learn from India. It was Müller who asked Shápurjí to carry out the translation, and in gratitude he wrote a personal preface to Shápurjí's latest publication.[2]

Martin Haug's admirer and collaborator, E. W. West, would write in 1883 that as a translation of a translation, Shápurjí's work lost some of the meaning of the original; West himself had had a major influence on the study of Pahlavi literature in Bombay and may have known Shápurjí personally.[3] Whatever the quality of the translation, its publication in 1870 is the last evidence we have that Shápurjí felt some lingering affinity with the religion of his birth. That he should have been interested in a text which contained admonitions as to a man's moral duty is significant. His Christian learning may have made him see Zoroastrian moral teaching in a new light, both as of value in its own right and as an important influence on Christian ethics. The ancient Zoroastrian texts emphasised virtues such as truthfulness (Zoroastrians have had a reputation for honesty over the centuries) and liberality (the Parsis of Bombay were noted for their philanthropy, and they contributed to many civic and humanitarian projects, in similar ways to the Evangelicals of 19th-century Britain). Wisdom and learning were also stressed, and this made education very important in the life of a Zoroastrian; in later years Shápurjí made great sacrifices to ensure that his children were well educated. There is plenty of evidence of Shápurjí's strong sense of the morally correct in his later dealings as Vicar of Great Wyrley, sometimes to the point of cussed single-mindedness. It seems likely that this dimension of his value-system stemmed from his Zoroastrian

---

[1] Shápurjí Edaljí, *The Pand-Nameh, or a Book of Parsé Morality, translated into English from Gujarati.*

[2] W.S.L., 190/3/96, Shapurji Edalji to Rupert Sims, 25.2.1893, 'Letters to Rupert Sims', p. 21.

[3] Haug, M., *The Parsis, essays on their sacred language, writings and religion,* revised and amended by E. W. West, Kosmo Publications, New Delhi, 1978.

Parsi upbringing overlaid with Christian, particularly Evangelical, ethics.

****

The move from Burford to Holy Trinity in St Ebbe's parish in late 1869 was the first of a series of moves, from one curacy to another, over the next five years: St James', New Bury, in Farnworth in Lancashire (1870-2); St Thomas', Toxteth Park, Liverpool (1872); St Clement's, Toxteth Park (1872-3); St Levan in Cornwall (1873-4); St Thomas', Toxteth Park again (1874-5); and St Leonard, Bromley, in Middlesex (1875). In those five insecure years he passed before a series of vignettes of industrial England, and saw far more of the country than he was to see during his forty-two years as Vicar of Great Wyrley.

The problems newly-ordained priests faced in finding a living have already been mentioned. Shápurjí was, however, a committed and talented man, and the fact that he waited five years, was a curate in seven different parishes (in one of them twice), and eventually only obtained a living through the connections he acquired by his marriage, suggests that he faced more obstacles than most; when he applied for a curacy in Gateshead, for example, the incumbent wrote to St Augustine's to ask whether Shápurjí had 'any dialectic peculiarity'.[1] In every parish and diocese he passed through, Shápurjí had to recommence the awesome task of challenging popular beliefs about the world beyond its boundaries. It will be clear by now that he was tough enough to take on any such task.

The view from six pulpits

Generations have trod, have trod, have trod;
And all is seared with trade; bleared, smeared with toil

Gerard Manley Hopkins[2]

In March 1870 a *Bolton Chronicle* headline announced with excitement: 'A PARSEE APPOINTED TO THE CURACY OF ST JAMES'S, NEW BURY'.[3] No doubt prompted proudly by Shápurjí himself, the paper told its readers that he was the 'first

[1] C.A.C, U88 A2/7 C21A (Rev. John Day to St Augustine's College, 10 May 1875).
[2] Gerard Manley Hopkins, *God's Grandeur*, 1877, reprinted in W. H. Gardner and N. H. Mackenzie (eds), *The Poems of Gerard Manley Hopkins*, Oxford, 1967, p. 66.
[3] *Bolton Chronicle*, 12 March 1870.

ordained native Indian clergyman in England'. He had already conducted four burials at St James's on one day in January – a very practical form of interview process[1] – and his Evangelical leanings had helped to land him the job; the incumbent, the Reverend C. J. Stewart, was strongly opposed to the Oxford Movement and the ritualists. In April the *Bolton Chronicle* described Shápurjí's first day in office, when he preached 'an excellent and impressive extempore sermon to a full congregation'.[2] The environment in which he preached had been moulded by Stewart according to his Evangelical inclinations: the pulpit at which Shápurjí stood was more prominently placed than it is today; behind him, in the chancel, were the more prosperous members of the community; and before him sat the rest of the congregation of six hundred, with an unrobed choir in the gallery at the back of the church. Shápurjí's sermon, with its stress on the importance of seeking deliverance from the death everlasting, the death in hell, had a distinctly Evangelical tone.

The move from Oxford to New Bury in Farnworth in Lancashire had taken Shápurjí to the first of the series of scarred and smoking parishes which was to give him a comprehensive view of England's new industrial landscape. If one counts St Mary's in Ketley, seven of the nine churches he worked in from 1869 onwards had been built between 1838 and 1845 – his life was to be given to missionary work among the new working classes of the Midlands and North of England rather than among his compatriots in India. W. E. Gladstone, by 1870 Prime Minister, had led the way from Oxford to Farnworth: despite the support of Bishop Wilberforce, E. B. Pusey, and John Keble, he was defeated as M.P. for Oxford in 1865, and three years before Shápurjí's arrival in Lancashire became until 1868 M. P. for South Lancashire, the constituency in which Farnworth lay. At the opening of Farnworth Park in 1865 Gladstone gave some indication of the character of the town, complaining bitterly that the park would not be of much value until the 'labouring classes' of Farnworth could live in an atmosphere free of smoke.[3] In the springtime of Shápurjí's own arrival the problems faced by his parishioners were still only too clear: complaints about the noxious vapours from local chemical works were reaching a climax – indeed, the previous curate had left the parish for the good of his health,[4] and even today there are places where the land is still 'bleared, smeared' by 19th-century chemical waste. In April, moreover, two men were killed at one of the local

[1] St James' parish register (held by churchwarden).
[2] *Bolton Chronicle*, 9 April 1870.
[3] Bolton Archives and Local Studies Service, 906/CLA (H. Clare, 'The Farnworth of the Past', 14 parts, *Farnworth Journal*, 1935, part 8).
[4] *Bolton Chronicle*, 26 February 1870.

collieries, where accidents were frequent and often gruesome, and there was a dangerous fire in the engine room at one of the cotton mills.[1] Shápurjí had exchanged the spires of Oxford for a landscape overwhelmed by cotton-spinning mills, power loom mills, chemical works, coal mines, and an ironworks.

Farnworth was also Bridgewater territory. The Duke of Bridgewater, who in 1761 had opened Britain's first canal, from Worsley to Manchester, and linked it by subterranean waterways to his Farnworth coal mines three miles away,[2] was the owner of Farnworth Hall. In the early 19th century Farnworth became a cotton town too – it is now a satellite of Bolton, itself the home of Samuel Crompton, inventor of the spinning mule (1779), which helped to turn the Lancashire cotton industry into Britain's leading manufacturing industry. Indeed, it was the Lancashire cotton industry's new dependence on India for cotton during the American Civil War which had helped to create a boom in Bombay in the early 1860s, just before Shápurjí's departure for England. These circumstances led to even more direct connections between Bolton and Bombay, for by 1874 there were at least two Parsis working in the Bolton textile industry. One of them was to commit suicide in bizarre circumstances the following year. This 21-year-old man, Dorabjee Dashai, had travelled from Bombay to Bolton to study the new machinery of the textile industry with a view to setting up a factory in his home city. He managed to fall in love with a young Bolton woman to whom he had never spoken, but on making enquiries he was told he had no chance of winning her. Shortly afterwards his body was fished out of a local reservoir. The *Daily Telegraph* pulled out the usual stereotype of Parsis to make a meal of the case: 'Not for the world,' it declared, 'would we think that an English maiden could willingly see even a fire-worshipper perish for her sake.' This young man, 'bent on outvying Lancashire cotton-lords,' had fallen victim to a 'Lancashire witch'.[3]

In the 1830s, coalminers in the New Bury district of Farnworth employed by the trustees of the Duke of Bridgewater had become anxious about the lack of a church or even a Sunday school in their growing township. Two of them walked hundreds of miles, even cap in hand to the condescending Lady Francis Egerton of the Duke of Bridgewater's family, to collect money to build St James' National School, which opened in 1840.[4] The school was used for church services until St James' Church itself

---

[1] *Bolton Chronicle*, March-April 1870, passim.
[2] B. T. Barton, *History of Farnworth and Kearsley*, Bolton, The Daily Chronicle Office, 1887, p. 13.
[3] Cited in *Bolton Journal*, 23 October 1875.
[4] *Bolton Chronicle*, 16 August 1862; H. Clare, 'The Farnworth of the Past', part 7.

was built between 1862 and 1865 (the delay may have been due to the crisis in the cotton industry caused by the American Civil War), and by the 1870s there was a congregation of six hundred.[1] It was in fact in areas such as this that the Church often struggled hardest to maintain congregations. Miners who spent large parts of their lives underground, or textile workers, many of them women, caged in the mill for up to fifty-eight hours a week, had little time to consider the plea by Gerard Manley Hopkins that we should restore a sense of the 'grandeur of God' to a world which has become 'bleared, seared with toil'. In 1851 Bolton came in the bottom five in the country for Church of England attendance – the new industrial working class was interested in the Church for rites of passage but not much more.[2]

The Reverends Mr Stewart and Mr Edaljí did their best to maintain the profile of the Church in this unpromising environment, notably during the annual church procession, which they headed as it wound its way between the pit-shafts and smoking chimneys.[3] For two years Shápurjí learnt his trade here, though Stewart maintained control of some of the duties which many vicars left largely to their curates. Shápurjí conducted only about half of the baptisms and burials, some of the baptisms being of children born to unmarried mothers at the workhouse, and a substantial number of the burials being of people who died in the workhouse. He also conducted two weddings within four months of his arrival, and on both occasions signed his name with the Gujerati accents – 'Shápurjí Edaljí' – instead of the simple 'Shapurji Edalji' which he was to adopt soon afterwards as part of the gradual process of anglicisation. By November 1871 he was preaching his stern farewell sermon, on the text 'You then, my son, be strong in the grace that is in Christ Jesus' (2 Timothy, chap. ii, v. 1).[4] His eighteen months in Farnworth had taught him much: he was no radical, but the humanitarian concern of the Evangelicals for the suffering of the working classes was needed more acutely there than in his first two parishes.

****

Carrying his newly accent-free name along with him, Shapurji Edalji passed to the next leg of his round-England tour. His journey took him westward, where he was to be sucked into another famous Evangelical net in another sea of religious

[1] Canon H. O. Fielding, *The Parish of St James, New Bury, Farnworth*, 1965, p. 4.
[2] Leslie Gent, *Bolton Past*, Phillimore, 1995, p. 59.
[3] *Bolton Chronicle*, 18 June 1870.
[4] *Farnworth Observer*, 25 November 1871.

ferment – Liverpool. The controversies stirred by Oxford dons from their cloisters in the 1830s and 1840s had taken on another dimension when they reached Liverpool. Here bitter conflict between Evangelical and ritualist was fuelled by the huge Irish presence, particularly after the potato famine of 1845-1846. Ulster Protestants filled the pews of the mainstream churches, whilst new Roman Catholic churches sprang up across the city. Pillar of the Evangelical cause for decades was Hugh McNeile, the Irish Protestant demagogue; he had recently left to become Dean of Ripon after thirty-three years in Liverpool, but his shadow still fell across all that Shapurji did during his stay in the city. McNeile, who condemned popery 'as a religious heresy and as a political conspiracy,'[1] had been at the heart of the campaign against the ritualists; a whole generation of working class Protestants in Liverpool was reared on a diet of anti-Catholic, anti-Irish rhetoric, and this led to some nasty scenes. In 1869 a mob gathered to abuse the congregation at St Margaret's in Toxteth, where services were clearly ritualist; one group broke inside the building and tried to rush the clergy conducting the service.

Shapurji had been nominated to a city centre curacy, at St Mark's on Upper Duke Street, next to the site of today's enormous Anglican cathedral.[2] The Irish incumbent, Rev. Drummond Anderson, labelled by a local journal as having an 'open, Celtic audacity about him', was very much in McNeile's camp; he was said 'in appearance, manner, delivery, method, thought and belief' to bear a striking likeness to his former leader.[3] For some reason Shapurji's nomination as curate was not confirmed and he had to spend five anxious, impecunious months looking for a new appointment. In the meantime he involved himself in the life of St Mark's and thus got a first taste of the cosmopolitan Christianity of England's second port.

A few hundred yards below the church the river Mersey flowed towards the sea, carrying thousands of ships to their worldwide destinations and back; 19,186 entered Liverpool in the year ending in July 1874.[4] Lines of docks stretched north as far as the shipyards, and south through Toxteth; one of the nearest to St Mark's was the Duke's dock, built by the Duke of Bridgewater in the 1760s to handle goods travelling along his

---

[1] P. J. Waller, *Democracy and Society in Liverpool 1868--1939*, Liverpool University Press, 1981, p. 11.
[2] The nomination papers (November 1871) are included in L.D.R.O., 283 DIO 233/26 (nomination and letters testimonial of Rev. Shapurji Edalji to stipendiary curacy of St Thomas, March 1872).
[3] *The Porcupine*, 8 April 1865.
[4] *Official Guide and Album of the Cunard Steamship Service*, Sutton Sharpe, 1876, p. 107.

canal, the canal whose eastern end was linked with his Farnworth coal-mines. It was here, by the river, that Liverpool's Irish population was concentrated: 'The whole line of docks, extending nearly six miles, swarms with Irish life,' as one contemporary put it.[1] One of the Rev. Mr Anderson's passionate concerns was with the downside of Liverpool's sea-carried wealth. A city dependent on sailors for its well-being was also a city full of orphans, and the Seaman's Orphanage Institution struggled to pick up the pieces for children whose fathers had been lost to the all too frequent shipwrecks, or to disease or injury, or to the impoverished insecurity of many sailors' lives. Shapurji watched as Anderson gathered anguished accounts of individual cases to try to prod Liverpool's more prosperous citizens into action.[2]

After this brief induction into the world of Liverpool, Shapurji's cause was adopted by a man who was to help transform his life; in April 1872 Rev. Reginald Yonge welcomed him as curate at St Thomas on Warwick Street in Toxteth.[3] The church was further south from the centre than St Mark's, but its clear view of the river provided constant reminder of the Bombay scenes of Shapurji's childhood and youth. Within the parish lay Brunswick Dock. St Thomas was a marine parish.

The estate which the church largely served was filled with people of so many nationalities that one journalist described it as a 'Lilliputian principality'.[4] Indeed quite apart from the Irish community Liverpool as a whole was Britain's most cosmopolitan city outside London, though far from being a Bombay. Its involvement in the slave trade meant there had long been an African presence, but the opening up of routes to South Asia in the second half of the 19th century, after John Gladstone (father of W. E. Gladstone) had sent the first ship from Liverpool, led to the arrival of lascars (Asian sailors) from the sub-continent. Joseph Salter, a Christian missionary working among people from beyond Europe who had landed in Britain, met nine of them during his investigations of 1867,[5] and perhaps Shapurji met some of them too. As Toxteth was close to the dockland there were also many Irish immigrants there. Shapurji, who was appalled by the way the Roman Catholic

[1] Hugh Heinrich, 'The Irish in England', in *The Nation*, 1872, cited in Graham Davis, *The Irish in Britain 1815-1914*, Gill & Macmillan, p. 118.
[2] *The Porcupine*, 27 January 1872, 4, 11 and 25 July 1874.
[3] Chester Record Office, CRO EDA 1/X (licensing of curates).
[4] 'South End Etchings', *The Liverpool Critic*, 3 February 1877.
[5] Joseph Salter, *The Asiatic in England; Sketches of Sixteen Years' Work among Orientals*, Seeley, Jackson, and Halliday, 1873, pp. 230-233.

Church was still ground down by the 'yoke of ceremonies',[1] joined McNeile and other Ulster Protestants in clenching his teeth at the strength of the opposition in his new home town.

Toxteth itself was one of the suburbs of Liverpool which were mushrooming as a result of the city's rapid development. The 18th century growth, based on tobacco, sugar, and the slave trade, was now giving way to development based on the industrial expansion of Lancashire – raw cotton from the USA and finished goods from the cotton mills of Farnworth, Bolton, and the rest of Lancashire passed through Liverpool. There were some prosperous corners with elegant houses in the burgeoning suburbs of Liverpool east of Parliament Street and Upper Parliament Street. There was also massive poverty, with some appalling working-class housing rushed up in the decades before Shapurji's arrival. Much of this housing has now disappeared, as has St Thomas itself.

It has often been said of Liverpool that every brick in the city was cemented with the blood of a slave,[2] and that included bricks for churches. St Thomas had been built in 1840-1 by Sir John Gladstone and humbly named after his own father.[3] The money he so kindly gave for church-building came from the labour of his slaves on his sugar plantations in the West Indies (some were flogged to death after an insurrection in 1823) and from the growing imperialism of the east – he owned the first ship from Liverpool to trade directly with India.[4] His commercial drive did not give way to other-worldly piety when he passed through the doors of his new churches; these churches appeared in his balance-sheets as part of his capital, and his pew rents brought him a 5% return on his investment.[5] His son, William Ewart Gladstone, used his maiden speech in the House of Commons in 1833 to defend his father against the accusation that he had systematically worked his slaves to death. This younger Gladstone was in fact one of those who signed the deed of endowment for St Thomas in 1841, and as patron of the church thirty-one years later might perhaps have heard of Shapurji's appointment, though he did have other things on his mind: a month before Shapurji moved to St

---

[1] Shapurji Edalji, *Lectures on St Paul's Epistle to the Galatians*, Midlands Educational Company, 1879.
[2] Peter Fryer, *Staying Power*, p. 33.
[3] *V.C.H. Lancashire*, vol. iii. p. 43; S. G. Checkland, *The Gladstones: a family biography 1764-1851*, Cambridge University Press, p. 294.
[4] Sarah Searight, *Steaming East*, p. 123.
[5] E. J. Feuchtwanger, *Gladstone*, Allen Lane, 1975, p. 5.

Thomas, Gladstone had been defeated after what was to be the first of his four terms as Liberal Party Prime Minister.[1]

Shapurji was left by the Reverend Mr Yonge to conduct most of the baptisms, marriages, and burials. The parish registers show that he did now see himself as 'Shapurji' – he never used the signature 'Shápurjí' again. His entries trace the lives of the families of workers connected with the docklands and shipbuilding yards – dock labourers, sailors, shipwrights, riggers, joiners.[2] Most members of these families lived short, strenuous lives; the labour of a dock worker was even more wearing than that of workers in a foundry or a mine, and many were dead by the time they were fifty

****

After six months, Shapurji moved on again – though not very far. His next curacy was not much more than a mile away, at St Clement's, also in Toxteth. The parish of St Clement's had some wealthy corners, but a great deal of extreme poverty too. Although it was slightly further from the river than St Thomas and had a rather more varied economic base, its destinies were still tied to shipping and the docks. Several rope-making businesses opened during the 19th century,[3] and parishioners included mariners, shipwrights, and sail-makers.[4]

St Clement's church was built in 1840, with room for over a thousand people, and was very much a hotbed of Evangelicalism in Shapurji's time. Even today the pulpit is still the dominant focal-point, partly obliterating the view of the altar and reflecting the Evangelical rallying-cry 'the word before the sacrament'. One of the key figures in the development of the church was Hugh McNeile, the famous Irish Evangelical, who was incumbent of a nearby parish until 1868. As a trustee at St Clement's, McNeile had been involved in 1857 in the appointment of the incumbent of Shapurji's time, Herbert Woodward, whose staunchly Protestant Evangelical preaching packed the church each week.[5] Despite the fact that he was nearing retirement, Woodward kept control of many of the occasional offices, particularly weddings, with Shapurji getting the leftovers.[6]

---

[1] L.R.O., 283 Dio 233/1 (deed of endowment for St Thomas, 1841).
[2] L.R.O., parish register files THM (St Thomas's).
[3] David Pope, 'History of the church, parish and schools of St Clement's, 1841-1991' (copy in L.R.O.), pp. 7-8.
[4] L.R.O., parish registers 283 CLE (St Clement's).
[5] David Pope, 'History of the church, parish and schools of St Clement's', p. 23.
[6] L.R.O., parish registers 283 CLE (St Clement's).

So it was that Shapurji served his time in yet another parish still with no clear future. Aged thirty, unmarried, living on a stipend of £120 per year,[1] he had no guarantee of ever securing his own living. A life as a lonely curate beckoned, not only cut off from his family in India but also eternally crossing England, from one parish to the next.

[1] Chester Record Office, CRO EDA 1/X (licensing of curates).

3. Looters and conquerors

10. 45 a.m., 11 November 1997. Staffordshire County Record Office is completely still. We waxwork researchers sit motionless at our desks, glued forever to parish registers, ancient village maps or, in my case, Edalji treasures. Then an archivist steps forward, creeps to each of us in turn. Her whispered words stir us from our trances one by one: 'We'll be having two minutes' silence for Armistice Day at 11 o'clock,' she announces.

The two minutes' silence does have a different quality; it is supposed to be reflective, and by now I am a Quaker of sixteen years' standing for whom periods of reflective silence are quite familiar. It is nevertheless the same silence, outwardly, as that which went before and that which comes after. It is a silence I need, like a drug. Having departed abruptly from the education system as a result of interacting waves of stress and ankylosing spondylitis I can bear neither to sit at home brooding nor to go out and mix with others. Silent record offices are cocoons, safe havens from the present. The Edalji family saves me from myself.

And so I find you, Maud. In the stillness of record offices across the land I find that it is you who holds all these stories together. More than that: I find that you can tell us things which no researcher has so far dreamed of.

Archivist

It was in Walsall Record Office that I had my first glimpse through the windows of that little house in Welwyn Garden City in which George and Maud lived out their last years. Here, in an unexpected memoir, an old girl of Queen Mary's High School in Walsall reported how 'Miss Connie', former art mistress at the school and sister of the Headteacher of Maud's day, used to visit her friend Maud in the 1930s. The author heard from Miss Connie how the walls of the tiny Welwyn Garden City drawing-room were covered with family pictures, and how Maud would proudly point them out to visitors: 'This is my cousin, my Grandmother, my uncle, another cousin, my aunt, my Grandfather, and so on.' According to Miss Connie, her 'mother's people were exceptionally English' in appearance.[1]

There they all were on the Welwyn walls: the photographs of pre-1903 George, a George without glasses, the young lawyer looking calmly towards his promising future; the photograph of the Edalji family at Easter 1892, just weeks away from the start of the troubles which would darken the rest of their lives; the photograph of Shapurji, the fresh-faced young priest; the charcoal and colour-wash portrait of Reverend John Compson of Great Wyrley, Charlotte's uncle, drawn by Charlotte in her youth; the miniature painting of the Reverend Edward Bate Compson, John Compson's brother, the man who had conducted Charlotte's and Shapurji's wedding service; the childhood samplers by Charlotte and her sister, the reds and greens of the embroidery still bright and fresh; the Stoneham coat-of-arms; and the treasured portraits of earlier Stonehams, including one of her great-great-grandfather, Thompson Stoneham, who was a J.P.[2]

The mother and grandmother of this Thompson Stoneham had in the mid-18th century moved upmarket from their Stepney roots to make Little Baddow in Essex the family seat for generations to come. So it was that when Maud prepared for death by arranging for the dispersal of her family archive she turned to Essex Record Office. She offered not only the portraits from the Stoneham side, but also nigh on two hundred and fifty years' worth of documents inherited via her mother from the Stonehams and two related clans, the Thompsons and the Swans. Sadly the Record Office could not accept the portraits; they were too large, and were later destroyed. The document collection was kept though, and when I finally went to Chelmsford to inspect it the full significance of the lives of Maud's English ancestors tumbled out. The fulcrum of the whole story was the Thompson Stoneham of the beloved portrait.

---

[1] W.L.H.C., 246/38 ('Queen Mary's High School, Miss Barbara Foxley, and The Edalji Case').
[2] E.R.O., D/DU 226/30, 31 (lists of children of Catherine and Thompson Stoneham, 1849).

Mariners and their money

This tablet is placed here
As a tribute of duty and affection
By Lieut Colonel A Stoneham of the Hon,ble East India
Companys Service
To the memory of his much beloved father and mother
whose remains are interred
In the family vault in this Chancel.
THOMPSON STONEHAM Esq
late of Whitwells in this Parish
and one of His Majestys Justices of the Peace
for this County
who died July 20th 1780 aged 48
and CATHERINE his widow
who died Nov 19th 1800
aged 62

Inscription in the chapel of St Mary the Virgin church, Little
Baddow, Essex, c.1830

Even in his scarlet tunic, ten-year-old Thompson Stoneham would scarcely have caught the eye in the streets of 1740s Bombay. That youthful rainbow of a town, flung together in just eighty years by the ambition of the British East India Company, was simply built out of colour. The seven boggy islands acquired by the British in 1662 when Charles II married a Portuguese princess had soon become an urban magnet. Most of the 50,000 or more inhabitants of Thompson Stoneham's time had flocked in from elsewhere, bringing with them a vivid diversity of dress, language, and religion, most as yet largely untainted by western influence. On the streets, alongside young Thompson, were thousands of settlers from the Bombay hinterland – Hindu bankers and traders, Muslim weavers from Ahmedabad, Jains, Parsi shipbuilders from the Gujerat; particularly distinctive were the Parsi men, with their smocks, trousers, small slippers, shawls, and stiff turbans. Overseas migrants were there too, from along the world trade-routes which radiated from Bombay's harbour – Chinese, Jews, Arabs, and slaves from East Africa and Madagascar imported by Arab traders. As for the Europeans,

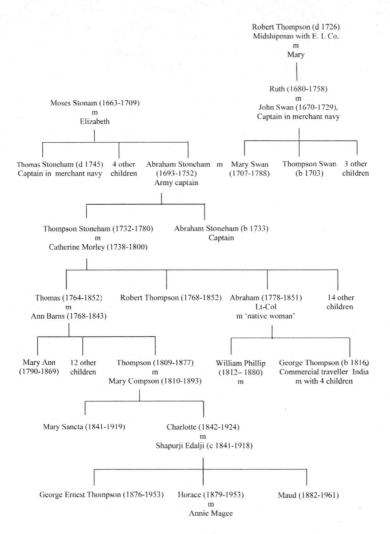

Robert Thompson (d 1726)
Midshipman with E. I. Co.
m
Mary

Ruth (1680-1758)
m
John Swan (1670-1729),
Captain in merchant navy

Moses Stonam (1663-1709)
m
Elizabeth

Thomas Stoneham (d 1745)   4 other   Abraham Stoneham m Mary Swan   Thompson Swan   3 other
Captain in merchant navy   children   (1693-1752)   (1707-1788)   (b 1703)   children
                                           Army captain

Thompson Stoneham (1732-1780)   Abraham Stoneham (b 1733)
m   Captain
Catherine Morley (1738-1800)

Thomas (1764-1852)   Robert Thompson (1768-1852)   Abraham (1778-1851)   14 other
m   Lt-Col   children
Ann Barns (1768-1843)   m 'native woman'

Mary Ann   12 other   Thompson (1809-1877)   William Phillip   George Thompson (b 1816)
(1790-1869) children   m   (1812– 1880)   Commercial traveller India
                       Mary Compson (1810-1893)   m   m with 4 children

Mary Sancta (1841-1919)   Charlotte (1842-1924)
m
Shapurji Edalji (c 1841-1918)

George Ernest Thompson (1876-1953)   Horace (1879-1953)   Maud (1882-1961)
m
Annie Magee

Thompson, Swan, Stonam/Stoneham
and Edalji families

they included the descendants of the Portuguese residents of pre-British days, along with a more recently arrived Greek community. They also included the British themselves, described by Myriam Kaye as 'perhaps the least prepossessing ingredient of this melange', at least in the early days of the colony.[1] The British contingent was made up largely of merchants (like Thompson's uncle, Thomas Stoneham), sailors (one of Thompson's great-uncles had sailed on an East India Company ship), soldiers (Thompson's father, Abraham, was a captain in the service of the Company), and other personnel supporting the Company's drive to exploit Bombay's strategic advantage as an entrepot along its trade-route to the East[2]; these included attorney John Morley, friend of Thompson's father and member of Bombay Council, whose five-year-old daughter Catherine had been born in the city.[3]

However much his small frame may have merged into Bombay's vivid bustle, young Thompson was far from faceless in his own family. Indeed, the family had some years earlier begun the process of investing its whole future in this one boy. His great-uncle, Robert Thompson of Stepney, a mariner with the East India Company, had left him money in his will; his father's brother, Captain Thomas Stoneham, also of Stepney, had made such a pile as a Bombay merchant that he could leave him the huge sum of £5,000; and his grandmother, Ruth Swan (née Thompson), was later to bequeath him half her South Sea stock, acquired largely through her husband's career as a mariner based in Stepney.

The investment in Thompson Stoneham was not just financial; his very name pinned to him the pride and hopes of two ancestries. The use of the surname Thompson as a first name was not an act of eccentricity. His great-grandfather, Robert Thompson, grandfather of his mother Mary, was a man the family wished to remember, a treasured symbol of a breeding-ground of mariners, the stuff of the East India Company's success. As for Abraham Stoneham, in passing on his surname to his son he was passing on several hundred years of pride, for the family traced the name Stoneham back to ancestors who fought in the Crusades.

On his death in 1780 Thompson Stoneham left no rupees, no medals, no sailor's mementos. He did, nevertheless, leave a

---

[1] Myriam Kaye, *Bombay and Goa*, Collins, 1989, p. 31.
[2] Except where indicated, references to the Thompson and Stoneham families in this chapter are from E.R.O., D/DU 226 (deeds of the Stoneham family).
[3] *East India Company Registers, Page: FHL Film 052382*, B.L.

life worthy of a plaque in the parish church in Little Baddow. The boy who had walked the streets of Bombay in a red tunic had married the Catherine Morley he had known since his Bombay childhood and had ended his days in another world, as landowner, gentleman farmer and respected J. P. in the Essex countryside. The mercantile wealth of his ancestors had allowed his grandmother Ruth and mother Mary to move out of London in the 1750s to take possession of a new family estate. As a result, Thompson's legacy to his family included three horses, five cows, seventeen pigs, and over forty-three acres of land. Catherine survived him, as did twelve of their fourteen children. One carried the famous ancestral name, Robert Thompson. There was also another Abraham, born in 1778.

****

Forty years later a notable birth was registered in Gorakhpur in north east India. Like his grandfather, the J.P. of Little Baddow, the baby in the registry office carried the name Thompson – George Thompson Stoneham. Unlike his grandfather, however, George did not bear the hopes of a dynasty. Indeed, he was already nearly two years old and yet it was only then, in 1818, that his father, the 40-year-old Captain Abraham Stoneham, had arranged the christening. The reason for the baby's near two years of oblivion was suggested in the register of births: the parents, it announced baldly, were 'Abraham Cpt 29th N.I. and a native woman'.[1] Little George had an older brother, William Phillip, and the register entry for his birth had described their mother in exactly the same way.

According to family legend, she was a maharaja's daughter who had once nursed Abraham after he had been badly injured, and they did actually marry.[2] Whether this is true or not, the disdainful anonymity bestowed on her by the authorities reflected the growing British feeling of superiority over the peoples of South Asia in the early 19th century: Charles Grant, a British historian, had in 1792 described the Indian people as 'a race of men lamentably degenerate and base, retaining but a feeble sense of moral obligation... governed by a malevolent and licentious passion...'[3] Abraham himself was quite willing to smother his son's origins in a western name. Indeed, despite the shame attached to the circumstances of his new paternity,

---

[1] B.L., Oriental and India Office Collections, L/Mil/9/107/F89 (Cadet 1799).
[2] Inf. via Liz Thompson (Stoneham descendant) from the daughter of Ivy Genevieve Stoneham, 5 May 2006.
[3] Cited in Dilip Haro, *Black British, White British*, Grafton Books, 1991, p. 5.

all his family pride flowed into his choice – George Thompson Stoneham.

Abraham Stoneham's ancestors, whether Thompson, Swan or Stoneham, had been 'looters and conquerors' according to Salman Rushdie's description, collaborators in the establishment of empire: as mariners and merchants they had built commercial links with India, and as sailors and soldiers of the East India Company they had helped maintain the first British bases such as Bombay. Now, in the early 19th century, Abraham's role was that of conqueror and ruler as the British extended their sway over large parts of the sub-continent. He had been wounded in the war against the Mahrattas in 1803; thanked by General Sir George Hewett for killing, dispersing or subduing members of a band of dacoits (robbers) in April 1809; made Captain in 1812; and then appointed superintendent of the Pindarry chiefs and superintendent of the northern border from Gorakhpur to the Nepal territories. His career progressed further after his sons were born; he was made Lieutenant-Colonel of the 69th regiment in 1825, and appointed to the command of the 53rd regiment Bengal native infantry in 1828.[1]

Abraham's family and Little Baddow roots always remained important, however, despite his quarter-century in India, as his choice of name for his son George Thompson Stoneham showed. On his return to Little Baddow as Lieutenant Colonel he gave expression to his pride again, this time by paying for a plaque to be erected in the parish church; it was in memory of his father, the Thompson Stoneham who as a boy had walked through Bombay in his red tunic, and his mother, Catherine, herself born in Bombay.

What did you make of all this, Maud? Would you say, with Salman Rushdie, that these 'years of looting and conquest 'left a stain upon' your family? I don't think so. You looked at Thompson Stoneham's face on your wall, so 'exceptionally English' in appearance, and you were proud of him and all your forebears, not ashamed of the long-term consequences of their deeds. You had understandings of many worlds, and your experiences in George's case made you more aware of the effects of British imperialism than most, but you were no critic.

---

[1] *Essex Herald*, 29 April, 1851.

Growing up

It was in July 1842 that the Reverend Thompson Stoneham, nephew of Lieutenant Colonel Abraham Stoneham and grandson of the Thompson Stoneham who had served as a magistrate in Little Baddow, stood at the font of St Mary's church in Ketley to wet the head of his second daughter and baptise her Charlotte Elizabeth Stuart Stoneham; this was the future Charlotte Edalji. Near to him, no doubt, were Charlotte 's mother, Mary (née Compson), and Charlotte's sister, Mary Sancta. On the front pews were other members of the Compson and Stoneham families – among them perhaps the William Phillip Stoneham and the George Thompson Stoneham whose Indian mother was not worthy of a name in British eyes. Behind them were the parishioners of Ketley. Whereas the Compsons and Stonehams at the front were descended from gentry, the parishioners further back were mainly from families connected with the local coal mines, ironworks, and associated trades.[1]

The church in which these two social worlds met had opened only four years earlier, as part of the 19th century outburst of new church-building which sought to bring Christianity to England's new industrial communities.[2] The patron, the 2nd Duke of Sutherland, had not only had the church built but also appointed the Reverend Mr Stoneham as the first incumbent. He was not disappointed by his choice; after attending a service incognito in 1839, he recorded his opinion that Stoneham's sermon was fair and unexaggerated, and that the singing was reminiscent of the Kirk – a hint at the Evangelical flavour of the Vicar's Anglicanism.[3]

Although much of Ketley's land was still owned by this one aristocratic dynasty, most of the congregation at St Mary's owed their way of life to a rather different set of magnates – the famous Darby family from near Dudley in Staffordshire. After taking over an ironworks at Coalbrookdale in Shropshire in 1708 this family had led the transformation of an area with a four mile radius into Britain's most important iron-making region, the cradle of the Industrial Revolution. In the cradle lay Ketley, where in the 1750s the Darbys, members of Britain's growing entrepreneurial class, leased coal mines from Earl Gower, of the old aristocracy, one of whose descendants was to become the 1st

[1] Details of the Stoneham and Compson families are from S.S.R.C., P149 (Ketley parish registers).
[2] John Hassell, 'Ketley Township 1838-1988', 1988 (copy in S.R.R.C.).
[3] *V.C.H. Shropshire* xi. p. 274.

Duke of Sutherland.[1] In 1756 they constructed two iron furnaces in the village, again on land leased from Earl Gower.[2]

A third furnace had been added by 1768,[3] and a forge was built in 1785. A new community of coal miners and iron workers sprang up around these enterprises. In 1818 a new company, the Ketley Company, took over the furnaces and the forge,[4] and so Ketley, where 80% of employed people in 1821 were miners or industrial workers, remained in the grip of one small clique.[5] By 1838 Thompson and Mary Stoneham, both the children of gentry, found themselves in Ketley serving the spiritual needs (as they saw them) of the new industrial working class of the Midlands.

Thompson Stoneham's feelings about his family's place in the world were eventually to be passed on to the daughter he baptised in 1842. Having an ancestor as a J.P. cemented the Stonehams' sense of belonging to England's ruling class, and their sense of being English was underlined by their Church of England roots, though in Charlotte's case it was to be made more acute by her marriage. Equally important was their feeling that their family had always been on the side of the true faith, from as long ago as the period of struggle with Islam over the 'Holy Land' in the Middle Ages – described by Alfred Crosby as 'Western Europe's first imperialistic attempts in Asia'.[6] When Charlotte's family became involved in the 'looting and conquest' of India from the late 17th century they were building on existing family foundations.

With such origins, the route to a clerical career enjoyed by Charlotte's father, the Reverend Thompson Stoneham (1809-1877), had been a traditional one. His own father, Thomas, inherited much of the first Thompson Stoneham's Essex estate, and with this springboard the younger Thompson Stoneham carried the family name into new fields. The south-east was the centre of gravity for recruitment to the Anglican establishment, and from Little Baddow he went to study at Peterhouse College, Cambridge; ordination was the expected destination of over half of all Oxbridge graduates at that time.

---

[1] Barrie Trinder, *The Darbys of Coalbrookdale*, Phillimore, 1974, p. 20; *V.C.H. Shropshire* xi. p. 271.
[2] *V.C.H. Shropshire* xi. p. 271.
[3] Barrie Trinder, *The Darbys of Coalbrookdale*, p. 27.
[4] *V.C.H. Shropshire* xi. p. 272.
[5] *V.C.H. Shropshire* xi. p. 269.
[6] Albert Crosby, *Ecological Imperialism: The Biological Expansion of Europe 900--1900*, Cambridge University Press, 1986, p. 58.

**Portrait of Rev. John Compson by his niece
Charlotte Stoneham, later Charlotte Edalji**

He was a shy man, but a leading scholar at his college, and won the theological prize for his year. He was much more than a traditionalist, however, for he was inspired by one of the most significant sources of renewal in Christianity in Britain at that time – the Evangelical revival.[1]

The Evangelical movement within the Church of England, spearheaded from the 1790s by Charles Simeon, Vicar of Holy Trinity in Cambridge, originated as a reaction against the slackness and indifference of the 18th century church, and had much in common with Methodism. It stressed the importance of faith in personal salvation as the essential basis of a religious life, and it called on the individual to be thrifty, sober, industrious, and self-sacrificing. Unlike Methodism, it spread amongst the upper and middle classes, and among Anglican clergy. Whilst at Cambridge University in the early 1830s, Stoneham could well have been one of the enthusiastic undergraduates who packed Holy Trinity church each week to hear Simeon's sermons; Simeon was one of the most famous Evangelical preachers of the day and provided training sessions in Cambridge for would-be clergymen like Stoneham. Queen Victoria herself, who had come to the throne five years before Charlotte Stoneham's birth, was no admirer of the Evangelicals, and yet she embodied many of their ideas: she was 'Low Church', distrusting any form of ritual, had very strong views on what was right moral conduct, and had an immensely powerful sense of duty.

Evangelicals were famous for their involvement in humanitarian reform, and Stoneham would perhaps have been inspired by the example of the most famous of the earlier Evangelicals, William Wilberforce (father of Soapy Sam, Bishop of Oxford), who died whilst Stoneham was at university; Wilberforce had been a leading campaigner against the slave trade (abolished in the British empire in 1807), and against slavery (abolished in the British empire in 1833, the year of Wilberforce's death). An Evangelical almost as famous as Wilberforce was to be Lord Shaftesbury, crusader for factory reform and many other causes, who in the year of Charlotte's birth helped to secure the passing of the Mines Act; this Act, which prohibited women and children from working in mines, changed the face of Ketley and Great Wyrley, and of dozens of other mining communities in the Black Country and Cannock Chase coalfields and beyond.

---

[1] *Wellington Journal and Shrewsbury News*, 22 September 1877.

As Thompson Stoneham, and no doubt Mary as well, were influenced by one of the most powerful currents in English Christianity of the time, it is perhaps more than coincidence that at her baptism their daughter was given names which were the pseudonym of a popular contemporary Evangelical writer – Charlotte Elizabeth. A year before Charlotte Stoneham's birth, Charlotte Elizabeth had expressed the view of many Evangelicals, in a dialogue between two cousins in her *Conformity: a Tale*, that only those who agreed with them were Christians:

> 'You admit that all mankind are divided into two classes –
> the Children of Light, and the Children of Darkness?
> 'Yes.'
> 'The former you allow to be those exclusively to whom we
> apply the Apostle's words, "But ye are washed, but ye are
> sanctified, but ye are justified in the name of the Lord
> Jesus, and by the Spirit of our God?"'
> 'Precisely those, and none other.'
> 'The children of darkness you comprehend under that
> term from every class of human beings: as Heathens who
> never heard of Christ; Jews and Infidels, who reject Him;
> Nominal Christians, who have a form of godliness, but
> deny the power thereof...'
> 'To all this I fully assent.'[1]

Influenced by such world-pictures, the Stonehams had, they believed, the terrifying responsibility of providing for the eternal welfare of those working-class parishioners who sat in church during Charlotte's baptism. Many of the residents of the parish were to them 'the children of darkness', unredeemed sinners; on Stoneham's death, the local paper was to describe sympathetically how in his first post as a curate he was to be found 'labouring among the teeming population of Malinslee', near Ketley.[2] In giving their lives to 'the Heathens', the Stonehams were missionaries seeking to divert the working classes from the revolution which the ruling classes still believed possible at that time. Charlotte Elizabeth showed clearly that she shared this belief in her other works: her novel *Helen Fleetwood*, for example, which was one of the first to devote itself entirely to the life of a working-class family in a northern industrial town, has been described by Patrick

---

[1] Charlotte Elizabeth, *Conformity, A Tale*, W. H. Dalton, 1841, pp. 18-19. Charlotte Elizabeth (née Browne), 1790-1846, is also known as Charlotte Elizabeth Tonna – Tonna being the name of her second husband.
[2] *Wellington Journal and Shrewsbury News*, 22 September 1877.

Brantlinger as 'a piece of social hysteria'.[1] William Cobbett was scathing in his analysis of the social aims of the Evangelicals, which he saw as being to: 'Teach the people to starve without making a noise, and to keep the poor from cutting the throats of the rich.'[2]

It was, however, another dimension of Evangelicalism which was key to the origin of the British Edalji family, namely the crucial role which Evangelicals played in missionary activity abroad. S. C. Carpenter has suggested that 'It was the Evangelicals who taught the Church of England to be missionary,'[3] and William Wilberforce, for all his liberal anti-slavery campaigns, himself played a key role in the 19th century outburst of religious imperialism. He saw the conversion of India to Christianity as 'the greatest of all causes', which he placed even 'before abolition' (of slavery). The Hindu gods, he told the House of Commons, were 'absolute monsters of lust, injustice, wickedness and cruelty. In short their religion is one grand abomination.'[4] He, Charles Simeon, and other Evangelicals played a key part in establishing the Church Missionary Society (1797), and in persuading Parliament to allow the evangelisation of India and the establishment of an episcopate there (1813). These developments helped to create a world in which the meeting of Charlotte Stoneham of Ketley and Shápurjí Edaljí of Bombay became possible.

Charlotte's mother, Mary (née Compson), had two brothers, perhaps present at Charlotte's baptism, who were curates – John (who was to be Shapurji Edalji's predecessor as Vicar of Great Wyrley) and Edward Bate (the man who would conduct the Edalji wedding in 1874). Both had studied at Oxford University. Mary's sister, Sarah, was also married to an Oxford-educated clergyman, James Murray Dixon (they were the great grandparents of Freda Shimmin, whom I visited in Peterborough in 2004). Charlotte was thus not just a Sunday churchgoer; she was related to at least four men in the lower reaches of the Anglican establishment. Despite its respectably orthodox background and against the grain of contemporary prejudice, the whole family years later welcomed Charlotte's marriage to an Asian whose route to the priesthood was not merely unorthodox but unique at that time.

---

[1] Patrick Brantlinger, *The Spirit of Reform*, Harvard University Press, 1977; G. Kitson Clark, *Churchmen and the Condition of England 1832-1885*, Methuen, 1973, p. 12.
[2] Cited in Ian Bradley, *The Call to Seriousness: The Evangelical Impact on the Victorians*, Jonathan Cape, 1976, p. 111.
[3] S. C. Carpenter, *Church and People 1789-1889*, S.P.C.K., London, 1933, p. 428.
[4] Rozina Visram, *Ayahs, Lascars and Princes*, p. 223.

Typically for a girl of her background, Charlotte Stoneham was educated within the walls of her own home, and the samplers she and her sisters produced in childhood were symbols of the life to come. There was no expectation that they would have a career. Girls of their class were usually taught to sew, knit, and embroider, and to develop further 'accomplishments' such as playing the piano and painting in watercolours – the kinds of skills which would attract a husband and help to make his home-life more pleasant. Within these constraints Charlotte was still able to show talent, from the childhood sampler embroidered in 1850 or 1851 to the charcoal and colour-wash portrait of her uncle, John Compson, Vicar of Great Wyrley from 1850 to 1875, which nearly a century later was bequeathed to the parish by her daughter and has graced the wall of the vestry at St Mark's since I recently had it reframed.[1] This drawing may have been produced during one of the many visits Charlotte paid to Great Wyrley, for from her childhood onwards her family often travelled the twenty-five miles to the village which was eventually to become her home; such visits were among the highlights of a limited social life. She was also musically gifted – she helped with the choir in church and was organist for many years.[2] As a young woman she became involved in good works too, as befitted the daughter of an Evangelical clergyman; her particular interest was in the Ketley National School.[3] This school opened at the Duke of Sutherland's expense in the year of her birth. Its roll rose steadily as the number of coal miners and ironworkers in Ketley climbed – there were about one hundred and fifty children there in 1851.[4] Charlotte grew up alongside them and waited for a husband to appear.

****

And you, Maud, you were inheritor of this history, half a Stoneham and last curator of the complete Thompson/Swan/Stoneham family archive. We know you loved the pictures on your Welwyn drawing room wall. How often did you pore over the package of family documents, now in Essex Record Office? Hundreds of years of your past were there, including one reference as startling as any. It's a piece of paper detailing your family's claim to a distant connection with royalty: 'Lady Katherine Howard gt gt grand-daughter of Robert

---

[1] *Express & Star*, 21 July 1962.
[2] *Shrewsbury Chronicle*, 14 March 1924.
[3] *Wellington Journal and Shrewsbury News*, 20 June 1874.
[4] *V.C.H. Shropshire* xi. p. 275.

Stoneham of Great Stoughton and wife of Lord William Howard of Effingham. Lord William Howard was half-brother to Lord Edward Howard whose daughter Katherine m Henry VIII.' You had this claim, too, Maud, a claim to an indirect family connection to Henry VIII's wife. All this you had behind you, and yet when the western world started to stare at you after 18 August 1903 it saw only the origin of your father and the colour of your skin.

4. Partners

1997. For over a decade, work and the multiculturalism of the 1980s and 1990s have diverted me from the line of inquiry which had consumed Michael Harley's energies; the lives of the Edalji family in general have come to seem more important than George's case in particular. Now, finally, I have followed Michael Harley on the trail to the Home Office files in the Public Record Office – but more to find insights into the doings of the family than to help resolve the question of George's guilt. There is one immediate delight – the discovery of how Charlotte met Shapurji.

****

I already knew that in 1872 Charlotte was still living with her parents at St Mary's vicarage in Ketley. As for Shapurji, he was curate to the Reverend Reginald Yonge at St Thomas in Liverpool, the sixth parish in which he had served, and there was no sign that his career would ever advance further.

It was a letter written by Charlotte in 1904, now held in the Home Office files, which revealed how everything changed in 1872. The change was the result of a visit made to Reverend Reginald Yonge by an old friend, the Reverend Thompson Stoneham of Ketley. Stoneham had been an undergraduate at Cambridge with Yonge, and the latter had been for twenty-one years vicar of Wrockwardine Wood, near Ketley, before moving to Liverpool. With Stoneham came the rest of his family, including Charlotte.[1] For Shapurji the courtship with Charlotte which followed must have been quite an adventurous experience, for if he had remained a Parsi in Bombay he might have enjoyed the security of an arranged marriage; Dadabhai Naoroji, the future M.P. in the British House of Commons who had attended Elphinstone College ahead of Shapurji, had been engaged to a seven-year-old girl at the age of eleven.

Charlotte and Shapurji were both already thirty when they first met, and all concerned were no doubt relieved that each had found a potential spouse, especially as Charlotte's older sister, Mary Sancta, was unmarried too. The Reverend Thompson Stoneham was however genuinely impressed with Shapurji, for after the Stonehams had made a second visit to Liverpool in 1873, he invited him to preach in Ketley.[2] In May 1873, in transit

---

[1] P.R.O., HO 144/984, no. 48 (letter by Charlotte, January 1904).
[2] P.R.O., HO 144/984, no. 48 (Charlotte Edalji, January 1904).

from Toxteth to his next curacy, at St Levan in Cornwall, Shapurji conducted a baptism at St Mary's;[1] the Reverend Mr Stoneham had faith in his future son-in-law. This was only the start, for Shapurji went on to carry out more of Stoneham's duties, both before and after the wedding – he conducted a further baptism and four burials in September 1874. Some indication of the feelings of the Stoneham family at this point was provided by Charlotte 's sister years later, in 1904, when she told a Birmingham M.P. that 'Our friends at that time too felt as we did that Parsis are of a very old and cultivated race, and have many good qualities.'[2] Evidently not everyone saw Parsis as 'fire-worshippers' or believed that black and minority ethnic citizens could not play an important part in British life, though Mary Sancta clearly did believe that 'racial' groups existed and could be given ratings.

Travels

The curacy at St Levan, near Land's End, brought Shapurji separation from his fiancée, but also an interlude between his industrial parishes, a taste of unspoilt natural beauty which he was rarely to experience again.[3] It was a magnificent spot – the cliff scenery at St Levan, especially at Logan Rock and along the coast towards Land's End, was described by a contemporary as the finest in the county.[4] The human landscape was also very different from that of the rest of England – the Celtic influence on Christianity in the south west was ancient, unlike that in Liverpool, and was reflected in the very name of the church in which Shapurji served; it derived from the 6th century Celtic saint, descended from a king of Cornwall, who first established a Christian community there.[5] Outside the church porch today there is still a great stone, split dramatically into two. Pre-Christian Celts may have worshipped the stone, whilst legend has it that St Levan himself liked to sit on it and that it was he who divided it with one mighty blow.[6]

In this poor, remote spot, within earshot of the solemn swish of the sea, Shapurji entered into a new kind of controversy. St Levan Church itself, most of it over five hundred years old,

[1] S.R.R.C., P149/2 (Ketley parish registers, christenings 1856-1891).
[2] B.R.L., 370795 (letter by Mary Sancta Stoneham, January 27 1904, in 'A Collection of MSS Formed by Sir J. B. Stone').
[3] Devon Record Office, Chanter 105, Curate Licences (licence granted to Shapurji 10 June 1873).
[4] Joseph Polsue, *A Complete Parochial History of the County of Cornwall*, 4 vol., William Lake, Truro, 1867-72.
[5] Jeffery C. Burr, *A History of the Church of St. Levan*, The Patten Press, 1994, p. 3.
[6] Ibid., p. 8.

was in a dreadful state when he arrived. The parish had been so neglected earlier in the century that there were periods when the church was not used at all, and by the 1860s it was so run-down and damp that one writer described it as having 'the atmosphere of a vault'.[1] At an emotional meeting in 1866, parishioners voted by eleven to seven to take the momentous step of building a completely new church. The new rector in 1868, however, had other ideas. Rev. Charles Anstey had just returned from seven years' service as chaplain at Faizabad in north east India, near the birthplace of Charlotte Stoneham's Anglo-Asian uncles. Anstey's heart was set on retaining and restoring the medieval building in St Levan rather than starting afresh, and it was at the height of the controversy, in 1873, that he appointed Shapurji as curate. Anstey's residence was near his other church at St Buryan, and when he needed to go to St Levan he would travel over by carriage. Shapurji was the man on the spot in St Levan itself, working in the damp 'vault' of a church, and here he conducted the usual round of baptisms, marriages and burials, whilst the more distant Anstey fought the battle to keep the building alive. Anstey won, and restoration work started soon after Shapurji departed for his next curacy, back in Liverpool. Thanks to his trusty patron, the Reverend Reginald Yonge, Shapurji was returning to the familiar territory of St Thomas, Toxteth. He had three months left to get ready for marriage.

Lessons

Preparations for the wedding, in the church in which Charlotte had been baptised by her father, gave Ketley parishioners the opportunity to show some recognition of the part Charlotte had played in the affairs of the parish. A timepiece and gold bracelet were presented to her, and she also received gifts from children of the National School, in which she had taken a deep interest.[2] The wedding itself was a happy one, but when the couple walked out of St Mary's church after the ceremony that day they carried a burden on their shoulders; they were pioneers, pioneers who would have to rise above the weight of prejudice which unions such as theirs aroused.

In recent times a new kind of weight has been put on the shoulders of their marriage. In a study of mixed heritage relationships published in 1992, Yasmin Alibhai-Brown and Anne Montague mentioned the Edalji marriage as one of the fairly limited number of Anglo-Asian marriages in Victorian

---

[1] Ibid., p. 19.
[2] *Wellington Journal and Shrewsbury News*, 20 June 1874.

Britain for which evidence still remains.[1] This evidence has become material for understanding attitudes to such relationships in the present. The interviews reported in this book contain many signs that British society at the end of the 20th century was still infected with the same prejudices as those the Edaljis had to face. Zerbanoo Gifford, for example, was born in Poona, seventy-eight miles from Bombay, and was, like Shapurji Edalji, originally a Parsi. She came to England in the 1950s, and in the 1980s was twice a candidate in parliamentary elections.[2] She described attitudes to her own marriage, to an Englishman, in the following terms:

> *We have had racial attacks, police guards, break-ins, death threats, telephone-calls, my car nearly pushed off the road at the last election. I was spat on in the road and called 'nigger-lover' and I was asked what it was like sleeping with someone like him.*[3]

The experiences of the Edaljis are evidence that the shame of these recent horrors is the product of a stain which had oozed through centuries.

There is, on the other hand, much to celebrate about the Edalji marriage. There is, admittedly, little direct evidence on Shapurji's view of marriage in general or of his own in particular, but so far as gender roles were concerned the influences upon him were clear. The tenets of Zoroastrianism with which he had been brought up made Parsi women pioneers of female emancipation in India. The Parsi community had never assumed the traditional Asian customs of polygamy and prohibition of the remarriage of widows, and the inspiration of the teachings of Zoroaster, with their emphasis on the importance of good thoughts, good words, and good deeds, fostered a social conscience and involvement in public life. Parsi women were the first non-British women in Bombay to receive a western education. Indeed, in 1842 (about the time of Shapurji's birth) a nine-year old Parsi girl, who later became Mrs Dossibai Cowasjee Jehangir Jassawalla, was even sent by her parents to be educated in Britain; she became a highly respected campaigner for women's rights in India, and her efforts were

---

[1] Yasmin Alibhai-Brown and Anne Montague, *The Colour of Love*, Virago Press, 1992, p. 10.
[2] Ibid., p. 42.
[3] Ibid., p. 46.

ST. LEVAN CHURCH.

St Levan Church, near Land's End in Cornwall

Courtesy of
Porthcurno Telegraph Museum

praised by Queen Victoria. The first South Asian woman to go to university in Britain (in 1889), Cornelia Sorabji, was a Parsi too; she later practised law in England at the time that George Edalji's legal career was getting under way. Another Parsi, Bhikhaiji Cama, was imbued with the Indian nationalism nurtured by Dadabhai Naoroji and others, and became a virulent critic of British imperialism; at the second International Socialist Congress in Stuttgart in 1907 she rose from the audience to become the first person outside India to unfurl the Indian national flag in public. [1]

Charlotte was always more open about her feelings than Shapurji, even in letters to the Home Secretary or the Queen, and it is clear not only that she was strongly loyal to Shapurji throughout their lives but also that her experience of marriage to him taught her a great deal about British attitudes on race. 'As an English woman,' she sighed in the thirtieth year after her first meeting with Shapurji, 'I am grieved & shocked about prejudice against the non-English.' In her letter to the Queen in February 1904, she commented bitterly: 'I have often been grieved to notice that an Asiatic is despised or disliked.'[2] A year later she told the Home Secretary, in terms which despite its sense of outrage still (in its use of the word 'only') admittedly implied a belief in racial hierarchy: 'I am an English woman & my blood boils at the continued injustice as it seems to be because my husband is a Parsee and my son therefore only half English.' Whatever her experiences in the parish which Conan Doyle described as 'rude' and 'unrefined', Charlotte had some insight into the fact that the stain of British racism was not created in the minds of Great Wyrley 's working class. By the time that Shapurji had arrived in England in 1867 racist ideas had infiltrated all sectors of British society and were at the heart of its institutions and imperial order.

Apart from such insights from Charlotte there is no evidence on the more private aspects of the Edalji marriage, except for the unusual family sleeping relationships about which there was gossip in the locality from 1903 and, after Conan Doyle's intervention, around the world in 1907.

The City

After the honeymoon Shapurji picked up the reins again in Toxteth in Liverpool, and so Charlotte moved home for the first time in her life. They were there for a year and then, in June

[1] Zerbanoo Gifford, *The Golden Thread – Asian Experiences of Post-Raj Britain*, pp. 30-34.
[2] P.R.O., HO 144/985, no. 69 (Charlotte Edalji to Queen Alexandra, February 1904).

1875, moved to London. Shapurji had been appointed to what would be his last curacy, at St Leonard's in Bromley.

Their journey from central London to their new home in Bromley was not glamorous: the East End reeked of slums. On the southern side of their route, hundreds of ships jostled in the wharves and docks stretching along the Thames from London Bridge to Limehouse, and from the West India docks on the Isle of Dogs to the swathe of south east Bromley which had been submerged by the building of the East India docks seventy years earlier. Between them the West and East India docks obliterated all trace of the quays which had once been the stepping-stone to Bombay for the 17th and 18th century Thompsons, Swans and Stonehams of Charlotte's ancestry. Funnels of steam ships and the stately masts and rigging of clippers like the Cutty Sark now stared inland from the East India docks, where the riches of India – tea, silk, indigo, spices – were gathered in.

North of the dock-ridden river bank, London's urban tide was still bursting eastward beyond Whitechapel and Spitalfields in a gigantic mid-19th century swell. Charlotte's gaze over the sea of yellow-brick terraces in Stepney and Mile End traced only snatches of the landscape her ancestors had once inhabited; now this was territory for the soup-kitchens of William Booth, on the brink of founding the Salvation Army, and for Dr Barnardo's rescue missions for homeless children. Further east, the Bow Road out of Mile End had in the days of Robert Thompson, Ruth Swan and Abraham Stoneham scythed through pleasant meadows, parted politely for the medieval church of St Leonard in the picturesque hamlet of Bromley-by-Bow, and departed via an ancient arched bridge over the river Lea en route to the later Stoneham homeland in rural Essex. The Bromley which now welcomed the Edaljis had been hastily drowned by gerry-builders – in the 1850s alone the population had risen from 11,000 to 24,000. One of Britain's earliest canals, the Limehouse Cut, sliced south-westwards through Bromley from Lea to Thames, gathering rows of brickfields, smoking factories and fuming chemical works on its way, along with a crossing-point known locally as 'Stink House Bridge'. On the eastern side of Bromley St Leonard parish, the river Lea had long been the Thames's channel to London's East Anglian food chest; by the 1870s its remote banks were an out-of-sight repository for the city's gasworks. The biggest employer in the area had built on a site just north of St Leonard church: here the later-famous 'match-girls' were among the 5,600 who risked 'phossy-jaw' as they slaved for match-makers Bryant and

May so that the nation could light its coalfires, gaslamps, and cigarettes.

The seaport atmosphere to the south of the parish revived Shapurji's memories of rainbow diversity in Bombay and Liverpool. The long-established Jewish community of Spitalfields was gradually creating new outposts in Stepney, Mile End, and then Bromley itself, whilst a century of Huguenots was already buried in St Leonard churchyard. There was a strong Irish presence too: the area alongside the Limehouse Cut was labelled locally as the 'Fenian Barracks', whose residents were imputed with putting more police in hospital than any other community in London.

As in Liverpool, new colours were added to the ethnic rainbow in the mid-19th century, when hundreds of lascars sailed into London on ships from the east. Many were not taken on for an immediate return voyage, and had to live abject lives in some of the most squalid streets and lodging-houses of the East End. Christian horror at their situation was based partly on humanitarian concern and partly on the sense that heathens were sitting on London's doorstep: Joseph Salter, the missionary amongst Asians who had worked with lascars in Liverpool, asked anxiously: 'Who will descend into the pit of mire and clay to rescue these perishing ones...?'[1] Thanks to the initiative of Henry Venn, Secretary of the Church Missionary Society, a 'Stranger's Home' was opened on the West India Dock Road in 1857; it served partly as a lodging house for foreign sailors, but was also used to ensure that 'the heathen' would not 'leave a Christian land without being brought into contact with its Christianity'.[2] It seems likely the Edaljis visited this establishment, which lay so close to their new home.

Sir Arthur Conan Doyle was later to use this distressed dockland landscape, unknown to middle class readers though they enjoyed the benefits of London's seafaring trade, as a backdrop for a Sherlock Holmes story. The focal-point of 'The Man with the Twisted Lip' is a cavernous den in a 'vile alley' behind the wharves east of London Bridge; the date is June 1889, the year after the Jack the Ripper murders in nearby Whitechapel. The den is run by a 'rascally Lascar', known to be 'of the vilest antecedents', who employs a 'sallow Malay attendant' to attend to opium-smokers in 'the vilest murder-trap on riverside'.

---

[1] Joseph Salter, *The Asiatic in England; Sketches of Sixteen Years' Work among Orientals*, p. 22.
[2] Rozina Visram, *Ayahs, Lascars and Princes*, pp. 48-49.

Unloading tea ships in the East India Docks, 1867

Courtesy of National Maritime Museum

Asian London had another face than this, one which never emerges in the impressions of the metropolis provided in the Sherlock Holmes collection. No Shapurji Edalji ever treads the stairs of 221B Baker Street, no Dadabhai Naoroji, no Cornelia Sorabji, no Mohandas Gandhi, and yet Asians had been making their mark on London since the middle of the century. As usual, the Parsis were in the fore – the Parsi company Messrs Cama and Co, of which Dadabhai Naoroji was a director, helped to pay for the Stranger's Home in Limehouse. In 1861 Dadabhai Naoroji was involved with the foundation of the London Zoroastrian Association, for the well-being of the estimated fifty Parsis in Britain.[1] The Association had its own burial-ground, without vultures, in Woking, and it was during the Edaljis' time in Bromley that Dorabjee Dashai, the Parsi who committed suicide in Bolton, was buried there; it may be that the Edaljis knew something of this event, for a group of members of the London Zoroastrian Association went to the inquest, and one of the witnesses, a Parsi mill operative in Bolton, was actually called Sorabjee Eduljee.[2] Dadabhai Naoroji was also involved in the foundation in 1865 of the London Indian Society, which aimed to spread knowledge of India.[3] Perhaps Shapurji was attracted.

The man with the twisted lip in Conan Doyle's story is in fact an ex-actor and journalist who (like George Edalji in real life) falls into debt after standing security for a friend. Using the den as his base, he disguises himself as a down-and-out beggar and several prosecutions barely dent his fat profits. Holmes unmasks him, but detective and police collude to hush the matter up on the grounds that the man was only protecting his family's middle class fortunes and respectability. In the meantime Asians belonging to the real poor of dockland are type-cast as opium-dealing scoundrels of sinister eastern heredity.

By the Edaljis' day the Church of England had adapted radically to Bromley's immersion in the East End brick terrace tide. The original church of St Leonard, marooned in the middle of Bow Road, was medieval: a Benedictine convent was founded on the site in about 1100 and the lady chapel was turned into the parish church when Henry VIII dissolved the monasteries. The church was completely rebuilt in 1842-3 and rededicated as St Mary's,[4] Bromley St Leonard, under the

---

[1] John Hinnells, *Zoroastrians in Britain*, Clarendon Press, 1996, p. 107.
[2] *Bolton Journal*, 16 October 1875.
[3] John Hinnells, *Zoroastrians in Britain*, p. 157.
[4] James Dunstan, *The History of the Parish of Bromley St Leonard, Middlesex*, Hunt & Son, 1862, p. 115.

guidance of the curate, Rev. George Augustus How. As numbers in the parish mushroomed, a north aisle was added in the year before the Edaljis' arrival.

The Rev. Mr How eventually became the incumbent, and it was he who welcomed the Edaljis in 1875. There were two other curates as well, and Shapurji worked hard with the unusually large team to meet the spiritual and social needs of a parish densely packed with mariners and match-girls, brick-makers and factory labourers. He performed some of the occasional offices, but his main preoccupation was increasingly with his last career move – to become Vicar of Great Wyrley in Staffordshire. In September 1875, testimonials to his character were sent from Bromley to the Bishop of Lichfield (George Selwyn), in whose diocese the parish of Great Wyrley lay, and in November the Bishop formally accepted the resignation of Charlotte's uncle, John Compson.[1] There were other candidates for the post, which was in the gift of the Vicar of Cannock,[2] and Shapurji's success may have generated jealousies in individuals or the wider ruling group in Staffordshire which help to explain the later hostility of figures such as Chief Constable Anson. For the moment, though, Charlotte and Shapurji enjoyed a heady time. It was not just that they faced the excitement of their new life at St Mark's vicarage in Great Wyrley. There was now something else to look forward to: Charlotte was expecting their first child.

In December Charlotte and Shapurji left Bromley to its precarious future: St Mary's was to be crushed in the 20th century, first by bombs and then by cars and their concrete in the shape of the northern approach to the Blackwall Tunnel. Amid the despoliation, traffic still dodges either side of the remnant St Mary's, under the reproving gaze of an imposing monument – the 1882 statue of W. E. Gladstone, paid for (according to the Fabian Society's famous call for action in 1888) by a one shilling wage-cut imposed on Bryant and May's impoverished match-girls.

Charlotte and Shapurji travelled north to Staffordshire, and when they passed through the door of St Mark's vicarage in early December 1875 they were entering what was to be their home for forty-two years. Shapurji was immediately immersed in a round of duties which was to occupy most of his energies until his death; he conducted his first baptism on 6 December, and by the end of the month had already officiated at three

[1] L.D.R.O., B/A/3 (presentation deeds), and B/A/1/33 (bishop's register 1867-77).
[2] *Cannock Advertiser*, 31 October 1903.

baptisms, three marriages, and four burials, including a baptism, two marriages, and a burial on Christmas Day.[1]

---

[1] S.R.O., D1215/1/1, F1215/1/9, and F1215/1/16 (Great Wyrley parish registers, baptisms 1845-86, marriages 1846-97, burials 1846-87).

5. Newcomers

September 1971. Great Wyrley Comprehensive School, created out of the former Great Wyrley Secondary Modern, is just a few days old. I sit in the Head's office along with a clutch of other bright-faced staff appointed for the new era. Here, on the site of what once was John Hatton's Brook Farm, we listen to the Head's welcome. 'These are village children,' he tells us, a line he uses regularly for newcomers and visitors. It is certainly true that the community still retains something of its rural atmosphere, despite the 1960s mass migration from the rest of the West Midlands to this new commuter-belt territory. Cows and horses still wander the fields which divide us from the West Midlands conurbation. Names like Hatton, Farrington, Badger, Green, Sambrook, Perks, Dace, Ridgeway, Bullock and Whitehouse still appear on the school rolls, alongside new ones with no local connection. But whatever the balance between old and new, it is now our task to create the future. The 1944 Education Act made free secondary education available to all, but in most parts of the country secondary provision has been divisive; until now the 11+ exam has separated Great Wyrley's children into those who go to Cannock Grammar School, just as George, Horace and Maud Edalji went off to grammar school in Rugeley or Walsall, and those who came to Great Wyrley Secondary Modern. Now we are here to make out of this community one which provides equality of opportunity for all of its own.

Standpoints

It is my belief, Watson, founded upon my experience, that the lowest and vilest alleys of London do not present a more dreadful record of sin than does the smiling and beautiful countryside.

Arthur Conan Doyle, 'The Adventure of the Copper Beeches.' [1]

---

[1] Arthur Conan Doyle, 'The Adventure of the Copper Beeches', first published in *The Strand Magazine*, 5-20 April 1889, reprinted in William S. Baring-Gould (ed.), *The Annotated Sherlock Holmes*.

**Statue of W. E. Gladstone in Bromley, allegedly paid
for by Bryant and May match-girls**

Courtesy of English Heritage

Sir Arthur Conan Doyle, I learned in the year after my arrival, had seen more sin than beauty in the parish in which I now worked: 'Perhaps some Catholic-minded patron,' he wrote in his memoirs in the 1920s, 'wished to demonstrate the universality of the Anglican Church. The experiment will not, I hope, be repeated, for though the Vicar was an amiable and devoted man, the appearance of a coloured clergyman with a half-caste son in a rude, unrefined parish was bound to cause some regrettable situation.'[1] Conan Doyle was not the only outsider to find the area unprepossessing. One of the more colourful of the Midlands journalists who covered George Edalji's case in 1903 bluntly summed up Great Wyrley as 'an eerie spot': it was 'as uninviting and as uninteresting as a coal-cellar, and just about as picturesque... Great Wyrley,' he sighed, 'generates depression by day and bronchitis by night.'[2]

It was galling, as a contributor to the life and work of this community for fifteen years, to learn that its image had been defined for a century by one Conan Doyle phrase: 'that rude, unrefined parish'. The Hattons, Badgers, Sambrooks, Edmunds and Farringtons of Conan Doyle's time and their descendants had, after all, helped to shape the community our new school was trying to shape further. It was painful to find that no histories of the village had been written to challenge Conan Doyle's putdown, though a start was made in the booklet *Great Wyrley 1051-1951*[3] produced by Homeshaw and Sambrook for the Festival of Britain celebrations (and Cheslyn Hay now has its own attractive full-length history thanks to the reworking of Roland Ridgway's research by Trevor McFarlane[4]). Great Wyrley's part in the Edalji story seemed to deserve more rounded coverage than that offered in all the accounts derived from Conan Doyle.

Arrival

When Charlotte and Shapurji themselves arrived in this unadmired landscape on that December day in 1875 the St Mark's complex on Station Road was already complete – church, vicarage, schoolroom, master's house. It was the centre of their world and a main focal-point for the striving community they had come to serve.

---

[1] Arthur Conan Doyle, *Memories and Adventures*, p. 216.
[2] *Express & Star*, 11 November 1903.
[3] Since supplemented by material in *Great Wyrley Millennium Souvenir*.
[4] Roland Ridgway, *The Bygone Days of Cheslyn Hay*, John Goodman & Sons, Birmingham, 2002.

Charlotte, of course, knew St Mark's well, having visited her uncle the Reverend John Compson many times. On that day in 1875, however, she sized up the vicarage with other eyes. Now she was its manager, and she knew not only that her husband's living was worth less than £250 a year, but that £70 12s of this would go for her uncle John's pension. The Ecclesiastical Commissioners were to award Shapurji a stipend of £94 in 1884,[1] but his income was always limited. The Edaljis could afford a resident maid at the vicarage (including the maid, Elizabeth Foster, who in 1888 allegedly helped to launch the years of crisis for the family), but otherwise their life-style was quite modest for a family of their class. In one of her flood of letters following her son's arrest in 1903 Charlotte hinted at what she had lost by marriage to Shapurji: 'He has no private means. He paid for... coming and... college out of the sale of his Dictionary. His desire to educate our children well made it impossible for us to enter into society as our means were so small.'[2]

To most of the 2,500 or so inhabitants of the parish, on the other hand, the Edaljis were rich and their home was a mansion. Their roomy palace was the Victorian redbrick expression of the fact that the Edaljis were people of rank. By the mid-19th century the title of clergyman was, it is true, generally no longer defined by the incumbent's status as a gentleman, as had been the case in the past. Shapurji was seen, rather, as someone with an occupational role, and he had status because of his theological training and pastoral skills. He was crucially responsible for the spiritual welfare of his parishioners, who looked to him above all for help in coming to terms with their greatest preoccupations – death, judgement, heaven, and hell. Beyond this, despite increasing emphasis in the 19th century on the clergyman's narrowly ecclesiastical role, he still had many secular responsibilities, at a time when the union between the Church of England and the state continued to be seen as a protection against subversion; like other Victorian clergymen, he was much involved in such activities as planning and financing schools (which, in part at least, aimed to teach the working classes to accept their station in life), supporting self-help groups (in the days before the welfare state such groups reduced the need for charity), and, increasingly, helping to make public health provision.

---

[1] S.R.O., D1215/2/12 (copy of *London Gazette*, 12 December, 1884).
[2] B.R.L., 370795, copy of letter from Charlotte Edalji 'to all who have given this case of gross injustice their attention', 26 January 1904, in 'A Collection of MSS Formed by Sir J. B. Stone').

Charlotte's class background and Shapurji's role and achievements as a clergyman would later confer status on their children as well. The ex-pupil of Queen Mary's High School in Walsall who wrote in the 1960s about her friend Maud Edalji was quite clear on this:

> There was never any question of Maud Edalji being discriminated against... in the social climate of more than 60 years ago the Vicar's daughter automatically had a certain social status. Even the poorest vicarage had at least one resident maid. Maud's brother was to enter the legal profession and she herself was accepted as an assistant at Queen Mary's, itself a social passport as some cachet attached to schools of this type. Maud would in fact be regarded by most people as belonging to the more fortunate minority of the population.[1]

Within the wider Staffordshire community the Edaljis were much smaller players, for they lived in a county in which in the 1880s 29% of the land was owned by just twelve landowners.[2] St Mark's church itself, a few yards from the Edaljis' vicarage home, was largely the creation of this ruling elite. Henry Ryder (1777-1836), brother of the 1st Earl of Harrowby, belonged to one of these twelve powerful families – as late as 1907 his family still owned 13,000 acres. When he was made Bishop of Gloucester in 1818 Ryder was the first bishop from Evangelical ranks, and when he was translated to the bishopric of Lichfield in 1824 he set about a huge programme of church-building; this programme led to the building of St Mary's in Charlotte's home village of Ketley in Shropshire and, a few years after his death, of St Mark's in Great Wyrley.[3] Much of the land in Great Wyrley was owned by an even more powerful landowner than the Earl of Harrowby – the Duke of Sutherland, who was the lord of the manor there as he was in Ketley.[4] The 2nd Duke of Sutherland, who had spied on Charlotte's father as he preached in Ketley in 1839, was also a leading benefactor of St Mark's in Great Wyrley, which opened in 1845.

Figures from two contrasting Staffordshire dynasties had actually planned the opening. One of them, the first Lord Hatherton (1791-1863), married to the Duke of Wellington's

---

[1] W.L.H.C., 246/38 ('Queen Mary's High School, Miss Barbara Foxley, and The Edalji Case').

[2] Pamela A. Sambrook , 'Aristocratic Indebtedness: The Anson Estates in Staffordshire, 1818-1880', University of Keele Ph.D. thesis, 1990 (copy in W.S.L.), p. 83.

[3] Kenneth Hylson-Smith, *Evangelicals in the Church of England 1734-1984*, T. & T. Clark, Edinburgh, 1988, p. 70.

[4] *VCH Staffordshire* v. p. 80.

niece, was a member of the Littleton family of Teddesley Park near Penkridge; the Littletons still owned 14,901 acres in Staffordshire in 1883.[1] His views about the importance of his own class were quite clear: 'In every district the able, intriguing, the enterprising are on the alert... penniless but clever knaves rushing up to the front. Thousands are taught that they have only to will to be somebody to be so.'[2] Despite his fears, the local aristocracy, including his own family, were to control the destinies of the Edaljis and their flock for years to come: his successor (1815-1888) provided the land on which Cheslyn Hay National School was built in the 1870s; the next Lord Hatherton (1842-1930) was Chairman of Staffordshire Quarter Sessions at the time of George's appearance before Court No 2 in 1903;[3] and the latter's brother, who as a teenager was stationed on a British ship in Calcutta during the Indian Uprising of 1857, was the Rear-Admiral Littleton who sat as one of the magistrates in George's case.

Although he despised the upstart classes of industrial England, in 1840 the first Lord Hatherton invited to his mansion a representative of the new order, a member of the local Gilpin dynasty, to discuss the need for a church in Great Wyrley.[4] The Gilpins, a family of entrepreneurs from Wolverhampton, had established an edge tool works at Churchbridge at the northern edge of St Mark's parish in the early 19th century. Like the ironworks at Coalbrookdale and Ketley, Gilpin's works, whose staple products were tools and agricultural implements, formed one of the invisible building-blocks of the British empire: Gilpin's tools were used on South Asian tea plantations and West Indian sugar estates, and for forest-felling in Britain's interests around the world. By the time the Edaljis took up residence at St Mark's the Gilpins were people of status and importance in Staffordshire, representatives of the mining and manufacturing interests which challenged the old order. It was in fact the influx of edge tool workers to Gilpin's works from the Black Country which had made collaboration between Hatherton and Gilpin in the building of a church appear necessary.

---

[1] G.E.C., *The Complete Peerage*, vol. vi., The St Catherine Press, 1920.
[2] Journal (1817-66) of the 1st Baron Hatherton (*Express & Star* cuttings, Hatherton file, C.L.).
[3] George Rickwood and William Gaskell, *Staffordshire Leaders*, p. 34.
[4] Journal (1817-66) of the 1st Baron Hatherton (*Express & Star* cuttings, Hatherton file, C. L.).

A British view of the world, Walter Crane, 1886

Courtesy of Victoria & Albert Museum

Surroundings

Once the church was built, the vicarage, schoolroom and master's house were soon added, but it was between the church and vicarage buildings that some of Shapurji's most visible public work was to take place. It was here, until the graveyard filled up in the 1890s, that he officiated over one burial after another – there would be almost a thousand of them by 1892.[1] No aspect of his job gave more vivid evidence of the grim differences between his parishioners' lives and those of the ruling elites which controlled them and shaped their views of the outside world. He regularly had to bury babies who had not survived the first few hours of life: in 1881 a child who lived five minutes; in 1882 a child who died after thirty minutes; in 1883 a child who lived three hours. Indeed, his parish register entries on the sixty-three burials he conducted in 1876, his first full year in office, revealed appallingly poor levels of health: of the sixty-two people whose age at death he gave, fourteen were under two months old, a further twelve died before they reached one year, thirteen more died before the age of five, and only seventeen survived beyond fifty.[2] Poverty was widespread, and Shapurji's burials included people who had died destitute in the Cannock Union workhouse, such as Harriet Hubery (1881) and Charles Dace, aged fifteen (1882). He also buried many of those who fell victim to the dangers of living in a community whose adults and young people worked in mines, ironworks, and brickworks, on canals and on railways, in a landscape scarred with pit workings and the debris of industrialisation: George Whitehouse, aged thirteen, who died of his injuries when trapped between the rolls of a mill for grinding clay at a brickworks (1879); Henry Bowen, aged seventy, killed at the Nook Colliery (1879); Charles Spragg, aged three, killed by a canal swingbridge whilst on his father's barge, a few weeks after Shapurji had buried the boy's three-month-old sister (1880); J. Dudley, a sixty-five-year-old miner, fatally injured by a fall of rock at Cannock and Leacroft Colliery (1881); William Perks, killed crossing the railway line (1881); Thomas Hubery, deputy manager at the Cannock-Wyrley Colliery, fatally injured when a fall of coal crushed him into some timber (1883); and George Holden, aged twenty-three, killed at the Great Wyrley Colliery Company when a lump of coal fell on him (1884).[3]

---

[1] *Cannock Chase Courier*, 8 October 1892.
[2] S.R.O., D1215/1 (Great Wyrley parish registers).
[3] *Cannock Advertiser*, 1876-1887, passim.

****

Of the actual buildings on the St Mark's site the church was clearly the key, but the others would be important for the Edalji story too. From the inner recesses of their vicarage home the Edaljis were reminded constantly of the rhythm of work in the building next door: from high up in a steeply-pitched roof, a bell tolled out the key times of the day in the National Schoolroom. This building (today the parish hall) had been opened by the National Society in 1849, and like much of the rest of Great Wyrley's social and economic landscape it was local magnates who were in immediate control of the change. The schoolroom was to play a part in some of the more turbulent episodes in the Edaljis' forty-two year stay; Conan Doyle was to suggest that Shapurji's decision to let the Liberal Party use the room during an election campaign might have helped spark off the outburst of letters and hoaxes which afflicted the Edalji family after 1892.

St Mark's was not just the focal-point of the Anglican Church's spiritual empire in Great Wyrley; it also lay on the area's main economic axis. The next building to the vicarage on the western side was the stationmaster's house, and beyond that lay the station, on a railway carried high over Station Road by a sombre brick bridge. This railway, opened in 1858, connected Great Wyrley with Walsall, Birmingham, and the Black Country of South Staffordshire and North Worcestershire in the south, and with Cannock, Rugeley, and the heart of the Cannock Chase coalfield in the north. It scythed Shapurji's parish in two – the township of Great Wyrley on the one side and the village of Cheslyn Hay beyond it on the other. Next to the railway lay the community's two largest places of employment: the first, a quarter of a mile north of the vicarage, was Gilpin's edge tool works; the second, half a mile to the south, was the Plant colliery – the scene of the outrage in 1903 which brought the Edalji family to its knees. The Great Wyrley Colliery Company which opened the site had been established a few years before the Edaljis' arrival with the assistance of one of their nearest neighbours – Great Wyrley's leading citizen, John Hatton.[1]

This colliery was Great Wyrley's greatest contribution to the development of the Cannock Chase coalfield, a coalfield which in 1850 was probably producing no more than 100,000 tons per year.[2] Aristocratic landowners in the Cannock area

[1] C. H. Goodwin, *The Chase for Coal*, p. 18.
[2] *V.C.H. Staffordshire* ii., p. 77.

such as the Marquess of Anglesey and Lord Hatherton were anxious to make the most of the black gold on and under their land; other mining magnates, such as the Harrisons, wanted to extend their empires;[1] industrialists such as the Gilpins needed coal; and prosperous farmers such as the Hattons of Great Wyrley saw the opportunities for investing their profits within their own localities. Expansion was rapid in the second half of the century, and by 1900 Cannock Chase was producing 4.5 to 5 million tons of coal per year, roughly equivalent to the declining rate of the Black Country.[2] At the time the Edaljis arrived in 1875, a large proportion of the men of St Mark's parish were already engaged in coal-mining.

As Station Road passed by the vicarage and under the railway bridge it entered Cheslyn Hay and climbed the hill to the centre of gravity of a community with a claim to its own distinctive character. Here the most important mines were controlled by an embryonic local dynasty, the Hawkins family,[3] and the most important factory was a tileworks. The village was also the nerve centre of the Methodist alternative to the establishment at St Mark's – Salem (the New Connexion chapel) and the Primitive Methodist Chapel.

The vicarage's south-facing windows looked over a more traditional ingredient of the local economy – fields planted with wheat, barley, turnips or mangolds, or grazed by cows, sheep or horses.[4] Some of the land was farmed by the Edaljis' nearest neighbours on the Great Wyrley side, Elizabeth and Thomas Green of High House farm. The Greens had long been one of the leading farming families in the village, though with surprising global connections: Elizabeth, a strong and energetic woman, who later in her long life corresponded regularly with relatives in different parts of the world, always boasted that she was a niece of Ulysses S. Grant.[5] The couple's son, Harry, was born in 1884, baptised by Shapurji, grew up alongside the Edalji children, and by allegedly killing his own horse at High House farm added a startling twist to the events of 1903.

Further along Station Road lived John and Mary Hatton of Brook House farm. John Hatton had been in a position to invest in the growth of coal mining in the area through profit from his farming interests. With such a portfolio he was also able to build a formidable array of civic responsibilities, making

---

[1] *V.C.H. Staffordshire* ii., p. 79.
[2] C. H. Goodwin, *The Chase for Coal*, p. 19.
[3] C. H. Goodwin, *The Chase for Coal*, p. 18.
[4] *Post Office Directory of Staffordshire*, 1876, p. 371.
[5] S.R.O., D3632/3/15, cuttings on the death of Elizabeth Green.

him almost squire to Shapurji's vicar for over thirty years. When the Edaljis arrived he was already a magistrate and a member of Cannock Board of Poor Law Guardians, and was serving as bailiff to the lord of the manor, the Duke of Sutherland. Under the Edalji regime he continued as chair of the Great Wyrley vestry meeting (predecessor of the parish council), as well as being chosen by Shapurji as minister's churchwarden at St Mark's in 1876. Shapurji baptised a succession of children born of the marriage between John and Mary Hatton, though not Christopher Hatton, the friend of Horace Edalji who had a cameo role in the events of 1903.

At its eastern end, Station Road met Great Wyrley's other north-south axis, the Walsall Road. From Gilpin's edge tool works in the hamlet of Churchbridge in the north, through the hamlet of Landywood, and towards the hamlet of Upper Landywood in the south, St Mark's parish straggled along two miles of this road. Strung along its length were many of the pubs which apart from the churches were almost the only centres for communal social life. At the Churchbridge end was the Robin Hood, where workers from Gilpin's had in the past paid for their beer with truck tickets. Further south came a pub with a little more prestige than the other beer-houses – the Swan had a licence to sell wine and spirits as well as beer and porter; for a time it acted as a temporary mortuary when there were fatalities in the local collieries,[1] and the parish vestry held some of its meetings there. Half-way along the Walsall Road was the Star, where the beer was served in the early years of the last century by the Maud and Henry Badger who were great-grandparents of one of my students at Great Wyrley High School.

One other building on the Walsall Road was of significance for the lives of the adults of the community, or at least for the lives of its men. The Working Men's Institute, opened in 1871, was the only centre for adult education,[2] apart from the churches. Here the Working Men's Mutual Improvement Society met regularly to hear lectures on a variety of subjects. The women of the parish were generally excluded from the Institute; indeed, they were also largely excluded from paid employment. In a study of women in the Cannock Chase coalfield in the 1880s, Mary Mills has pointed out that, in neighbouring Cannock at least, the 1881 census shows that only 2.6% of women from mining households had discernible

---

[1] Vivian Bird, *Staffordshire*, Batsford, 1974, p. 124.
[2] *Kelly's Directory of Staffordshire*, 1900, p. 545.

occupations.[1] Some women worked as servants in middle class or artisan homes, but this was usually before marriage. The average age at marriage was 21.93,[2] and afterwards women were generally tied to the home for the rest of their lives.

World views

Writers across the globe have been inspired by the 'rude, unrefined' label to pass sweeping judgements on the people of Great Wyrley. In his biography of Conan Doyle, Hesketh Pearson declared confidently that the villagers of Great Wyrley thought the world could learn nothing from Parsis, whilst Harold Parsons suggested that congregation and non-church folk alike must have been appalled by Shapurji's appointment.[3] Peter Costello explained parishioners' attitudes very bluntly: 'It was, after all,' he wrote, 'the duty of the English to evangelise the Blacks, not the Blacks to preach to the English.'[4] No author has however produced any explicit evidence on racial prejudices in the village, apart from the examples of racist abuse in the various outbursts of anonymous letter-writing after 1888. In fact the surviving sources only provide indirect glimpses of the impact of 'the stain' on everyday life. It is only possible, for the most part, to examine the influences which shaped attitudes rather than the attitudes themselves.

The churches had an important impact on people's world-views – attendance was still relatively high at St Mark's, which for some events was full to overflowing – and were often centres for the promotion of the notions about racial superiority which Salman Rushdie blamed for the 'stain' of racism in our own time. One Sunday in 1878 a special sermon was given at St Mark's by the Reverend A. A. Welsby, travelling secretary to the South American missionary society, who according to the *Cannock Advertiser* provided the congregation with an account of 'the fierce and idolatrous nations'. In the evening, Shapurji himself continued the process when he preached what the newspaper called 'an excellent sermon on similar subjects'.[5] The feelings of outrage towards non-Christian beliefs which he had learnt from the Evangelicals in Bombay helped him to pass on notions about the inadequacies of peoples beyond these islands.

---

[1] Mary E. Mills, 'Women, Family and Community in the Cannock Chase Coalfield in the 1880s', Wolverhampton Polytechnic M. A. dissertation, 1987, p. 53.
[2] Ibid., p. 46.
[3] Harold Parsons, *Murder and Mystery in the Black Country*, Robert Hale, 1989.
[4] Peter Costello, *The Real World of Sherlock Holmes*, p. 73.
[5] *Cannock Advertiser*, 5 October, 1878.

For members of the congregation who wanted to hear more there was, by the 1880s, the Cannock branch of the Zenana Missionary Society. Its purpose was to raise money to send missions to women in 'zenanas' (secluded apartments) in India. Many believed that it was the duty of Christian people to provide money to export the western civilisation which would save those women; the Zenana Missionary Society was the handmaid of the Church Missionary Society established by Wilberforce, Simeon, and friends. At a Zenana Missionary Society meeting in Cannock in 1881, Miss Neale, a missionary in India for seventeen years, showed her audience a view of 'an atrocious heathen festival' and expressed the view that the people of India were 'lovers of idols'.[1] The message was the same in 1886, when Miss Hamilton, a missionary in various zenanas in India, suggested that it was important to set Indian women free and 'give them a Christian religious place free of idolatrous darkness'.[2]

The other churches also promulgated pictures of the world created elsewhere. At the Primitive Methodist Chapel in 1882 there was a talk about phrenology, the 'science' which purported to demonstrate that people's characters, including the character of whole 'races', could be told from their skulls.[3] Such notions were building-blocks of the 'scientific' racism which became ever more elaborate in the 19th century and shaped attitudes to non-Europeans, mixed marriages, and mixed 'race' children.

Schools, too, were geared to promoting the views of empire constructed by the ruling elites of the south-east. According to one study of English history textbooks in the 19th century the most frequent impression given of the peoples of India was that they were 'cruel and totally unfit to rule themselves'.[4] The primary schools in Cheslyn Hay and Great Wyrley in Shapurji Edalji's time certainly presented images of empire which did not put the world's people of colour in a favourable light. In his log book of 1891 the Head of Great Wyrley Board School noted nonchalantly that a 'nigger minstrel' group was due to visit;[5] such groups were popular at the time, and usually consisted of white people who blackened their faces, though occasionally black American groups toured Britain too. When George and

[1] *Cannock Advertiser*, 24 September, 1881.
[2] *Cannock Advertiser*, 16 October 1886.
[3] *Cannock Advertiser*, 14 October, 1882.
[4] Valerie Chancellor, *History for their Masters: Opinion in the English History Textbook: 1800-1914,* Adams & Dart, 1970, pp. 122-7.
[5] S.R.O., D4339/1/1 (Great Wyrley Board school log book, 1883-1904).

Horace Edalji attended Rugeley Grammar School in the late 1880s and early 1890s the curriculum was utterly Christocentric and Eurocentric, not to say Anglocentric, the subjects taught being scripture, English grammar, English history, geography, English literature, arithmetic, algebra, Euclid, Latin, French, and chemistry.[1] An examiner's report in 1892 suggested that in geography (Great Britain and her dependencies) 'the weakest part of the paper was the description of Hindoostan (India).'[2]

Activities at the Mechanics' Institute also played their part. On the whole the lecture topics were not about the remote world beyond Britain at all – usually members of the society themselves provided the talks, often on topics relating to science and technology such as 'heat', and 'steam boilers'. The few speakers who did cover the wider world, however, generally provided a negative view. In 1880 a G. H. Clifford of Hatherton Hall spoke on New Zealand where, he claimed, 'the natives were cannibals of the fiercest type' when Cook went.[3] There were also social entertainments at the Institute, with women allowed into the men's den: in 1892 a concert was given by the Hednesford Christie Minstrels, whose repertoire included 'The Jolly Old Nigger', which according to a local paper they 'sang in character'.[4]

It can certainly be assumed that the result of the constant repetition of such messages was that the Edalji family was always viewed through a foggy mix of ideas about supposed racial difference, and about British genetic and cultural superiority. Most revealing are reactions to George's conviction in 1903. Large parts of the press, including the papers most likely to be read in Great Wyrley, now felt free to unleash their prejudices on the proven criminal. Everywhere, his 'Eastern extraction' was used as an explanation for his seeming criminality. The *Express & Star* ran an editorial which suggested:

> *If Edalji did perpetuate those horrible outrages he might have been actuated by feelings which were originally born in the breast of a Parsee ancestor, and by the law of heredity transmitted to the present generation.*[5]

---

[1] S.R.O., D5408/7/6 (Cambridge examination report, 1897, in Rugeley grammar school file 1875-1951).
[2] S.R.O., D5408/7/4 (Cambridge examination report, 1892, in Rugeley grammar school file 1860-1898).
[3] *Cannock Advertiser*, 13 March 1880.
[4] *Cannock Advertiser*, 26 November 1892.
[5] *Express & Star*, 24 October 1903.

The same *Express & Star* journalist who saw Great Wyrley as 'an eerie spot' reported that a cab taking George to the courtroom was attacked by a crowd and the door torn from its hinges. The reporter put this down to George's 'nationality', suggesting that 'the average rustic can see no good in a foreigner, and to him an Asiatic comes in the guise of an emissary of the devil'. [1] This same writer had been in Great Wyrley during 1903, and noted later that 'many and wonderful were the theories I heard': a local explanation for the outrages was that George was making 'nocturnal sacrifices to strange gods'. Elsewhere, the 'Oriental' love of mystery was commonly seen as a likely motive for George's alleged secret work of the night.[2]

Another person whose feelings about race were unleashed by George's conviction was his mother. The conservative Charlotte, so imbued since childhood with traditional ideas about her own Englishness, knew now, from the years of her marriage to Shapurji in general and the treatment of her son in particular, that Englishness had another face: 'As an English woman,' she sighed in the thirtieth year since her first meeting with Shapurji, 'I am grieved & shocked about prejudice against the non-English.' [3] Whatever her experiences in the parish which Sir Arthur Conan Doyle had described as 'rude' and 'unrefined', Charlotte had some insight into the fact that British racism was not born in the minds of Great Wyrley's working class. By the time that Shapurji had arrived in England in 1867 racist ideas had infiltrated all sectors of British society and were at the heart of its institutions and imperial order.

Celebrations

This fact makes Shapurji's personal career achievements all the more remarkable. Perhaps his greatest moment was the day in January 1876, a month after his arrival, that he stood in St Mark's Church facing Bishop Hobhouse to be instituted as Vicar of Great Wyrley. It was twenty years since his rebellion against the faith of his birthright community in Bombay, and for the last nine years he had struggled grittily to establish himself in England. Now he could savour the celebration of his installation as Vicar of St Mark's in Great Wyrley in Staffordshire. The significance of this moment has never been made apparent in Great Wyrley, the West Midlands, the

[1] *Express & Star*, 14 January 1907.
[2] *Daily Mail*, 24 October 1903.
[3] P.R.O., HO 144/984, no. 48 (Charlotte Edalji to the Home Secretary, January 1904).

Church of England, the United Kingdom, South Asia, or beyond. If Shapurji really was the 'first ordained native Indian clergyman in England' then it is very likely that he was the first 'native Indian clergyman' to be preferred to an English living, something to be celebrated. He was, admittedly, an awkward man, a man whose inner resources and brand of Christian commitment were so strong that he could be stubbornly resistant to authority and moral pressure of all kinds. As he once wrote: 'It is the duty of Christ's ministers always to do only that which they in their consciences believe to be good for their people without thinking whether they would thereby become popular or unpopular.'[1] It was nevertheless because of this very awkwardness that he achieved so much. The career of this talented and immensely resilient pioneer should be reported and remembered.

The institution ceremony was on the one hand watched by a perhaps bemused congregation of coal-miners, ironworkers, farmers, and their families, and on the other led by a bishop who was closer to the origins of 'the stain' than the allegedly 'rude, unrefined' people before him. Bishop Hobhouse had in fact been delegated the task of conducting the institution by a man he had also served in a previous existence, George Selwyn, Bishop of Lichfield; the lives of these two pillars of the establishment had been entwined since Hobhouse's period of service as chief aide to Selwyn whilst the latter was Bishop of New Zealand and Melanesia. Selwyn himself had been born into the highest reaches of England's ruling classes – at Eton he was co-editor of a school magazine with William Ewart Gladstone, and Gladstone was to act as coffin-bearer at his funeral in Lichfield Cathedral.

Selwyn and Hobhouse had returned from their time in New Zealand and Melanesia six years before Charlotte and Shapurji arrived in Great Wyrley. In some excruciating verses the magazine *Punch* took the opportunity of Selwyn's appointment as Bishop of Lichfield to gush contempt for the 'savagery' of both the indigenous peoples of New Zealand and the working classes of the Black Country:

THE RIGHT BISHOP IN THE RIGHT PLACE, OR, SELWYN AMONG THE BLACKS...

...Long, long, the warm Maori hearts that so loved him
May watch and may wait for his coming again,
He has sowed the good seed there, his Master has moved him

---

[1] Shapurji Edalji, *Lectures on St Paul's Epistle to the Galatians*, p. 18.

To his work among savages this side the main,
In "the Black Country", darker than ever New Zealand,
'Mid worse ills than heathenism's worst can combine,
He must strive with the savages reared in our free land,
To toil, drink, and die, round the forge and the mine!

Say if We'nsbury roughs, Tipton cads, Bilston bullies,
Waikato can match, Taranaki excel?
Find in New Zealand's clearings, or wild ferny gullies,
Tales like those Dudley pit-heaps and nailworks could tell.
A labour more brutal, a leisure more bestial.
Minds raised by less knowledge of God or of man,
More in manners that's savage and less that's celestial,
Can New Zealand show than the Black Country can?

A fair field, my Lord Bishop – fair field and no favour -
For your battle with savagery, suff'ring and sin,
To Mammon, their god, see where rises the savour
Of the holocausts offered his blessing to win.
Your well-practised courage, your hold o'er the heathen,
From, not to, New Zealand for work ought to roam;
If it be dark, what must the Black Country be then,
What's the savage o'er sea to the savage at home? [1]

Both Shapurji's compatriots in South Asia and his working class parishioners in Great Wyrley, close to the Black Country, clearly had a lot to contend with. The 'heathen' Parsi of 1856 and the Christian alone among the 'savages' on the mission to the Waralis of the rainforest in 1866 was by 1876 the Asian alone among the 'savages' of the Cannock Chase coalfield.

Such pictures of the world were not confined to the minds of writers for *Punch*. Like much of the establishment, Selwyn himself held views about the empire and race which presaged Kipling's notorious injunction to 'Take up the White Man's burden – Send forth the best ye breed'.[2] At a large missionary meeting in the United States in 1874, the year before he appointed Shapurji, Selwyn urged 'the good comfortable rectors' of New York to go and convert the Indians in the West. He suggested that the English and American churches should act in union, for 'there is no nation now upon the earth that can be put in comparison for one single moment of real missionary power to our English-speaking race'.[3]

---

[1] Punch, 14 December, 1867, cited in Rev. H W. Tucker, *Memoir of the Life and Episcopate of George Augustus Selwyn, D. D.*, William Wells Gardener, 1879, vol. ii, pp. 242-3.
[2] 'The White Man's Burden', 1899, *The Works of Rudyard Kipling*, pp. 323-324.
[3] J. H. Evans, *Churchman Militant*, p. 181.

The building which was Selwyn's seat, Lichfield Cathedral, itself celebrated the forcible spread of empire with a series of memorials to the armed forces of South Staffordshire. One such monument had been erected to perpetuate the memory of those in the 80th regiment who helped destroy Sikh resistance to British rule in the 1840s. Selwyn's successor was to be Bishop Maclagan, who had himself served as a soldier in the British army in India in the 1840s, and drew a military pension for the rest of his life, even when he became Archbishop of York in 1891.[1] It was in 1886, during his period in office, that the colours of the 38th Battalion of the South Staffordshire Regiment, which helped suppress the 1857 Indian Uprising, were installed in the cathedral.[2] The fabric of this glorious building was impregnated with pride in British imperialism. The fabric of the establishment to which Shapurji committed his fate in January 1876 was in much the same condition.

****

In the following month parishioners gathered in St Mark's for a second happy event in the Edaljis' new lives; Charlotte had given birth to the couple's first child and now was the time for the christening. The service was led by Shapurji himself, and it was therefore he who formally bestowed on the baby boy a combination of names – George Ernest Thompson Edalji – which provided poignant commentary on the Edaljis' view of their son's identity. Shapurji was now so heavily westernised that he and Charlotte quite naturally used the surname Edalji for their son, though if Shapurji had remained a Parsi in Bombay the baby's last name would have been Shápurjí. The name Thompson honoured not just the baby's English clergyman grandfather, but also a family tradition stretching back beyond the boy in the scarlet tunic in Bombay in the 1740s to the family of mariners which helped secure the British foothold on the west coast of India and loot some of its riches in the first place. As for the name George, this was a reminder of the two-year-old christened in Gorakhpur in 1818 during a new phase in British imperialist expansion – the George Thompson Stoneham whose name obliterated all trace of his Indian mother.

To the congregation, these allusions to the baby's heritage were no doubt a complete mystery. For them, whatever the

[1] F. D. How, *W. Dalrymple Maclagan, Archbishop of York*, Wells, Gardner, Darton & Co Ltd, 1911, p. 14; *V.C.H. Staffordshire* iii, p. 81.
[2] *The Military Forces of Staffordshire in the Nineteenth Century*, reprinted from *The Staffordshire Advertiser*, 1901, p. 7.

baby's English names, the bundle Shapurji held above the font was simply the child of a mixed marriage, and they had not been brought up to view such marriages or such children as anything but a problem. Still, after entering all the baby's names in the parish register, Shapurji himself proudly added the baby's date of birth in the margin, a practice he did not follow with other baptisms.[1]

George Edalji''s English grandparents were enthusiastic about their first grandchild. In March, the Reverend Thompson Stoneham was to be found conducting a burial and two baptisms in Great Wyrley, whilst Shapurji was in Ketley officiating at a burial.[2] The exchange of parishes allowed Mary and Thompson Stoneham to spend a few days with the baby. Sadly for this closely-knit family, Thompson Stoneham died the following year. Ejected from the vicarage by her husband's death, Mary moved from Ketley to nearby Much Wenlock. Her new home was that of her other daughter, Mary Sancta, and of Thompson Stoneham's sister, Elizabeth. Typically for women of their class, the three members of the household lived from incomes provided by their dead male relatives. George was later to travel to the Much Wenlock house many times, to visit his grandmother, who died in 1893, and his aunt, Mary Sancta. George Ernest Thompson Edalji was a family man.

---

[1] S.R.O., F1215/1 (Great Wyrley parish registers).
[2] S.S.R.C., P149/2 (Ketley parish registers, christenings 1856-1891).

6. Citizens

One thing which drove Conan Doyle on in his campaign on George Edalji's behalf, he once suggested, was the sight of 'the coloured clergyman in his strange position, the brave, blue-eyed, grey-haired wife, the young daughter, baited by brutal boors...'[1] By the 1990s this presentation of the Edalji family as helpless victims of racial prejudice seemed to me as one-sided as his description of Great Wyrley as a 'rude, unrefined parish'. Many of the pupils I had taught in the 1970s and 1980s had grandparents and great-grandparents who had been baptised by Shapurji, and some had relatives who had been married by him. Shapurji had also been at the centre of the community's efforts to provide elementary education for all, as envisaged by the 1870 Education Act; some of the infrastructure created then was still there in the 1970s, including Great Wyrley Primary School which sent children to us. Between them the Edaljis had used their talents and energies to help make Great Wyrley what it was in my own time. They were a real, living, achieving family, not the one-dimensional stuff of a Sherlock Holmes story

Roles

From the moment of arrival the Edalji marriage partners worked conscientiously to serve the St Mark's flock. The Reverend John Compson had had a curate to assist him in his later years, but Shapurji had to carry out all the routine duties of the parish on his own. In his first full year, 1876, he conducted forty-six baptisms, eleven marriages, and sixty-three burials, and the numbers of these occasional offices stayed at roughly the same level into the 1880s.[2] He was more, however, than just a competent manager of his parishioners' rites of passage. He soon came to be known for the quality of his sermons, and this, along with the attractive decoration of the inside of the church for special occasions, left a local journalist so impressed that he announced boldly that St Mark's 'may be truly stated to be one of the best Churches in this neighbourhood'.[3]

One small reason for this journalist's high regard for St Mark's was the contribution made by Charlotte. He delighted at the profusion of fruit and flowers at the harvest festival of 1883,

---

[1] Arthur Conan Doyle, *The Strange Case of George Edalji*, George Newnes, c. 1925.
[2] S.R.O., 1215/1/1 (Great Wyrley parish register, baptisms 1845-1886).
[3] *Cannock Advertiser*, 27 October 1883.

pointing out that Charlotte was one of those responsible for the decorations; in 1886 his paper again commented on the bright decoration of St Mark's for the harvest celebration – Charlotte had decorated the font. There were severe limits, though, to the contribution Charlotte could make to the life of the church. She did prepare some female candidates for confirmation, but for the most part her role outside the vicarage did not include parishioners' spiritual welfare. If she left the vicarage on church business it was most likely to be to decorate the church, to help with catering on some special occasion, or to visit the sick. Even the three female friendly societies in Great Wyrley in this period were run by men. Members paid regular subscriptions to these societies, and received benefits for themselves and/or their families in the event of illness or death.[1] Shapurji allowed one such body, the Great Wyrley Female Friendly Society, free use of the schoolroom for meetings. Charlotte sometimes attended, but men took all the leading roles.[2]

The shackles on Charlotte's use of her talents were the same for many women at that time, though the shackles were different in kind for middle class as opposed to working class women. The Evangelicals, with their emphasis on female submission as supposedly laid down in the book of Genesis and the writings of St Paul, had done much to reinforce a view of women as wives, mothers, and home-makers. A favourite passage in collections of 19th-century family prayers was St Paul's Epistle to the Colossians: 'Wives submit yourselves unto your husbands... Husbands, love your wives and be not bitter against them.' The Victorian idealisation of the woman as 'the angel in the house', which restricted Charlotte's role largely to the home, was widespread. Sir Arthur Conan Doyle, for example, was brought up on these notions of womanhood; when votes for women became an issue he was altogether opposed to the idea, and his notions of chivalry once caused him to hit his own son because he said a woman was ugly.[3] In 1892 he created his own model 'angel in the house' in Mary Holder, a character in the Sherlock Holmes story 'The Beryl Coronet'.[4] Mary is described by her adoptive father as a 'sunbeam' in his house, 'sweet, loving, beautiful, a wonderful manager and housekeeper, yet as tender and quiet and gentle as a woman could be'. Many middle class

---

[1] Mary E. Mills, 'Women, Family and Community in the Cannock Chase Coalfield in the 1880s', p. 70.
[2] *Cannock Advertiser*, 22 June 1878, 21 June 1879, 24 June 1882.
[3] Julian Symons, *Portrait of an Artist: Conan Doyle*, Whizzard Press/André Deutsch, 1979, p. 119.
[4] Arthur Conan Doyle, 'The Beryl Coronet', *The Strand Magazine*, May 1892, reprinted in William S. Baring-Gould (ed.), *The Annotated Sherlock Holmes*, 2 vols, John Murray, 1968.

women such as Charlotte lived in the strait-jacket of such role expectations.

One consequence of this was that men and women played distinct roles in religious life. The pews at St Mark's may have been dominated by females, but it was men who were in control: God was widely seen, after all, as being simply the epitome of a Victorian gentleman. There was nevertheless some redefinition of the role of women in this period, when the purely domestic role assigned to them previously was extended into the public sphere by an increasing emphasis on philanthropy: the qualities which appeared to equip women for home-making were also the qualities needed for social reform. There was an explosion of charitable endeavour in the Victorian Church, much of it carried out by upper and middle-class women, many of them from vicarages. Whether their energies sprang from compassion or from a conscious or unconscious belief that the working classes at home and 'fluttered folk and wild' abroad[1] were monsters in need of taming is a matter for debate, but their sphere of activity expanded enormously. Charlotte had first become involved in philanthropic activity because her father was a clergyman; her involvement in the church school in Ketley before her marriage was part of a general pattern – clergymen's daughters and wives were doing the same all over the country. Her marriage did not change anything. From 1874 until Shapurji 's death, her role outside the home, apart from the occasions after 1903 when she entered into other worlds because of George's case, was entirely shaped by society's limited expectations of a clergyman's wife. Within these limits she had much success, and won the affection of many.

Conflict

It took more than fine sermons and a well decorated church for Shapurji to win the confidence of members of his congregation. This was particularly the case with the group of men involved in running the affairs of the parish. In the months which followed the Edaljis' arrival this group and their minister circled round each other, searching for pattern in the new relationship.

---

[1] Rudyard Kipling, 'The White Man's Burden', 1899, in *The Works of Rudyard Kipling*, The Wordsworth Poetry Library, 1995, p. 323.

Shapuri Edalji as Vicar of St Mark's

There was one person in the congregation who was more likely than any other to determine the outcome of this shadow dance. The Edaljis' neighbour, John Hatton, leading farmer, driving-force behind the establishment of the Great Wyrley Colliery Company, magistrate, frequently-elected chair at meetings of Great Wyrley vestry, bailiff to the Duke of Sutherland, and member of the Cannock Poor Law Board of Guardians, was a pillar of the establishment whose support would help guide Shapurji through the uncertainties. Shapurji opted for stability by reappointing him as minister's churchwarden at the Easter vestry of 1876. The fact that the ratepayers nominated Hatton as chair, however, is an indication of where the balance of power lay in village affairs and Shapurji was in the long run not as accommodating towards these vested interests as Compson had been.[1]

Within two years the continuity between the regimes of John Compson and Shapurji Edalji had been shattered, and the parish was rent with controversy. The first sign that all was not well came in April 1878, when John Hatton chaired a vestry meeting which found itself considering some embarrassing news: a letter had arrived from Cannock District Gas Company which coldly threatened to remove the gas meter from St Mark's Church and to take proceedings for arrears.[2] The meeting decided to ask for Shapurji's help, and John Hatton was dispatched to the vicarage with the other churchwarden to ask him to attend. Shapurji bluntly refused, and the meeting was reduced to making a humiliating resolution: for the foreseeable future the churchwardens must wait in the porch after church services and beg for extra contributions from the congregation so that the gas bill could be paid. Shapurji's stubborn unwillingness to help the churchwardens in the discharge of their duties was a token of an ominous coolness between himself and some of his key parishioners: one church-goer was to claim later that at one point churchwardens Hatton and Munro were 'abused from the pulpit'.[3] The die was cast, and at the Easter vestry Shapurji appointed a Richard Webb, not John Hatton, as minister's churchwarden, whilst Donald Munro, manager at the Great Wyrley Colliery Company and along with Hatton one of the most powerful men in the parish, was reappointed parishioners' warden. Shapurji then objected to a vestry meeting decision that the churchwardens should be allowed to make a collection at the

[1] S.R.O., D144/A/PV/1 (Vestry minute book, 1833-1993, 17 April, 11 May 1876).
[2] S.R.O., D144/A/PV/1 (Vestry minute book, 1833-1993, 11 April 1878).
[3] Letter to *The Birmingham Gazette*, 21 February 1907.

church to cover the expenses of a previous churchwarden, and Webb and Munro had to stand in the street to collect instead.[1]

One factor in these developments, no doubt, was the impact of British racism on the mindsets of the players in the drama; Charlotte, Shapurji, and George and Maud all referred later in general terms to the racial prejudice they had met. It may well be that the Edaljis' first few years were the most critical in this respect, as Shapurji had to do far more than any white minister to prove his capability, and earn affection and support. There is, however, no direct evidence to link racism to the shaping of the early troubles.

Whatever the precise causes, by the time of the Easter vestry of 1879, parish affairs were in turmoil. The churchwardens appointed the previous year were grunting about the misery they had suffered: the honour and pleasure of the office, they felt, was now outweighed by the 'unpleasantness and increasing troubles which seem to surround it at Great Wyrley'.[2] As a result, Richard Webb was replaced as minister's churchwarden by Edward Sayer, and Donald Munro was replaced as parishioners' churchwarden by Thomas Thacker. Some time later, however, Sayer and Thacker compounded the crisis by refusing to take up office. Shortly afterwards Shapurji presided over another, distraught, vestry meeting. Without Shapurji's blessing, the meeting tried to find candidates willing to take over from Sayer and Thacker, but no-one would accept what was now seen as a poisoned chalice – even John Hatton refused to come back into the fold. As for Shapurji, he only succeeded in pouring oil on troubled waters: not for the last time, he put procedure before sensitivity to mood and tried to insist that this particular meeting had no power to make new appointments anyway. As the temperature rose, his own alleged weaknesses were thrown back at him – his failure to publish the annual statement of accounts on time or to keep up with home visits.[3] The latter issue was far more important than the gas bill: not only were times of sickness seen by the Church as the best opportunity to strengthen a parishioner's consciousness of the awful prospect of meeting God face to face, but also regular visits were important for encouraging church attendance.

Events reached a climax in June, when a specially-called vestry meeting made a desperate decision: a deputation consisting of John Hatton and John Greensill was delegated to

---

[1] Letters to *The Birmingham Gazette*, 21 and 26 February 1907.
[2] *Cannock Advertiser*, 3 May 1879.
[3] *Cannock Advertiser*, 3 May 1879.

go to the Bishop of Lichfield himself to discuss the troubled state of affairs in the parish. There is no record of the outcome, but never again in Shapurji's time was there such a prolonged period of dissatisfaction.[1]

Whatever the attitudes of members of the 'rude, unrefined parish', Shapurji's own fundamental commitment to standing for truth as he saw it was never going to ensure an easy passage. It was in 1879, at the time that relationships in the parish were at their lowest ebb, that he published his *Lectures on St Paul's Epistle to the Galatians*, which contained his uncompromising statement that 'It is the duty of Christ's ministers always to do only that which they in their consciences believe to be good for their people without thinking whether they would thereby become popular or unpopular.'[2] One ingredient in the difficult early years, then, was his stance as a man of principle, at times in overzealous fussiness over procedural matters but on other occasions in fearless struggle over issues which were central to his fundamental beliefs.

Schooling

One of these central issues was his commitment to church control over education, and it was this commitment, however consistent with the principles underlying his life's mission, which sparked much of the heat in the conflicts of the late 1870s. Communities all over the country were grappling at this time with the provisions of the Education Act passed by Parliament in 1870 during W. E. Gladstone's first ministry. Until 1870 all elementary schools had been provided by voluntary organisations, mainly the Church of England National Society and the nonconformist British and Foreign Society. From 1833 the government had provided grants to the voluntary societies to help to finance their schools, but the rapid growth of population in the 19th century, particularly in areas of heavy industrialisation such as the Cannock Chase coalfield, still left many children with no chance of going to school. Direct intervention by the state in 1870 came at a time when there was an increasing feeling among Britain's rulers that she would be overtaken by her economic competitors if a system of education for all were not provided, whilst for reasons of social and political control it was also considered important to educate the new working classes.

---

[1] S.R.O., D144/A/PV/1 (Vestry minute book, 1833-1993, 5 June 1879).
[2] Shapurji Edalji, *Lectures on St Paul's Epistle to the Galatians*, p. 18.

**Great Wyrley's image in the 1970s – a cartoon from
the Black Country Bugle**

Kind permission of the Black Country Bugle

The only surviving picture of the Edalji family, taken in c.1892

Kind permission of Trevor McFarlane

The 1870 Act allowed local communities to set up School Boards, which could raise money from ratepayers to establish and run Board schools if existing voluntary schools did not provide for all children in the area, or to take over and develop existing schools in negotiation with the voluntary societies. The aim was to make education compulsory for all, and by 1880 the work of the new School Boards had advanced enough for an act to be passed compelling all children between the ages of five and ten to attend school. These developments were accompanied all over the country by some fierce struggles, with the Church of England and its National Society in particular fighting to keep a large proportion of the schools under their control. Often, as in Great Wyrley, the church could not afford to provide new buildings, but still opposed the provision of schools by the School Boards.

In Great Wyrley parish a stubborn and uncompromising Shapurji Edalji was at the heart of a struggle which was to last, on and off, for thirty years, and end with him facing the Attorney-General in court in London for a final showdown. As late as 1963 an official in the legal branch of the Ministry of Education read through the file on the case and was so horrified at the way Shapurji had been treated that he considered the affair still merited attention from a local historian.[1] The file, he said, reveals 'a sorry story of official rigidity, even cruelty,' in which every solution proposed by Shapurji in the late 1870s and early 1880s for the old National School of Cheslyn Hay was rejected, and he was left to look after the property without any money. Some of Shapurji's contemporaries were not quite so charitable about his role in the struggle.

In Great Wyrley parish two schools had been provided by the Church of England by the mid-1870s. Great Wyrley's National School, built next to St Mark's vicarage in 1849, has already been mentioned. Shapurji had closed this school by the late 1870s and the bell which rang out the rhythm of the school day over the vicarage had been silenced. The National School in Cheslyn Hay, St Peter's, was built in 1871 on land provided by Lord Hatherton,[2] in the six-month period allowed by the 1870 Education Act for church schools to be built in ill-provided areas before a School Board was established. There were two nonconformist schools – the British School in Cheslyn Hay and the Wesleyan School in Landywood.[3]

---

[1] W.S.L., CB/EDALJI/2 (J. L. B. Todhunter to J. H. P. Oxspring, 5 February 1963).
[2] *V.C.H. Staffordshire* v. p. 102.
[3] Ibid., p. 82, 102.

Shapurji's burning desire was to keep open the two National schools, and thus to maintain the role of the Church of England in shaping the minds of the community's children. His churchwardens and the trustees of the two schools were inevitably drawn into the conflict, and the pressures on them no doubt contributed to the tensions which led to the sending of a deputation to the Bishop of Lichfield in 1879. The parish vestry itself was more concerned with the overall problem of providing schooling for all children in the area as required by the 1870 Act, and by the late 1870s was considering whether to establish a School Board. Whilst the trustees of the school at Landywood were happy to hand over their school buildings, during 1878 and 1879 Shapurji battled with sceptical ratepayers to persuade them to provide him with the funds to re-open the Great Wyrley National School next to the vicarage, whether a School Board was set up or not. He also had problems with St Peter's, the National School in Cheslyn Hay, which he was forced to close in 1879 for lack of a competent teacher.[1]

At this point he weakened temporarily. Parents in Cheslyn Hay were complaining to him about the shortage of provision for their children, particularly for girls. As it did not seem likely that he could raise the money from the ratepayers to re-open St Peter's School he decided his best option was to arrange a handover to the School Board for Great Wyrley and Cheslyn Hay,[2] which was eventually elected in September 1880. The new School Board found it easy enough to reach agreement with the trustees of the Landywood School and the British School in Cheslyn Hay for them to be taken over, but when it came to Shapurji and the two National schools the path was much less clear. In negotiations with the board he demanded, impossibly, that if he handed over St Peter's all future teachers must be members of the Church of England and trained in a Church of England college. He also wanted to retain clear control over religious instruction.[3] As the Board of Education would not allow the condition that teachers should be Anglicans he broke off negotiations.

Even if the National schools had been available, the School Board would not have had enough space in existing buildings to provide for the children of the parish, but now it had no choice but to rely on the building of two new Board schools, one on Walsall Road in Great Wyrley (the site of Great Wyrley

---

[1] P.R.O., ED2/397 (Shapurji Edalji to Board of Education, 18 January 1880).
[2] P.R.O., ED2/397 (Shapurji Edalji to Board of Education, 18 January 1880).
[3] *Cannock Advertiser*, 27 September 1879.

Primary/First School in my time at the High School in the 1970s and 1980s) and one in Cheslyn Hay. Shapurji, however, would not accept defeat easily. When a vestry meeting was called in February 1881 to discuss the application from the School Board for land to build a school in Great Wyrley, those present were surprised to see Shapurji arrive and use his authority to take the chair. Members were even more startled when he launched into a lecture about the role of the National School in making provision for children in the area. When he was coldly informed that this was not the purpose of the meeting he burst into derogatory remarks about members of the School Board. Burnett, chair of the Board, responded sharply, and Shapurji was forced to apologise. He still tried to read a motion to the meeting which it did not want to hear, was ruled out of order, and walked out.[1] His brave but single-minded struggles on behalf of the Church did not always win friends.

He succeeded in arousing similar reactions in Cheslyn Hay where during the rest of 1881 he was under more pressure to give up St Peter's National School. Whilst the School Board wrote to the Board of Education in London for support in the battle, Shapurji actually threatened to re-open the school. In March one of Her Majesty's Inspectors of Schools, who had seen Great Wyrley at first hand, informed the Board of Education that Shapurji was 'an impracticable man'.[2] Then in May the vestry, chaired by John Hatton, recorded that it wanted to express 'in the strongest terms its disapprobation of the Vicar in attempting to reopen the Cheslyn Hay National School'.[3] So it was that whilst the School Board proceeded with plans to build a new Board School in Cheslyn Hay, Shapurji, in June 1881, defiantly reopened St Peter's. There was little chance of this school surviving in the face of the new competition. In 1882 the two new Board schools, in Great Wyrley and Cheslyn Hay, were opened, and by 1884 Shapurji's school in Cheslyn Hay had closed and he was humbly offering to sell the furniture to the opposition. However, he was not finished. In 1885 he re-opened the National School next to St Mark's vicarage, and the head of the Great Wyrley Board School noted in his log book that attendance had dropped because of the Vicar's action.[4] Again, Shapurji was acting on the basis of principle rather than practicality and his school was closed within months.[5] For the time being he accepted surrender.

[1] S.R.O., D144/A/PV/1 (18 February 1881, St Mark's vestry minute book, 1833-1893).
[2] P.R.O., ED2/397 (letter from Mr Yarde, 18 March 1881).
[3] *Cannock Advertiser*, 14 May 1881.
[4] S.R.O., D4339/1/1 (Great Wyrley Board School log book, 1883-1904).
[5] P.R.O., ED2/397 (letter from T. R. Dolby, 6 March 1886).

Picture

It was in his first years in Great Wyrley that Shapurji also prepared his last published work, a series of lectures into which he poured his Christian faith. The books which reflected his roots and earlier interests were behind him now – the Gujerati-English dictionary, the Gujerati grammar, the translation of Johnson's *Rasselas*, the lecture on the westernisation of Hinduism, the translation of the Zoroastrian Pandnameh. His last book, in 1879, revealed how far he had been brought by John Wilson and the Wilson College in Bombay, by Henry Bailey and St Augustine's College in Canterbury, by the Evangelical circle in Oxford, and by all the other Christian influences upon his world-picture. In this new work, *Lectures on St Paul's Epistle to the Galatians*,[1] he wrote as a Christian minister in an English parish. He was probably the first South Asian to do so.

George was two, and Charlotte was expecting a second child, but the couple's domestic tranquillity and sense of anticipation in the third year after their arrival in Great Wyrley were not matched by the mood outside the protective walls of the vicarage. The churchwardens were becoming increasingly restless about the state of affairs in the parish, and the battle over the schools was leaving Shapurji more and more isolated. His work on the lectures provided some distraction.

Shapurji wrote. He did not intend these lectures to be controversial; he simply wanted to use the works of others he admired to provide a straightforward exposition of St Paul's epistle. Whatever his intentions, however, he could not contain himself entirely. Using as a vehicle Paul's criticisms of the churches of the Galatians for straying from the true path, he made it perfectly clear what he himself believed the true faith to be. He also took the opportunity to snipe at heathens abroad and papists at home. His Evangelical leanings rose to the surface as he stressed what he called the two 'great doctrines' for Christians, 'faith in Christ alone as our saviour, and purity of life and character by the power of the Holy Ghost'. We must come to God as we are, he proclaimed, as 'poor and miserable sinners', entreating him for 'mercy through Christ'.

---

[1] Shapurji Edalji, *Lectures on St Paul's Epistle to the Galatians*.

Dadabhai Naoroji, the Parsi who became known as the 'Grand Old Man of India'

Only too aware of current conflicts with some of his parishioners, he then made the heartfelt declaration which was the touchstone for his behaviour as vicar for forty-two years: 'It is the duty of Christ's ministers always to do only that which they in their consciences believe to be good for their people without thinking whether they would thereby become popular or unpopular.'[1]

Although a fully-fledged Anglican vicar, who thought, spoke, and wrote in the language of moderate Evangelicalism, his origins led him at least to acknowledge the aspirations of other world faiths, including those beyond Europe: 'There were wise men in ancient Greece and Rome, in ancient India and Persia,' he admitted, in part-allusion to the magi of Zoroastrian and Christian tradition, 'who exercised their minds to the utmost, for delivering the world from sin and hell.' However, though their books are still with us, he wrote (no doubt with the ancient Zoroastrian writings particularly in mind), we do not find in them anything like 'the simple truth that God had loved fallen sinners and sent His Son for their salvation...'[2] Indeed, for Shapurji, both non-Christian faiths and the Roman Catholic tradition were contaminated with that great obstacle to genuine faith, what he called 'the yoke of ceremonies'. Before their conversion, he said, the Gentiles were 'idolators and had their own heathen yoke of endless and cruel rites and ceremonies'. Paul's salvation was that he forsook ceremonial law and came to Christ. Now, in Shapurji's time, the 'yoke of ceremonies' was still 'grinding down' the Roman Catholic and Greek Orthodox churches. 'Let us not be entangled again,' he begged, 'with the yoke of Popish bondage.' How he must have shivered during his days with Richard Meaux Benson's Society of St John the Evangelist in Oxford.

It may not have been a conscious decision, but when he put down his pen after composing these lectures Shapurji was bringing his academic writing career to an end. When later asked for details of his writings for the *Bibliotheca Staffordiensis* he certainly wanted to prove that his pen had not become inactive, but the only works he could list after 1879 were *Hymns for Sunday Schools* (1887), produced for Great Wyrley's schools, and *Catechism Cards* (1890); Great Wyrley was clearly not as stimulating an environment for him as Bombay and Oxford had been.[3] There was one consolation, the

---

[1] Ibid., p. 18.
[2] Ibid., p. 20.
[3] W.S.L., 190/3/96, Shapurji Edalji to Rupert Sims, 28.3.1893, 'Letters to Rupert Sims', p. 24.

appearance of a new edition of his Gujerati-English Dictionary in London in 1884,[1] which Maud would claim in her last years was still being used in India in the mid-20th century.[2] And there was one last cause: in 1905 his elegant and powerful pen was called on to defend his son.

Children

On Good Friday 1879 Horace Edward was born. Maud Evelyn arrived three years later. All three Edalji children were educated at home at first, in a room which Charlotte and Shapurji set aside as the 'nursery'.[3] As the educational waters became calmer in the mid-1880s and Shapurji had no National schools to look after, he could invest much of his energy in another project dear to his heart – the education of his own children. Charlotte was involved as well, and as George did not go to school until he was eleven, Horace until he was eight, and Maud until she was fourteen, much of the children's personalities and world-pictures can be attributed to the influence of their parents. Even George's handwriting, so much an issue from 1892, took its shape from his parents' teaching.

Eventually the two Edalji boys were given a taste of the wider world. In February 1887, at the age of eleven, George started to attend the Grammar School in Rugeley, a mining town eight miles from Great Wyrley; the railway line from Rugeley to Birmingham passed through Cannock and Great Wyrley, and George could travel to school by boarding the train at the station next to the vicarage. The notorious 'Rugeley Poisoner', Dr William Palmer (1824-56), had attended Rugeley Grammar School half a century earlier, but it was much changed by George's time. The jovial Headteacher, Richard Boycott, had started his headship in the year that Shapurji was instituted as vicar, 1876, and had increased numbers from eighteen to seventy-three. Regular exams assessed by outside external examiners became a feature during his time, whilst in 1886 an assembly hall was added to the school. Boycott seems to have started boys wearing school caps; the only remaining photograph of the Edalji family, taken at Easter 1892, shows the two boys in caps, perhaps their school caps. In his attempts to imitate the public schools Boycott also encouraged sport,

---

[1] J. F. Kirk, *A Supplement to Allibone's Critical Dictonary*.
[2] Letter from Maud Edalji to Hesketh Pearson, 28 August 1956, Hesketh Pearson Papers, The University of Texas at Austin.
[3] *Cannock Advertiser*, 19 January 1889

including the playing of cricket.[1] It is unlikely that George, described by his father as studious and unathletic, made much use of the facilities.[2] Indeed, George's eyesight was already a matter of concern to his parents, though he was not to wear glasses until after his troubles of 1903. In a letter to the *Daily Telegraph* in 1907 Charlotte wrote that George always held reading close, and did not recognise people outside: 'When I met him anywhere I always felt I must look for him, not he for me.'[3] George himself reported that he sometimes could not see well enough to identify his numbered desk in examination rooms.[4]

Having released one son upon the world, the Edaljis had the confidence to let go of another. Six months after George started at Rugeley Grammar School, Horace joined him on the daily train. He was only eight.[5]

It was around the time that the two boys started school that there occurred the curious development in the family's domestic arrangements which was to have dramatic consequences later. Maud, at the age of four or five, was seriously ill for a time. As 'the angel in the house', Charlotte's role included self-sacrifice for the sake of the children, and she shared her daughter's bedroom during the illness so that she could look after her; George moved in with Shapurji. There was much more to the episode than this, for when Maud recovered the old pattern was strangely not restored: for reasons which it is impossible to know now, Charlotte and Shapurji continued to sleep apart. A year or two later, in 1888, there began the train of events which was to end in 1903 with the family's unusual sleeping arrangements a matter of national knowledge, whilst a dispute about those arrangements led in 1907 to a furious clash between Staffordshire's Chief Constable and Britain's most famous contemporary writer.

[1] S.R.O., D144/A/PV/1 (potted history of Rugeley grammar school).
[2] P.R.O., HO 144/984, no. 45 (declaration by Shapurji Edalji).
[3] Cited in *Express & Star*, 18 January 1907.
[4] *Daily Telegraph*, 17 January 1907.
[5] S.R.O., D5408/2/1 (Rugeley grammar school admissions register 1872-1909).

7. Players

Abusive letter-writers and animal-slashers: like every other available account, the first part of this book might give the impression that this was all that the people of Great Wyrley thought about in the years 1888 to 1907. The 'rude, unrefined parish' was actually concerned of course much more with the business of living than with providing material for a kind of Sherlock Holmes story. Charlotte and Shapurji, despite their nineteen years of travail, were at the heart of this enterprise throughout, real players in a real-life drama.

Education was a case in point. The letter-writing episode of 1888 which led to the arrest of Elizabeth Foster may have hit the headlines but behind the scenes Shapurji was not distracted from his energetic involvement in the community's efforts to provide a decent education for all its children. Having seemingly given up hope for the re-opening of the National schools, he actually went over to the enemy he once reviled, the School Board. He was elected as a member in 1886[1] and re-elected a number of times, the size of his vote (he came third in 1892)[2] being testimony not just to his status but also to the respect which fellow-citizens had for him. He was appointed vice-chair in 1890.[3]

During their years of adversity Charlotte and Shapurji pushed on with equal determination with their own children's education. Maud stayed at home, her learning still directed by her parents in the 'nursery', whilst George (who celebrated his 13th birthday a week after Elizabeth Foster was bound over in 1889) and Horace continued to step out of the vicarage each day to board the train for Rugeley.

As the first of the siblings to go to school George had been the first to face the brunt of the wider society's wild and often brutal notions about 'race' and 'racial' identity. One of his school contemporaries later mentioned in a letter to Charlotte that George had had to suffer a great deal of teasing at school – predominantly racist, presumably, though he did not say so explicitly.[4]

---

[1] *Cannock Advertiser*, 25 September 1886.
[2] *Cannock Chase Courier*, 24 September 1892.
[3] *Cannock Chase Courier*, 15 November 1890.
[4] P.R.O., HO 144/984 (J. Darge to Charlotte Edalji, 1903, in R. D. Yelverton's submission to the Home Secretary, December 1907).

should lose all my clients, I am,
as a last resource, appealing for
aid to a few strangers.

My friends can only find
me £20, I have about £20 myself.
I shall be most thankful for
any aid, no matter how small
as it will all help me to meet
my heavy liability.

Apologising for troubling you &
trusting you may assist me as
far as you can,

I am,

Yours respectfully,

G. E. T. Edalji

Rt. Hon Sir J. B. Stone

**Part of George Edalji's begging letter to
Sir J. B. Stone, 1902**

Courtesy of Birmingham Central Library

His memory was that George had not shown anger or pain in face of the taunts. Like many in the same situation – as a person of colour in a sea of white faces – George's strategy was to keep quiet and try to fit in. Mild-mannered and good-natured, steeped in the Christian piety of the Edalji household, and with middle-class expectations of success in life even in a white society, George was a conformist, not a critic. A. D. Denning, who taught at Rugeley Grammar School in George's time and later became Headteacher,[1] remembered him as 'a thoroughly principled and upright youth'.[2] George's sister Maud, with whom he had a very close relationship, even described him as timid.[3]

He left school at Christmas 1891 with an undistinguished record in the Cambridge local examinations: '1891 Edalji G Satisfied'.[4] The following January he went to study at Mason College (now Birmingham University) and it was then that he began to blossom academically. He did so despite the fact that for the next four years his family was tormented not just by further floods of anonymous and often vicious letters but also by a plague of infuriating hoaxes.

****

Conan Doyle's brief investigation into the day-to-day affairs of Great Wyrley led him to offer two passing suggestions as to the motive for the persecution of the Edalji family in these years. The first was that those behind the letters and hoaxes of 1892-5 were perhaps allies of the former maid Elizabeth Foster seeking revenge. The second was that the decision to appoint an Asian to the 'rude, unrefined parish' was bound to cause some difficulty. The only example of the latter problem he could produce, however, was an incident in the course of the election campaign of June 1892 which ended with W. E. Gladstone enjoying his fourth and final innings as Prime Minister. Conan Doyle noted that during the campaign there was indignation among some of the 'baser local politicians' when Shapurji lent the National schoolroom for a Liberal party meeting which he himself chaired.[5] It is true that the letter-writing started after this incident, but there is no reference to it in the letters. Indeed, if the role Shapurji played in the

[1] S.R.O., D5408/2/1 (Rugeley Grammar School admissions register, 1872-1909).
[2] P.R.O., HO 144/984, no. 25 (letter from A. Denning, in R. D. Yelverton's submission to the Home Secretary, 9 December 1903).
[3] P.R.O., HO 144/984, no. 45 (letter from Maud Edalji, in R. D. Yelverton's submission to the Home Secretary, 5 January 1904).
[4] S. R. O., D5048/7/4 (Rugeley grammar school file, 1860-98).
[5] *Daily Telegraph*, 11 January 1907.

community did have any bearing on the persecution there are many more causes of conflict which might be examined. Ever since the Edaljis' arrival there had been tensions of one kind or another, and these continued in the years immediately before and during the troubles of 1888 and 1892-5.

One source of division had always been the clash between the attempts of the more powerful members of the community to assert their own interests and Shapurji's belief that it is 'the duty of Christ's ministers to do only that which they in their consciences believe to be good for their people'. At a School Board meeting in 1889 he made a brusque challenge to the nomination of Charles Browell (manager of the Great Wyrley Colliery Company) as chair, predicting that Browell would be 'harsh in his dealings'. Browell was elected anyway, but Shapurji then supported the suggestion that a William Rogers should be made vice-chair, in preference to Thomas Hawkins, the son of the proprietor of the Old Coppice colliery and probably the most powerful citizen in Cheslyn Hay;[1] Shapurji's argument was that one of the two top offices should be held by a working man.[2] Again he was defeated.

His liberalism was however humanitarian, not radical, and in the same year he managed to antagonise miners pressing for mines reform, a matter of great concern for many members of his party, and for hundreds of residents in his parish. Certainly he believed that the parliamentary system could and should bring reform on behalf of working class people; at a Liberal party meeting during the 1892 general election campaign he spoke warmly of the Liberal parliamentary candidate, John Kempster, as having 'a heart that felt for the toiling masses'.[3] The new unionism of the 1890s, however, which followed the match-girls' strike of 1888 and the dockers' strike of 1889 (both closely connected with Bromley, where Shapurji had once served as curate), reflected greater confidence amongst unskilled workers in their capacity to organise themselves for effective action. As elsewhere, the miners of Great Wyrley and the rest of the Cannock Chase coalfield were becoming increasingly assertive in their demands for concerted action over their appallingly low wages and outrageous working conditions. In 1889 Shapurji willingly allowed miners to pack into the St Mark's schoolroom to discuss their response to a catastrophic explosion at the Mossfield colliery in Longton in North Staffordshire; sixty-six men and boys had been killed in

[1] C. H. Goodwin, *The Chase for Coal*, p. 18.
[2] *Cannock Advertiser*, 5 October 1889.
[3] *Cannock Chase Courier*, 2 July 1892.

the blast, as well as twenty-five pit ponies.[1] Shapurji chaired the meeting, and was cheered when he spoke with feeling about the need to improve wages and conditions for the miners. When local miners' trade union agent Albert Stanley spoke of strike action, however, Shapurji went cold.[2] For all his sympathy with his parishioners' problems he could not contemplate the kind of action which might do anything radical about them. An acrimonious correspondence about his stance followed in the local press, with one writer accusing him of belonging to 'a class whose opinion is ever wavering and who side with one party and apologise to the other for doing so'.[3]

As if all this were not enough, in the same year Shapurji revived the old school issue. His determination to defend the interests of the church so far as the educational system was concerned had always been passionate and sometimes impractical. Now, after the years of truce, he decided to try to sell the National School in Cheslyn Hay but failed in the face of opposition from parishioners wanting to keep the school for the church, from Lord Hatherton, and from the Bishop of Lichfield.[4]

****

Attitudes to the Edalji family by 1892 had therefore been shaped by seventeen years of parish politics, not just one incident in an election campaign. None of these episodes is mentioned in the anonymous letters of 1888 and 1892-5 but the authors may well have been influenced by the climate they created. The climate in Great Wyrley was however shaped by something much more than Shapurji's role and personality, and here there certainly are lessons to be learned from the election campaign of 1892.

The eventual winner, the Liberal Party, contained some strange bedfellows. The new Prime Minister, W. E. Gladstone, may now be famous and respected for his high-minded moral convictions but the fact remains that in his earlier career he had spoken in Parliament in favour of his father's slave-owning interests. One of his newly-elected MPs, Dadabhai Naoroji, had very different roots. Like Shapurji a Parsi who once attended Elphinstone College, in 1885 he became a founding father, alongside Shapurji's former schoolmate Dinsdale Eduljee

[1] *Cannock Chase Courier*, 9 November 1889; Fred Leigh, *Lest We Forget*, Rose Bank Publications, 1994, p. 59.
[2] C. H. Goodwin, *The Chase for Coal*, p. 72.
[3] *Cannock Advertiser*, 16, 23 November, 7, 14 December, 1889.
[4] P.R.O., TS 18/251 (Shapurji Edalji to Charity Commissioners, 14 January 1892).

Wacha (another Parsi), of the Indian National Congress in Bombay and was made president in 1886. His defeat as Liberal candidate in Holborn in the 1886 British general election led Conservative Prime Minister Lord Salisbury to make his notorious comment that 'however great the progress of mankind has been, and however far we have advanced in overcoming prejudices, I doubt if we have yet got to the point of view where a British constituency would elect a black man'.[1] Then, in the lead-up to the 1892 election, an extremely illiberal caucus in Naoroji's own local Liberal party bitterly opposed the nomination of an Asian as candidate. With attitudes such as this across the political spectrum it is hardly surprising that the Edalji family faced problems in their own parish. The letters of 1892-5 contained much racist abuse.

****

If only I had got to Great Wyrley 10 years earlier, Maud, perhaps I could have talked to you as you tended your father's lonely grave. What would you have told of the real world behind the vicarage walls in those painful years? The change in family sleeping arrangements resulting from your childhood illness did admittedly become the subject of worldwide gossip after Conan Doyle published his *Daily Telegraph* articles, but apart from that we know nothing about your life until the troubles of 1892-5 were over. And yet you were at the centre of everything, you and your mother. You slept in the same room, and you spent much of each day together whilst your father was carrying out his duties and your brothers were at school or college. You were there when the postman or intruders stuffed abusive letters through the door, when letters and other objects were strewn about the grounds, when police officers lurked outside in the night, when tradespeople called with unordered goods, and when hoodwinked professionals from across the land appeared on the doorstep. You must have heard the bewilderment and outrage of your parents as they responded to each new invasion. And you must have learnt from their unwavering reaction to adversity: fight not flight.

---

[1] Rozina Visram, *Ayahs, Lascars and Princes*, p. 83.

Dinshaw Edulji Wacha, former classmate of Shapurji Edalji, who along with Dadabhai Naoroji was one of the founders of the Indian National Congress

****

The Home Office files do provide some insights into life inside the vicarage walls of which earlier writers were unaware. Most startling is the material about Horace. One typically candid letter from Charlotte to Conan Doyle in 1908 revealed something about her second son which has never been reported: he had, she said, been a youth with a 'singular brooding temper'. Most notable was the astonishing occasion on which a minor dispute with Maud led him to refuse to speak to her for the whole of the next four years.[1] This was a boy with a will of his own. Already he was isolated by the family sleeping arrangements from the Charlotte-Maud and Shapurji-George axes, and he was also increasingly excluded from the easy understanding which obtained between his two siblings. A more gregarious person than George, he reacted by looking outside the vicarage for social contact and was particularly friendly with Christopher Hatton, one of the children of John and Mary Hatton of Brook House. He also had to cope with the fact that George was turning out to be the academic achiever of the family; in 1893 he was articled to Messrs King and Ludlow and his successes started to multiply, whilst Horace's academic career ended when he left school in 1894. His independence of spirit, part cause and part consequence of the strained relations of these years, would lead later to more explosions and eventually to exile.

Lull

At last, in December 1895, the letters and hoaxes stopped, and at last, at the age of fourteen, Maud was sent to school. Shapurji believed so passionately in the importance of education that it seems unlikely that he thought it only of value for his sons. Perhaps he and Charlotte delayed releasing Maud on to the world because of fears aroused by the troubles; to get to Queen Mary's High School in Walsall she had to travel the same route as the boys going to Walsall Grammar. Certainly Shapurji's birthright Parsi community in Bombay had produced many women who played a significant part in public life and, as the age of the Suffragettes dawned in Britain, he as a Liberal might be expected to have some openness to the possibility of greater opportunities for women.

---

[1] P.R.O., HO 144/989 (Conan Doyle to Home Secretary, 2 February 1908).

255

Maud's closest role-model, Charlotte, had had a much more limited life-experience than her husband, thirty-two years in St Mary's vicarage in Ketley and twenty years in St Mark's vicarage in Great Wyrley. She nevertheless continued to pour energy into the roles which were allowed her during these formative years for Maud's development. In 1897 Great Wyrley prepared cheerfully for the celebrations marking Queen Victoria's Diamond Jubilee, and Charlotte played her part. In the twenty-one years since 1876, when Shapurji was instituted as Vicar of Great Wyrley and Queen Victoria became Empress of India, much of the map of Africa had been coloured red. The Diamond Jubilee represented the last blaze of imperial glory, though Kipling, in his poem 'Recessional' was one of the few to suggest this possibility at the time.[1] After a further four years had passed, during which time the Boer War had taken some of the gloss from Britain's sense of invulnerability, Queen Victoria was dead. In 1902 the all-male Great Wyrley parish council formed a committee to plan the celebration of Edward VII's coronation, and graciously resolved that 'the ladies be asked to help'. Special invitations to join in went to those, including Charlotte, who had been involved in the preparations in 1897. 'Helping' meant, on the whole, catering, but Charlotte tried to be more creative when she attended the committee meetings, suggesting for example that special coronation mugs should be provided for the children – in the end eight hundred were ordered from Burslem in the Potteries in North Staffordshire. All the preparations were made: special teas were to be served by 'the women and some men' to children and older people; there was to be a bonfire; balloons, four of them 'grotesque', were to fly above the revellers; and there were to be races, sports, and a choral competition. Then, with two days to go, an emergency committee meeting had to be called to decide what to do about some sudden news: the king had had an operation for appendicitis, with the foreign guests already arriving for the coronation on 26th June. Charlotte seconded a motion that if the coronation was postponed (which it was), so should all plans, apart from the special teas.[2]

What did Maud take from all these influences? When she started school she was already a keen naturalist, and the fact that she would eventually acquire items of specialist equipment – a microscope, a vasculum (a case for holding flowers), and a small trowel which she carried in a sheath during her expeditions – is an indication that she had more than a passing amateur's interest; the trowel was to be briefly suspected as the

[1] Rudyard Kipling, 'Recessional', 1897, The Works of Rudyard Kipling, p. 328.
[2] S.R.O., D3148/1 (minutes of Great Wyrley parish meetings, 1893-1934).

horse-slashing weapon in 1903.[1] Miss Foxley, Headteacher at Queen Mary's at the time, described her as someone who not only had a strong bent for natural science but also a careful training in botany, physiology, and other branches of science. Much of her time was spent in outdoor work on natural history, and she had good powers of observation.[2]

In the end, however, all this activity never became more than a hobby. Despite her scientific talents, Maud remained first and foremost a home-maker and family support. Even the opportunity to become involved in the work of elementary schools in the parish was closed to her now that the National schools no longer functioned. Whatever the rising expectations which numbers of middle-class women had for themselves, she internalised some of the examples set by Charlotte, her role-model. Perhaps part of her saw herself marrying a clergyman and maintaining the family tradition of female submission to husband and Christ.

****

So far as Horace was concerned, these were the years of decision with regard to a profession. After he left school in 1894 he eventually opted for the Inland Revenue, though not with any great prospect of a highflying career: in 1899 he was placed twenty-sixth out of twenty-nine candidates in the examinations of the Department of Inland Revenue.[3] By 1901 he was nevertheless living in London and working as a surveyor of taxes.

As for George, the late 1890s seemed to promise a much dizzier career for him. Whilst he was articled to Messrs King and Ludlow from 1893 to 1898, he thrived as a law student. He won several prizes from the Law Society whilst he was studying, and in 1898 passed his final examination before the Law Society in London, with second class honours (there were no firsts, and only a dozen out of two hundred students achieved a second); he also won the prize of the Birmingham Law Society, along with the bronze medal, a treasure which he was to display in his various offices for decades.[4] In the same year he added the second speaking prize of the law students' society to his trophy-case – he was something of an all-rounder.

---

[1] Shapurji Edalji, *The Case of George Edalji*, p. 35.
[2] P.R.O., HO 144/985, no. 127 (testimonial on Maud Edalji by Barbara Foxley and L. Dawson, 18 January 1905).
[3] *London Gazette*, 15 December 1899.
[4] Shapurji Edalji, *The Case of George Edalji*, p. 7.

He started to practise as a solicitor in Newhall Street in central Birmingham, but still lived at the vicarage; he travelled to work each day on the same railway line as in his schooldays though in the opposite direction. From 1899 he even used the vicarage as a base for a local legal practice and played something of a role in the community, drawing up conveyances not just for private properties such as the Edmunds' house but also for land for a waterworks in Cheslyn Hay. Just as his father had begun his literary career young, so George, at the age of twenty-three, published a book, *Railway Law For The Man In The Train*.[1] The book was well-received: a *Manchester Guardian* reviewer commended him for making it interesting without 'falling into the puerilities one sometimes finds in the popular treatment of legal subjects.'[2] Within George's lucid and comprehensive survey there were many titbits for the serious traveller. He advised, among many other topics, on what would happen if a passenger's fingers were crushed when a railway employee closed the door,[3] and warned that anyone playing games of chance on a train risked three months' imprisonment.[4]

George's private life was remarkably unexciting. He was a teetotaller, did not smoke and his occasional stays away from home tended to involve walking in the countryside on his own – he liked the Shropshire hills his mother had known as a girl.[5] Sometimes he travelled over to Much Wenlock to see his aunt, Mary Sancta Stoneham, and his main activities there were walking and reading – he often sat and read to her in the evening. On occasion he would do some shopping for her in Birmingham and then visit her after work. To Mary Sancta, George was 'my favourite nephew' – though as she only had two this says as much about Horace as it does about George.[6] There were also times when he travelled further afield: his day trip to Aberystwyth with his sister in August 1903 was a key piece of evidence in his trial.

With the example of an increasing number of people of Asian or part-Asian origin before him, it seemed possible that George, like his father, would push forward the boundaries of

---

[1] George Edalji, *Railway Law For The Man In The Train*, Wilson's Legal and Useful Handy Books, 1901.
[2] *Manchester Guardian,* 26 March 1901.
[3] George Edalji, *Railway Law For The Man In The Train*, p. 88.
[4] Ibid., p. 98.
[5] P.R.O., HO 144/984, no. 49 (George Edalji to Charlotte Edalji from Church Stretton, September 1897).
[6] P.R.O., HO 144/984, no. 45 (letter from Mary Sancta Stoneham, included in R. D. Yelverton's submission to the Home Secretary, 5 January 1904).

Anglo-Asian achievement in Britain, despite the great barriers which remained for anyone trying to break into a world controlled by the likes of the Gladstones of Liverpool or the Ansons of Staffordshire. As Michael Harley first pointed out in 1983, however, evidence exists that by 1902, even before the troubles associated with the Wyrley outrages started, all was not well beneath the surface of George's promise.[1]

****

As he approached his sixtieth birthday, in 1902 (according to most evidence), Shapurji's duties were becoming in some ways more onerous. The rapid growth of population in the parish meant that he had to spend more time baptising, marrying, and burying people, with no curate to help. The changes brought about by the Local Government Act of 1894, on the other hand, changes which in the case of Great Wyrley involved the substitution of a parish council for the old parish vestry, meant that he had less responsibility in secular matters. There were also no longer any National schools for him to supervise. Still, he worked hard for the School Board, and there were new and difficult issues to grapple with as the community grew and changed. In 1892 he called a vestry meeting to ask what he should do about the fact that the churchyard was nearly full – nine hundred and ninety people had been buried there since his arrival in Great Wyrley.[2] The whole process of planning a new cemetery took five years, and as Cheslyn Hay parish council was also about to plan a cemetery of its own, Shapurji became anxious about the extra pressures on incumbents of St Mark's parish in the future. As a result he became entangled in another a difference of opinion, this time with Great Wyrley parish council, which proposed to reduce fees for gravestones. The Bishop of Lichfield, Augustus Legge, accepted the council's view over Shapurji's, and consecrated the cemetery in June 1897.[3]

Storm

The years of relative peace ended with the night-time slaughter of Joseph Holmes's colt in February 1903. Then came the further outrages, and after the attack on 17/18 August George hit the national headlines. He and his family remained

[1] Michael Harley, *Cannock Advertiser*, 19 August 1983.
[2] *Cannock Chase Courier*, 8 October 1892.
[3] S.R.O., D4397/5/3/5 (petition to bishop of Lichfield and correspondence re: cemetery, 1897).

a focus of media attention for the next four years, and in 1907, after Conan Doyle's intervention, his name became familiar in the international press too. When in 1997 I finally started ploughing through the Home Office files in the Public Record Office at Kew, however, I soon realised that there was much more to the lives of the Edaljis during these years of trauma than had ever been told.

In the months after that first, February, outrage, as the Great Wyrley community became ever more frantic about the stream of attacks on its precious horses, cows and sheep, the family maintained its usual routines. For George, each day started with the short climb to the station to catch the Birmingham train. As the train chugged through the fields towards Walsall he had in these months, however, more to occupy his thoughts than the message of his father's last sermon; his financial situation was desperate, as Michael Harley revealed in his articles of 1983. George's begging letter to the Birmingham M.P. Sir J. B. Stone in December 1902 announced openly that he had been reduced to absolute poverty after paying out money for a friend for whom he had stood surety. The Home Office files contain further details supplied by Chief Constable Anson on bankruptcy petitions presented against George in early 1903, when he was in danger of being struck off the Solicitors' Roll. The proceedings against him were however overtaken by the events of August; Anson described his arrest as a 'perfect godsend' for him.

Whatever he knew of his son's problems in the first half of 1903 Shapurji pursued his daily round with his usual vigour – services, baptisms (up to five at a time), marriages (three on 1 June alone), burials, home visits, administration and civic activities. As the crisis deepened – George was under suspicion from late June, arrested in August and convicted in October – Shapurji never failed in his duties, as witnessed by the fact that between July and December he conducted a further thirty-eight baptisms. George himself supported his parents' efforts to maintain normality: 'I don't think my affair should interfere with your harvest services,' he told his mother in a letter from Stafford Prison in September.

The Rev. Mr. Edalji, vicar of
Great Wyrley, whose son is now
in Stafford Gaol awaiting his trial

Photo of Shapurji Edalji taken for the *Illustrated
Mail* shortly before his son's trial

Charlotte and Shapurji may be forgiven however if by the autumn their minds were focused on their older son's fate. Ignoring the usual boundaries between public and private roles Shapurji used the pulpit week on week to preach George's innocence, and once R. D. Yelverton had picked up the gauntlet St Mark's vicarage became the local headquarters of a national campaign

****

The references to George's financial affairs in the Home Office files may reveal one unknown side of Edalji family life in 1903, but elsewhere there is a yet more startling secret. At last, in 1997, I discovered what Michael Harley had meant when in 1983 he reported that George had been incriminated by 'someone close to his own family'. That someone was George's own brother.

There exists a private memo which Home Secretary Herbert Gladstone wrote in June 1907 as a record of a meeting he had with Alfred Hazell, M.P. for West Bromwich in Staffordshire. Hazell told him that he had been with C. F. Vachell on the defence side at George's trial, and that during the trial a member of the Edalji family (he thought it was Horace) produced a letter (from 1895) which he said he had found in one of George's drawers so that they could examine George's handwriting. The letter, addressed to a maid, was full of 'unmentionable' language. Vachell decided to suppress it as damaging to the defence case.[1]

Horace did not confine himself to offering revelations to defence counsel. According to a police report he also told his friend Christopher Hatton that he believed that George had been involved in the letter-writing of 1892-5, and Hatton's reaction was to urge him to tell his father all he knew. Horace hesitated, for fear that his relations with his family were so fragile that they would disown him, but in December 1903 he did travel back to Great Wyrley with the intention of acting on Hatton's advice. When he arrived, however, he discovered that Yelverton was at the vicarage and so he kept quiet, preferring to let Shapurji know by post.[2] Charlotte responded with a furious thirty-two-page letter, demanding to be told why, if he thought he knew something in 1895, he had not said anything at the time.[3]

---

[1] P.R.O., HO 144/988 (note by Home Secretary on a conversation with Hazell, 6 June 1907).
[2] P.R.O., HO 144/985, no. 124 (Anson to Home Office, 1904).
[3] P.R.O., HO 144/989 (Horace Edalji to Christopher Hatton, 13 December 1903).

Horace also wrote to Christopher Hatton to present the view which was to be repeated in the anonymous letter to Anson in 1907: if George did carry out the outrages it must have been for money. He mentioned the bankruptcy petition against his brother at the beginning of 1903, and reported darkly that George spent a week in London at about the same time without giving any explanation. He made it clear, though, that he thought the evidence against George was not strong enough to convict, and he was clearly uncertain about the truth. He even suggested that a man named Warner might have been responsible for the killings.[1]

Whatever truth there may have been in his accusations, the Home Office files show that the man who as a youth had displayed a 'singular brooding temper' towards his family had now burnt his boats. From the end of 1903 he neared complete isolation.

****

Charlotte and Shapurji may have lost both their sons in the aftermath of that night in August 1903, one to prison and one to rejection, but what of their daughter? Here, at least, there is something positive to report. It was in 1903 that Maud took up the post of Assistant to the Kindergarten Mistress at her former school in Walsall. There was nevertheless no escape from being the sister of George Edalji. One day whilst George was in prison the Headteacher Miss Foxley announced mysteriously in assembly that nothing that might be happening outside the school at the moment was to make any difference inside it. One young girl vaguely realised that this had something to do with the 'very dark young woman (she was quite non-European in appearance) named Miss Maud Edalji' who was working in the Kindergarten. According to this girl, writing in later life, 'Miss Foxley must have needed all her firmness, guile and charm in order to carry the parents and Governors with her when she determined to continue to employ a partly coloured woman whose brother was in prison for a series of revolting offences.' Perhaps, she suggested, Miss Foxley believed George was innocent.

In contending with such prejudices, Maud, it seems, was as much a pioneer in going from Great Wyrley to work in Walsall as Shapurji had been in coming from Bombay to Great Wyrley. Still, with the usual Edalji resilience she took on the world and made friendships at the school which were to last long after she

---

[1] P.R.O., HO 144/989 (Horace Edalji to Christopher Hatton, 6 December 1903).

had left. One particular friend, Miss Connie Smith, who was second-in-command to Miss Foxley and took over the headship when the latter left, was to pay visits to the Welwyn Garden City house decades later.[1]

Confinement

Since August 1903 George had been ensconced in prison, his world in ruins. The move from Stafford prison to Lewes after the trial had left him a hundred and fifty miles adrift of his family. By 1904 he had been struck off the Roll of Solicitors. With six more years in prison ahead of him he might well have sunk into despair. He nevertheless later described his experience of life in four different prisons with an amused detachment which shows that he possessed the resilience characteristic of the rest of his family. His standard day during his time in Lewes Prison involved getting up at 5.45, slopping out at 6.15, work from 6.30, breakfast at 7.30 followed by the folding of bedding, then chapel and seventy minutes of exercise, confinement in his cell until 12.00, dinner, work until 5.30, supper, and bed at 8.00. Although he had been sentenced to seven years' hard labour, a prison doctor judged that his poor eyesight made him incapable of it, and for a period he was subjected to the irony of having to make horses' nose-bags. In his series of articles in *The Umpire* in 1906 he recounted in manner-of-fact fashion how some prisoners screamed and yelled incessantly, and noted that there were suicides from time to time, including one in a cell near to his own.[2]

During 1904 he was moved to the third of his prisons, Portland, which had a broadly similar regime. Despite all the hours spent alone, however, he did make some social contacts. Eustace Jervis, a prison chaplain, later remembered talking with George several times as each of them toured the prison circuit, and he commented admiringly: 'He took his gruel like a man.' He also noted how short-sighted George was.[3] Indeed, on arrival at Portland George was put in a special ward, because it was judged that his myopia and astigmatism made it unsuitable for him to go up and down stairs.[4]

He was allowed books, newspapers, and weekly visits, and his parents did travel to see him from time to time. Charlotte

---

[1] W.L.H.C., 246/38 ('Queen Mary's High School, Miss Barbara Foxley, and The Edalji Case').

[2] *The Umpire*, 9 December 1906.

[3] Eustace Jervis, *Twenty-five years in Six Prisons*, T. Fisher Unwin, 1925, p. 108.

[4] *Wellington Journal and Shrewsbury Gazette*, 19 January 1907.

would go all the way to Portland for meagre 20-minute interviews.[1] Back in the vicarage, all Maud could do was wait.

Campaign

George occasionally fired off petitions to the Home Secretary but it was impossible for him to orchestrate a campaign for his own release from prison. It was left to others to make the decisions, though Yelverton did visit him in Portland at one point to discuss plans. Yelverton's submission to the Home Secretary in December 1903 had in fact had no apparent effect; he received no response at all for months, and then his case was rejected out of hand. Charlotte and Shapurji however did not wait till then. From the start both of them were at the heart of the campaign to free their son.

Shapurji's protests may not have been quite as public as they had been in 1903 but they were equally as passionate. In a series of angry letters he battered at the gates of the citadel of empire in Whitehall, his efforts culminating in 1905 in his booklet *The Case of George Edalji*, a detailed and lucid analysis of the woeful police and prosecution case against his son.

For Charlotte these bitter years saw a temporary release from that imprisonment in the home to which she had been condemned by her gender. She was now freed to a much more public role, one in which she not only took on the world as a mother in defence of her son, but also was drawn as a near celebrity into wider campaigns. Her letters were always more revealing about her sense of family than were Shapurji's. In January 1904 she told the Home Secretary exactly who she thought she was:

> *My father and mother were both English people. My father's ancestors fought in the Crusades. I have... the portrait of my great, great, great, great, Grandfather, who was a Judge.* [2]

She might have been a little overenthusiastic here. If she was referring to the Thompson Stoneham of Little Baddow who had grown up as a boy in Bombay then he was only her great-grandfather and a J.P.

---

[1] P.R.O., HO 144/985, no. 103 (Charlotte Edalji to Home Secretary, 26 November 1904), HO 144/986, no. 134 (letter from Charlotte Edalji, 18 August 1905).
[2] P.R.O., HO 144/984, no. 48 (Charlotte Edalji to Home Secretary, January 1904).

265

In the same month she made her feelings about the reasons for George's troubles very clear to the M.P. for Birmingham: 'I am an English woman, and I feel that there is in many people a prejudice against those who are not English, and I cannot help feeling that it is owing to that prejudice that my son has been falsely accused.'[1] Although, her instincts were more conservative than her husband's, her ideas about Englishness had clearly been challenged by her family's direct experience of racism. Again, in a letter to the Queen in February 1904, she commented bitterly: 'I have often been grieved to notice that an Asiatic is despised or disliked.'[2] A year later she told the Home Secretary: 'I am an English woman & my blood boils at the continued injustice as it seems to be because my husband is a Parsee and my son therefore only half English.'[3]

Her letter to the Queen showed the rest of Charlotte's pain about George's plight: 'We are getting old and it is impossibly painful to be separated from him.' Queen Alexandra, as Princess of Wales, had at one time been the Princess Diana of her time, fashionable and dazzling, but abandoned by her husband for, among others, the great-grandmother of Camilla Parker Bowles. She also had Princess Diana's gift for supporting the afflicted, and appeared in some ways to be the right person to appeal to: her own devoted sons called her 'Motherdear'.[4] Charlotte, pursuing every avenue she could find, went on to appeal to the King, reporting anxiously that all the money they had intended to use to provide for Maud had now been spent on George's case.[5]

Charlotte must have worn out several pens on George's behalf between 1903 and 1907, but letter-writing was only the beginning. Her new public role also took her away from home, without Shapurji, in pursuit of her mission. In February 1904 she stayed for ten days in London (at 39, Woburn Place); this move was prompted by Yelverton, who vainly believed that the Home Secretary would agree to see her. Charlotte travelled with her sister, Mary Sancta Stoneham, who was still passionately involved in efforts to secure her nephew's release and gave a lot of her savings to help the cause. The gates of the citadel in Whitehall nevertheless remained firmly closed.

---

[1] B.R.L., 370795 (Charlotte Edalji to J. B. Stone, 26 January, 1904, in 'A Collection of MSS Formed by Sir J. B. Stone').
[2] P.R.O., HO 144/985, no. 69 (Charlotte Edalji to Queen Alexandra, February 1904).
[3] P.R.O., HO 144/985, no. 119 (Charlotte Edalji to the Home Secretary, 9 March 1904).
[4] Nancy Banks-Smith, *The Guardian*, 2 September 1997.
[5] P.R.O., HO 144/985, no. 94 (Charlotte Edalji to King Edward VII, 3 May 1904).

Portland Prison in the 1890s

Courtesy of Old UK Photos

Despite the silence of the Home Office the Edaljis' efforts helped in these years to make George a central figure in a wider campaign. In 1905, the radical paper *Truth* took up his case in a series of lengthy articles, comparing it with that of Adolf Beck.[1] Adolf Beck, a Norwegian, had been subjected to unjust imprisonment in chilling circumstances. The story began in 1877, when a man named Thomas Smith defrauded seventeen women of their jewellery by posing as a nobleman. He was convicted of larceny and sentenced to five years' penal servitude. In 1895 the crimes resumed, but this time one of the victims accused Beck on the street, and subsequently several others identified him as the man who had robbed them. Beck was in the middle of a horrific nightmare: in 1896 he was convicted of Smith's crimes and sentenced to seven years' imprisonment. At his trial, a handwriting expert – none other than the Thomas Gurrin who was the prosecution's 'trump card' at George Edalji's trial in 1903 – testified that documents supposedly written by Smith were actually in Beck's disguised hand. The hapless Beck petitioned the Home Secretary several times, but with as little success as George. He was released in 1901, but in 1904, astonishingly, was re-arrested and convicted on similar charges to those of 1896. The judge reserved sentence, however, and in the meantime Smith himself was also arrested and confessed to all the frauds. Beck received two free pardons and £2,000 compensation, later raised to £5,000.[2]

Pressure from the newspapers led to the establishment of a committee of inquiry into Beck's case, and in October 1904 Thomas Gurrin was compelled to appear before it to acknowledge that he had made a great mistake in his handwriting evidence of 1896. This, as Conan Doyle was to point out in 1907, cast even greater doubt on George's conviction in 1903. Other papers responded to the lead which *Truth* was taking on George's behalf, so that the names of Beck and Edalji became firmly linked in the public mind. In February 1905 a large public meeting in Essex Hall in London heard Yelverton, Beck, and others fulminating at the injustices which arose in a system with no Court of Criminal Appeal; the Home Office was described as a modern Star Chamber, and a resolution was passed demanding a public inquiry into George's case. With them on the platform were two other very contrasting figures – George Bernard Shaw and Charlotte

---

[1] *Truth*, 12 January to 23 February 1905.
[2] Rosemary Pattenden, *English Criminal Appeals*, Clarendon Press, 1996, pp. 28-9.

Edalji. Charlotte, there to answer questions, had turned from clergyman's wife into national celebrity.[1] She and her husband had helped to make their son's case a central plank of the campaign for a Court of Criminal Appeal in Britain.

****

An important detail which the Home Office files reveal is the process by which George's release was prepared. When George emerged from prison it was not quite the surprise for the family which it might appear to have been to outsiders, for in the autumn of 1905 Shapurji had received a letter from the Home Office which was rather different from the stonewalling responses he was used to. The Home Secretary, Akers-Douglas, had made half a decision. George's sentence, he declared, had been too severe, and Shapurji was informed that if George's good behaviour continued he would be released on licence after three years.[2] This meant the family still had a whole year to wait.

After the Liberal success in the general election of 1906, the new Home Secretary, Herbert Gladstone, confirmed the decision. George would be released, but on licence, still under a dark cloud of believed guilt. In October he was sent to Pentonville for discharge, and at 10.30 on 19 October he at last breathed a sort of freedom again, as he left Pentonville in a cab, with a warder and another released prisoner. In his pocket was the standard allocation of £2 19s 10d with which he was expected to start his new life. Charlotte was waiting in London to welcome him.[3]

He went to stay with a supporter, Miss Goode, in Mecklenburgh Square, but so long as he lived in London he was required to write each month to Scotland Yard. As he had not been declared innocent he could not be reinstated on the Roll of Solicitors and could not practise his profession. He had vowed never to return to Great Wyrley until he was declared innocent (his father even believed that Chief Constable Anson and the police might hatch a plot against him[4]), but he still had a lust to gather evidence which would help him and this conquered his antipathy. A few days after his release, therefore, he went to Great Wyrley with a legal friend in order to study the

---

[1] *Cannock Courier*, 11 February 1905.
[2] P.R.O., HO 144/986, no. 134 (home office notes on decisions about George's release, 1905-6).
[3] *Daily Chronicle*, 20 and 22 October 1906.
[4] Letter from Maud Edalji to Hesketh Pearson, 28 August 1956, Hesketh Pearson Papers, The Univerity of Texas at Austin.

scene of his alleged crime.[1] He only stayed for a few hours – even the reunion with his parents could not hold him – and returned to London to contemplate his next move. He was as effective a publicist for his cause as were his parents: by November *The Umpire*, a Manchester magazine, was publishing a series of well-scripted articles in which he described his experiences and declared his innocence.[2] He knew, nevertheless, that this was not enough. As well as a powerful pen, he needed powerful allies. The establishment needed to be shaken by someone even mightier than those who had been ranged against it so far. It was George who recruited Conan Doyle to the cause.

****

The media focus on the Edalji family since George's arrest had been fierce enough. During the furore cause by Conan Doyle's *Daily Telegraph* articles of January 1907 and his subsequent campaigns, however, the Edalji family was subject not just to national but to international scrutiny. During all these years, nevertheless, Charlotte and Shapurji continued to serve parish and community as faithfully as ever. They were already into their sixties when George was imprisoned, and they were to continue their work for fifteen more years, but their resilience and their faith in their son shone through until the end. One fascinated reporter, dispatched to Great Wyrley in 1907 to follow up the Conan Doyle story, shadowed Shapurji as he went about his work. He described his subject as a small, slight man 'with the vivacity of a 20-year-old' who 'bounded across the churchyard' and into the church. Shapurji led the service, his voice small and thin, and then mounted the pulpit 'with airy rapidity'.[3] On Shapurji's death another journalist was to paint an endearing picture of his devotion. No clergyman, he wrote, spent more time than Shapurji did in visiting – more especially his poorer parishioners. Shapurji would be observed 'plodding about in the evening in winter, in dark roads, carrying a lantern to direct him on his errands of mercy'.[4]

Shapurji's stamina and independent spirit were also called into play for one last great battle on the schools front, and on this occasion his bloody-minded tenacity led to an appearance of his own in front of the Attorney-General in the very year that his son was in the world headlines. Two years earlier, during

---

[1] *Cannock Chase Courier*, 11 January 1952.
[2] *The Umpire*, 11, 18, 25 November, 2, 9, 16 December 1906.
[3] *Daily Telegraph* report, cited in *Express & Star*, 3 September 1907.
[4] *Cannock Chase Courier*, 25 May 1918.

the darkest years of George's imprisonment, he had returned to the fray over Cheslyn Hay National School, his battling spirit undimmed. The school had been left unused since the stormy conflicts of the 1870s and 1880s, but it was now firmly in the sights of the new Staffordshire Local Education Authority, which had been established as a result of the Education Act of 1902 and had taken over control from the Cheslyn Hay and Great Wyrley School Board.

Shapurji and the other trustees simply ignored these moves, and proposed that the school should be reopened as a church day school which would also be used as a Sunday school. The County Council objected, saying that they needed the building as an overspill for their own County School, the former Cheslyn Hay Board School. When the Board of Education, the predecessor of today's Department for Children, Schools and Families, ordered an enquiry, Shapurji's stubbornly independent streak came to the fore once again; he and the other trustees refused to attend, saying that the County Council's proposals were incompatible with the terms of their trust. The Board of Education responded by presenting the case to the Attorney-General, with a view to taking proceedings against Shapurji and others of the trustees. By 1907 the Attorney-General was not only being consulted about George by the Home Office and helping to steer a bill to establish a Court of Criminal Appeal through Parliament as a result of pressure to which both George and his father had contributed; he also had to face Shapurji in court on behalf of the Board of Education.

So it was that in July 1907, when Parliament was still buzzing with questions about his son, Shapurji appeared in court in London himself.[1] The case of the Attorney-General versus Shapurji Edalji and the two churchwardens, William Wynn (father of the Fred Wynn of the 1892-5 letters) and James Bullock, was heard before Justice Swinfen Eady in the Chancery Division of the High Court of Justice. In his submission the Attorney-General was blunt about Shapurji's responsibility for the impasse in Cheslyn Hay. It was, he claimed, Shapurji's 'imprudent action' which had created the original problem of the 1880s, for at the time Shapurji was the only person who wanted to retain the Cheslyn Hay National School, which he had re-opened in 1881 after the closure of 1878. Those who wanted a Board School were still prepared to come to an agreement if Shapurji would make changes at the National School. He would not make a settlement, and the

---

[1] *The Times*, 5 July 1907.

Board School, which destroyed the National School's chance of recovery, was built nearby.[1]

The Attorney-General then put forward the proposal that the County Council should take over, maintain, and run the school as an infant school during the week, leaving the Vicar to use it on Sundays and during evenings. Justice Eady suggested that as an alternative the County Council could lease the buildings from the Vicar and the churchwardens. Shapurji, of course, would have no truck with any of this, and insisted that the trustees wanted to reopen the school for elementary education themselves. All the bitterness of the thirty-year struggle poured out as he described how the trustees had striven for several years to get a grant to re-open the school but had been refused by the Board of Education unless they accepted rate aid. They were unwilling to accept this condition, as the school would then be subject to the provisions of the 1902 Education Act, whereas the original loan from the Board of Education in 1874 had been given only on condition that the school was operated under the terms of the 1870 Education Act. The trustees had been overruled when they protested at the building of a Board School in the 1880s, which forced the National School to close. Now, with the growth of population, there was a need for the school to open again.

Shapurji's version of past events was not entirely misplaced: as late as 1963 an official at the Department of Education was to write to the Staffordshire County Archivist about the thirty years of struggle over the school, suggesting that Shapurji had been treated with 'official rigidity and unhelpfulness', not to say 'cruelty' by the Board of Education.[2] Justice Eady however ignored Shapurji's defiance. He pointed out that so far as the current situation went, Shapurji had no funds, no teachers, and no scholars. He thought the best way forward was for the trustees to let the school to the Local Education Authority on a ten-year lease. Therefore the school would be referred to Chambers to make inquiry. One can imagine Shapurji's look as he left the court with churchwardens Wynn and Bullock after this judgement. He had no intention of surrendering. Two years later he was left with no choice, when the trustees were ordered to execute the lease to the County Council. Defiant to the end, Shapurji was forced to pay tax at 4% to cover legal costs.[3]

---

[1] *Express & Star*, 4 July 1907.
[2] W.S.L., CB/EDALJI/2 (J. L. B. Todhunter to J. H. P. Oxspring, 5 February 1963).
[3] S.R.O., D1215/6/2 (Attorney General v Edalji, certificate of costs, 1909), D3749/7/2 (miscellaneous correspondence).

****

'Sir Arthur Conan Doyle Married Quietly. Name of Church Where Ceremony Took Place Had Been Kept Secret. Edalji at Reception.' This *New York Times* headline in September 1907 suggested a kind of happy ending to George's story, with George welcomed and honoured amongst Britain's elite.[1] My 1970s teaching may have ended here, but in reality the story had no ending. Despite his celebrity George was pained for the rest of his life by the failure of the Home Office to accept his complete innocence, and Charlotte, Shapurji and Maud suffered for him too. Still, there were important if lesser victories. In December 1907 George's face was to be seen staring out from the front page of the *New York Times*, this time against the headline 'Edalji once more a British lawyer'.[2] His restoration to the Roll of Solicitors showed a belief in his innocence on the part of one institution, and he was able to practise as a lawyer again.

It was not Conan Doyle's wedding but another one which brought a kind of closure to one aspect of the Edalji trauma. In his *The Real World of Sherlock Holmes* Peter Costello revealed in 1992 (unfortunately without acknowledgement) some remarkable information dug out by Michael Harley.[3] In 1910 Horace Edalji married an Irish woman, Annie Magee, in Hereford, and took what was for his time an extraordinary decision: he adopted her surname. It was the final step: in abandoning his family name Horace was abandoning his family, his origins, and all association with his brother's case. He may well also have been striving to cast off the guilt of betrayal and the pain of rejection. He and Annie, Michael Harley discovered, eventually went to live in Ireland. George's case drove both brothers into exile.

War

The last years of the Edalji regime in Great Wyrley were the years of the Great War. Dadabhai Naoroji, for all his radical criticism of imperialism, declared in 1914 that India should fight as part of the British empire. Thus the 'Grand Old Man of India' and Shapurji Edalji, in their final years, found themselves supporting the same cause, Shapurji from Great Wyrley and Naoroji from Bombay, where he died in 1917. Over one million Indian soldiers and 1,200 Indian nurses were shipped out to serve in the Middle East and on the Western Front, and at the

---

[1] *New York Times*, 19 September 1907.
[2] *New York Times*,1 December 1907
[3] Peter Costello, *The Real World of Sherlock Holmes*.

end 56,423, including 61 Parsis,[1] were dead or missing; the myth of Indian inferiority in battlefield courage was drowned in blood in the trenches of Flanders. That other child of Bombay, Rudyard Kipling, acknowledged the part Indians played in the War too:

This man in his own country prayed we know not to what Powers.
We pray to Them to reward him for his bravery in ours.[2]

Great Wyrley's own war-time roll of honour was erected in gardens by the Walsall Road in 1918 – unusually early – and was described by a visitor from Stoke as the finest he had seen.[3] Cheslyn Hay had its own memorial, which stands proudly at the focal-point of the old village. The lists of names on these lovingly created monuments bear witness to the remorseless carnage which the Great War visited upon the young men of those communities. Familiar names from this story appear among the three hundred or so men listed on the Great Wyrley memorial, including four Sambrooks and a Farrington. In Cheslyn Hay, inevitably, the name Hawkins appears.

In general, the War was still a remote affair for the people of Great Wyrley compared with more recent wars. Personal news of the devastation in the trenches came through official army letters announcing that sons, brothers, fathers, and husbands had fallen in action. Zeppelins did, however, sometimes reach as far as Staffordshire on their bombing raids – one attack on the Midlands killed fifty-nine people, and one of Shapurji's fellow-ministers in Staffordshire saw his church destroyed.[4] This war certainly seemed closer than any previous one.

The Great War also extended the range of demands on clergymen and their families. Those who lost family or friends in the war needed both material and emotional support, and a number of organisations were established in the Great Wyrley area to provide relief, in the tradition of the self-help groups which were so important in the days before the Welfare State. Despite her age (she was seventy-two when the War started) Charlotte was energetically in the thick of things, doing what she saw as her patriotic duty. She regularly attended meetings of the Local Relief Committee and Red Cross Society of Cheslyn

[1] John Hinnells, *Zoroastrians in Britain*, p. 104.
[2] Rudyard Kipling, 'Hindu Sepoy in France, Epitaphs of the War', 1914-18, in *The Works of Rudyard Kipling*, p. 387.
[3] *Cannock Chase Courier*, 16 February 1918.
[4] *Cannock Advertiser*, 5 February 1916.

Hay,[1] and helped to organise events run by the local committee of the Soldiers and Sailors Fund. Her contribution was to be spoken of with real gratitude by many members of the community after Shapurji's death. Indeed, she still cut a memorable figure in the village. One person who retained a vivid image of her throughout life was Marion Homeshaw, a keen local historian who helped me with my teaching about the history of the community in the 1970s. She described Charlotte as a 'true Victorian lady, in a little black hat and high collars... she was very small, trim and dainty.'[2]

Charlotte always believed that Shapurji's eyesight had been affected by his intense work on the book which paid for his journey to England in 1867, but it was not until the end of his life that the problem became really serious.[3] By 1916, his fading eyesight was turning to blindness. From August 1916 he was leaving others to fill in the details in the parish registers, whilst he simply added his signature. By December even his signature flopped down sadly and indistinctly, and from then on he left the signature column to others.[4] He was becoming physically weaker, too. Maud and Charlotte looked after him, with Maud in the leading role now – she even had to guide her father round his own church and lead him up the pulpit steps; he insisted on preaching, right to the end.[5]

Despite all this, he continued to serve. Parish affairs had entered another difficult period, for no one had been willing to act as churchwarden since 1911, throwing more of the burden on him. As so often in the past, Shapurji stood alone against attempts to rectify the situation. At a special vestry meeting in the National schoolroom in May 1916 at which he took the chair there was a heated discussion about the election of churchwardens. Eventually Tait and Rowley were appointed, but when Thacker proposed that the churchwardens and sidesmen should form a committee to further church work in the parish (perhaps because of Shapurji's increasing frailty), Shapurji objected and simply declared the meeting closed. The parishioners just ignored him, continued the meeting, and appointed a committee.[6] This was the last time that Shapurji minuted a vestry meeting; in 1917 one of the churchwardens had to do the job for him.

[1] *Cannock Chase Courier*, 22 June 1918.
[2] *Cannock Advertiser*, 23 May 1980. Marion Homeshaw's husband was the co-author of Homeshaw and Sambrook, *Great Wyrley 1051-1951*.
[3] P.R.O., HO 144/985, no. 69 (Charlotte Edalji to Queen Alexandra, 16 February 1904).
[4] S.R.O., D1215/1/4 (Great Wyrley parish register, baptisms 1908-20).
[5] *Cannock Advertiser*, 23 May 1980.
[6] *Cannock Advertiser*, 20 May 1916.

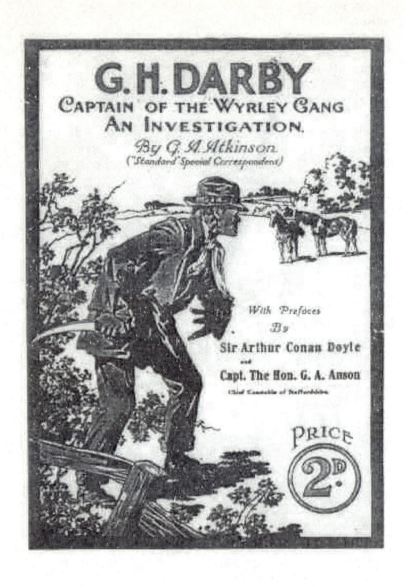

Cover of G. A. Atkinson's 1912 booklet on the identity of 'G. H. Darby'

At his final vestry meeting of Easter 1918, Shapurji, almost totally blind,[1] chaired the meeting and nominated the minister's warden as he had always done, though the minutes again had to be taken by Tait, one of the churchwardens. A week later Shapurji had a stroke which led to a bad fall. He was attended by Dr Butter, the eccentric Scotsman who had practised in the area since the 1870s,[2] and whose evidence had contributed to his son's conviction in 1903. Shapurji never recovered from the stroke and died a month later.

---

[1] *Express & Star*, 23 May 1918.
[2] *The Medical Register for 1916*.

The green spaces of Welwyn Garden City, the new town started in 1919

Kind permission of David Thorpe

Tuesday October 9th

I wish to make a statement of my own free will and I have been cautioned by Supt Hall I have been writing for over 25 years I have never done any of the outrages I have only wrote the letters and sent them to folks what I have seen in the newspapers have sent letters to Mr justice mackinnon and Lord Cadnam some time ago and lately I have been sending letters to Mr and Mrs ferris carlos [ray] ck Cannock and Mr and Mrs Jones choslyn and I have sent some to Mrs randle 141 cromford lane westbromwich my wife does not know anything about the letters and she had not seen me write any I am admit all what I have done and I am very sorry indeed I hope they will forgive me for the trouble what I have caused them for years for the sake of my wife and in future I shall not send any more letters to any more people

Signed Enoch Knowles

Confession of Enoch Knowles, 1934

Kind permission of Staffordshire Record Office

Photograph of George Edalji in the Daily Express,
November 1934

8. Passers on

It was on a beautiful summery day in late May that hundreds of parishioners and ex-parishioners gathered at St Mark's to pay their last respects to a 'faithful and devoted pastor', as a local paper warmly described him.[1] There were so many there, in fact, that the church was filled to overflowing and a crowd was left outside to watch the cortège as it passed along the path from the vicarage. Charlotte and Maud were joined by George, who had not returned to Great Wyrley since 1906, and by Horace, travelling back from Ireland; it was the first time the family had been together since the parting of the ways in 1903.

After the service, Shapurji's body was buried in that quiet corner of the churchyard which I visited so many times with my students in the 1970s and 1980s. Most of the churchyard has long been cleared of its graves, but in that corner under the trees, far from the vultures on the Towers of Silence in Bombay, the terse inscription on Shapurji's gravestone is still legible: 'Here lies Rev Shapurji Edalji, forty-two years Vicar of this Parish.' It is a sadly bald summary of the remarkable life of a talented son of the British empire.

****

As ever, the fate of the seventy-six-year-old Charlotte was decided by that of her husband. Within days of the funeral she was preparing to leave her home of forty-two years, taking Maud with her. Still, before she left there were warm expressions of affection and appreciation from members of the community. At a weekly meeting of one of the war-time relief groups, the combined Cheslyn Hay Relief Committee and Red Cross Society, the chair, F. W. Hawkins, referred with sympathy to Shapurji's death. Charlotte he described as an enthusiastic worker on the committee and a good lady for visiting people, especially 'poor folk'. As members stood in silence, a vote of condolence was passed.[2] When Charlotte went to a later meeting of the society to wish all her friends a 'happy goodbye', Hawkins and others again spoke appreciatively of her – she had been a member from the beginning, they said, and rarely absent.[3] In July the parishioners of St Mark's made their own farewells to Charlotte and Maud, in the schoolroom next to the vicarage which had been so much a part of the Edaljis' lives for so many years; Charlotte was presented with a wallet and

[1] *Cannock Chase Courier* and *Cannock Advertiser*, 1 June 1918.
[2] *Cannock Chase Courier*, 1 June 1918.
[3] *Cannock Chase Courier*, 22 June 1918.

£30 collected by the parishioners.[1] In their final tribute, the Cheslyn Hay Red Cross Society presented her with an inscribed leather purse with money. Hawkins was again fulsome in his praise: 'her beautiful disposition and the busy and practical work performed by Mrs Edalji had been an inspiration to the whole village'. Charlotte's response was that she had done her work for the heroic boys who had fallen.[2]

Mother and daughter moved to Coalbrookdale, close to Charlotte's Ketley roots, to live with Mary Sancta, her sister. Mary Sancta had moved to Coalbrookdale from Much Wenlock several years earlier, but unfortunately died within a few months of their arrival. The funeral took place in Ketley, and George and Horace again travelled to join their mother and sister as Mary Sancta was buried next to her parents in St Mary's churchyard.[3] Relations between Horace and the rest of family were very strained: Mary Sancta had left all her money to Charlotte and her 'favourite nephew', George.

Maud had been thirty-two when the war started and already unlikely to marry, but the deaths of so many men between 1914 and 1918 made marriage even less likely, quite apart from contemporary attitudes to mixed heritage relationships. Her traditional female role in life remained that of family carer, and she looked after her mother in her last years. When Charlotte's health became so poor that Maud could not look after her any more, Charlotte went into a nursing home in Shrewsbury, and she died there in March 1924. George, Horace, and Maud were again all at the funeral, and Charlotte's daughter-in-law too – the Magees were not so isolated from the family that they were unwilling to travel over from Ireland.[4] The meeting of the siblings was however as tortured as ever – as her sister had done, Charlotte had left Horace out of her will, and all her money went to her other two children. Funeral services, conducted by one of Charlotte's father's successors, Reverend C. B. Crowe, were held both in Coalbrookdale and at St Mary's in Ketley. Already in place in the churchyard at Ketley was a monument whose four faces were each devoted to one member of her family – Mary Ann Stoneham (her great aunt), the Reverend Thompson Stoneham (her father), Mary Stoneham (her mother), and Mary Sancta Stoneham (her sister). It was here that Charlotte Elizabeth Stuart Edalji was buried, and her name inscribed below that of

---

[1] *Cannock Chase Courier*, 13 July 1918.
[2] *Cannock Chase Courier*, 20 July 1918.
[3] *Wellington Journal and Shrewsbury News*, 3 March 1919.
[4] *Cannock Advertiser*, 15 March 1924.

her father. The monument still stands proudly at the entrance to the churchyard, smothered in ivy.

As for the three Edalji children, they strove to live out their later lives in a tranquillity not granted to them in their younger days. At first Maud stayed in Coalbrookdale after her mother's death, but in 1930 she moved to the secluded little house in Welwyn Garden City to be nearer to her older brother. Welwyn Garden City, planned as a new town in 1919 by Sir Ebenezer Howard, was a symbol of Britain's post-war attempts to create something different from the blighted and sprawling industrial landscapes Maud had grown up with in the Midlands. From time to time, in the 1930s at least, she met with her friend Connie Smith, the former Headteacher at Queen Mary's High School in Walsall, who reported on Maud's beloved family portrait gallery on the walls of the tiny drawing room.[1]

Since being restored to the Solicitors' Roll in 1907 George had maintained a practice in Borough High Street in Southwark, with bronze medal and other evidence of academic achievement on display. After Maud moved south he went to live with her, still travelling to his office in central London each day. It might seem that the two of them, like Horace, had escaped from their past. There was however no escape from the ghosts of the Wyrley Gang. In 1934 George was in the news again.

Ghosts

The pen of the most prolific letter-writer of all, 'G. H. Darby', had haunted the Midlands for years. He started writing after George's trial and the *Express & Star* was bombarded with letters, many of them gloating about his role as leader of the 'Wyrley Gang' and about the 'Gang's' further attacks on animals. The writings stopped after a few weeks but there were periodic outbursts in the following years; they included the letter found in a field near to where a horse had been maimed in Darlaston in 1906,[2] and the flurry which followed the last Wyrley outrage, of August 1907, just as the Edaljis were trying to creep offstage.[3]

There was a new cascade in 1912-13, and now 'Darby's' horizons stretched well beyond Great Wyrley and the *Express &*

---

[1] W.L.H.C., 246/38 ('Queen Mary's High School, Miss Barbara Foxley, and The Edalji Case').
[2] *Express & Star*, 26 October 1934.
[3] *Express & Star*, 18 September 1907.

Star; dozens of people became victims of his gruesome pen, which often claimed his involvement in crimes before the courts. A letter of June 1912 to a Mrs Poulton of Wednesbury announced that 'Darby' had forced her daughter to drown herself by telling her he would have her locked up for robbing him. In the same month Mrs Garmstone of Wednesbury was told that he had poisoned her daughter. In a postcard to Mrs Birch Lyndon in November 1912 he confessed to killing her daughter, informing her heartlessly 'while the other men held her I did the murder with a razor'.[1]

Great Wyrley was still a recurring subject. In January 1912 H. Bartle, the governor of Stafford prison, was promised £5,000 if he released Joseph Mellor (in prison for three months for assaulting a policeman) and £10,000 if he killed him. If Bartle refused he himself would be killed. This time the letter was signed 'Mr Smith, Royal Oak Inn, Great Wyrley' rather than 'G. H. Darby'. Confusingly the same 'Mr Smith' then received a letter threatening to have him arrested for the maiming of horses in Great Wyrley.[2]

'Darby' still linked the 'Gang' with attacks on animals in the Midlands, and during 1912 his threats seemed very real. In July of that year he proclaimed that the 'Gang' would carry out another maiming, only to report that the attempt, in Bilston, had failed.[3] A few days later however a young mare was found in Darlaston with its throat cut; it survived, but the police, rejecting rumours that the injury was made by barbed wire, saw this as a deliberate maiming. In August, after another horse was injured, this time in Walsall, a new 'Darby' letter claimed that the 'Gang' had been wagered £500 that it could not kill ten horses.[4]

The media were again agog at goings-on in the Midlands; *Truth* suggested that the various episodes since 1903 might all be linked to one person, someone whose attacks were spasmodic because he was away at certain times rather than because he was a maniac as some believed.[5] Anson and Shapurji were again pounced on for comment; Anson, whose view was that the attacks had nothing to do with the Wyrley outrages of 1903, reported that he and the Governor of Stafford Prison had themselves received threatening letters.[6] George

---

[1] 'G. H. Darby' letters, 1903-1912 (copies in S.C.P.M.).
[2] 'G. H. Darby' letters, 1903-1912 (copies in S.C.P.M.).
[3] *Cannock Advertiser*, 20 July 1912.
[4] *Cannock Advertiser*, 17 August 1912.
[5] Cited in *Cannock Advertiser*, 24 August 1912.
[6] *Cannock Advertiser*, 7 September 1912.

Edalji intervened at this point himself, this time with a letter to the *Daily Mail* which was as outspoken as anything he ever wrote.[1] A great many people, he said, had asked him if he had any theories about the latest maimings, but his main concern was what he called the 'ludicrous' efforts of the police over the previous nine years. He informed them bluntly that they should get rid of the notion that anyone whose name they were unable to spell or pronounce (the correct pronunciation of Edalji was Ee-dl-gee, with the accent on the first syllable[2]) was a foreigner, or that foreigners were most likely to commit such ferocious crimes.

Whatever the reason, the police certainly made no progress after this. In September 1912 'Darby' informed the *Express & Star* 'the next outrage will be at Wednesbury', and in the following month he predicted a maiming in Wolverhampton.[3] His identity remained a matter for anxious national speculation. The *Daily Express* ran a series under the headline 'Mystery that must be solved',[4] and in the following year the *Standard* also brooded over the evidence, in six daily articles.[5] The first article homed in on Darlaston near Walsall (where, it alleged, the Black Country landscape was fit only for Dante's *Inferno*) as a centre of 'Darby's' activity. By the end of the sixth article it could only suggest, helplessly, that everyone posting letters in Walsall should look out for a skulking figure waiting to sidle up to the box and furtively slip in his mail.

G.A. Atkinson, the journalist who produced the *Standard* articles, eventually had them published as a booklet. The cover illustration, showing a man approaching two horses with a fearsome-looking blade, gave visual form to the image of Great Wyrley which stuck in the public mind for decades.[6] Atkinson persuaded both Anson and Conan Doyle to write prefaces, and Anson, strangely, gave the name of Royden Sharp as the man Conan Doyle suspected of writing the pre-Darby letters – even Conan Doyle's biographers did not name Sharp until Pierre Nordon did so in 1966.[7] Anson pointed out that Royden Sharp had spent a period in prison at a time when letters were appearing, so he could not be Darby. As for Atkinson, his overall view was that Darby was involved in the continuing

[1] *Daily Mail*, 4 September 1912.
[2] *Pearson's Weekly*, 14 February 1907.
[3] 'G. H. Darby' to *Express & Star*, 12 September and 7 October 1912.
[4] *Daily Express*, 2, 4, 5 and 7 September 1912.
[5] *Standard*, 6, 7, 8, 9, 10 and 11 October 1913.
[6] G. A. Atkinson, *G. H. Darby, Captain of the Wyrley Gang: an Investigation*, T. Kirby & Sons, 1914.
[7] Pierre Nordon, *Conan Doyle*, pp. 125-6.

outrages and that the perpetrator must be in the circle of acquaintances of Harry Green, but he had little evidence to support his hunches.

Later in 1913 a *Daily Sketch* headline ran 'Wyrley Gang at work again'. The article linked another threat by 'G. H. Darby' with an actual cut, 10" long and 3" deep, to a pony in Darlaston.[1] Other papers made similar connections:

> *These outrages have been going on for ten years at varying periods. Every outrage has been preceded by letters or postcards signed "G. H. Darby, captain of the Wyrley Gang"... in July, August and October 1912, three horses were maimed at Darlaston, Walsall and Wednesbury. Once again they stopped, but now they have recommenced, two occurring last month at Darlaston and Wednesbury, and one a week ago at Bradley.*

Many places mentioned in the letters in these years, and the locations of the injuries to animals themselves, were towns in the Black Country, several miles south of Great Wyrley though still at that time part of Staffordshire – Walsall, Darlaston, Bilston, Wednesbury, Wolverhampton. It was a region filled with thousands of smoking ironworking foundries amid a landscape covered with dark spoil from the working of both shallow and relatively thick coal seams. As elsewhere, the use of motorised transport was expanding fast, but horses were still vital to the Black Country economy.

This was the world with which 'Darby' seemed to be associated, but still the press headed north. In September 1913 Shapurji opened the vicarage door to find yet another journalist hovering with questions about the ghosts of Great Wyrley. The man from the *Manchester Guardian* had already spent time in a pub quizzing locals on their theories about the identity of 'G. H. Darby'. Now he faced 'this brave-hearted gentleman of alien blood in the midst of a prejudiced flock'. Shapurji, he reported, described the crimes of the past as a mystery, but then smiled suddenly at the memory of some placards left outside St Mark's in 1909; these placards, attributed to 'Darby' by Shapurji, had announced that the vicar and his daughter would sing when the church's new organ was first used.[2]

Then the journalists drifted away again and the war came, a solution no nearer. In 1915, however, 'Darby' reappeared, in a

---

[1] *Daily Sketch*, 5 August 1913.
[2] *Manchester Guardian*, 1 October 1913.

strange new guise. Now he was 'Count von G. H. Darby', captain of a Wyrley Gang with members who had 'come over to the district on their holidays from the war as spys for the Germans'.[1] The gang seemed as murderous as ever. One letter predicted an outrage, and a few days later a horse was found maimed in Darlaston.[2] Soon afterwards there were further threats: 'If the bluebottles don't leave the force at once there will be further maiming outrages done, and there will be another murder done later on by the gang.' Two weeks later a bay gelding was found wounded at Hill Top in Wednesbury.[3] Then the shower of letters subsided. In early 1916 there was one last threat to murder the police, and afterwards the Darby pen was still. The unaccustomed silence suggested that the 'Count' really had gone to war.

It was shortly after Herbert Hunter started work as Chief Constable Anson's Deputy in 1919 that the letters and postcards cascaded forth again. The activities of the 'Wyrley Gang' were still the focus:

> *Warning notice*
> *Headquarters, Market Place, Wyrley*

> *Sir, the wyrley gang is giving the bluebottles a week notice to leave the bluebottle force in Staffordshire from now if not there will be another outrage at West Bromwich...* [4]

This letter, appearing shortly after a horse had been maimed in Wednesbury, provoked fury in the area. One *Express & Star* correspondent lambasted the 'vile scoundrel' 'G. H. Darby'.[5] Another exploded with a paranoia equal to 'Darby's', suggesting that 'Count von G. H. Darby' was probably a German agent, paid by the Kaiser to show up the impotence of England's police forces.[6] The weary Anson washed his hands of it all, leaving Hunter to deal with investigations into the identity of the murderous scribe. Indeed, the case was still high profile enough for him to appoint a team of particularly good officers. For the next fifteen years he also dealt with every case of

---

[1] *Express & Star*, 10 September 1915.
[2] *Express & Star*, 9 September 1915.
[3] *Express & Star*, 16 September, 4 October 1915
[4] *Express & Star*, 4 September 1919.
[5] *Express & Star*, 5 September 1919.
[6] *Express & Star*, 8 September 1919.

alleged cattle maiming in South Staffordshire, even after 1929, when Anson at last retired and Hunter replaced him.[1]

The tide of 'Darby' letters turned during the 1920s. In 1931, however, it suddenly poured forth again, and for three years there was a flood. All sorts of people received letters or postcards, and some of them received dozens. Then, in October 1934, Great Wyrley hit the headlines for the last time:

"WYRLEY GANG": AMAZING COURT REFERENCE
"POISON PEN" CASE AT WEDNESBURY

The sensational and mysterious Wyrley maiming outrages of 1903 were mentioned at Wednesbury Police Court today in a case which was described as "One of the most... remarkable prosecutions in this or any other court in the Midlands." Amazing allegations were made against Enoch Albert Knowles (57), labourer, of 8, Park-street, Darlaston. He was accused of sending obscene communications through the post.[2]

This was the man. 'G. H. Darby' had been found, and it was soon obvious that he had absolutely nothing to do with Great Wyrley. Born in 1877, Knowles had lived in Darlaston for the whole of his life, apart from his short spell in the army during the War. Since 1902 he had been employed as a labourer at the Darlaston firm Guest, Keen & Nettlefolds, which made nuts and bolts, and had always given the impression at the works that he could not write and could only sign with a cross.[3]

This strange man was an extraordinarily obsessive writer. His very first letter had been inspired by newspaper reports about George's trial in October 1903. Within a week of George's sentence he wrote to the *Express & Star*, stating that for the time being there would be a cessation of activities, but that they would start again later. As the 'Captain of the Wyrley Gang' he threatened further attacks on and off for years, and when maiming outrages actually took place, as in Darlaston in 1906, it appeared to the world that the letter-writer really was connected with them; there is in fact no evidence that Knowles had anything to do with the injuries to animals. From 1903 to 1916, when he joined the army, postcards and letters were sent to dozens of people, including magistrates, judges, prison governors, and even members of the royal family. His method

---

[1] Sir Herbert Hunter, 'My Real Life Adventure', unpublished manuscript (copy in S.C.P.M.)
[2] *Express & Star*, 26 October 1934.
[3] *The Birmingham Daily Mail*, 6 November 1934.

of working was simply to look through the press for reports of criminal cases and then select some important witness as his victim. That person would then receive abusive and often malicious letters, sometimes accompanied by threats of violence and murder.

When he went into the army in 1916 the writing stopped, but it resumed after his demobilisation in April 1919. His marriage in the same year seems to have been the reason for a curtailment in his maniacal hobby, but in 1931 a new, insatiable outburst began.[1] His victims included a Mr and Mrs Curtis, witnesses in the case of Mary Jarvis, indicted at Stafford with manslaughter in consequence of criminal damage whilst driving a car; Mr and Mrs Curtis, who were respectable licensees in Cannock, received fifty-two postcards and five letters between July and October 1934.[2] Another target was Mrs Randle, who had given evidence in a murder trial and was rewarded with fifteen Darby letters and twenty postcards. Other hapless Midlanders received similar treatment, and yet Knowles' wife Lizzie knew nothing at all of his relentless letter-churning, most of which was carried out on Sundays. After his arrest, writing materials and copies of the *News of the World* were found pushed up a chimney at the Knowles' home.[3]

The police had spotted 'Darby' through a lucky chance. By 1934 post offices in the area were on the lookout for mail with the 'G. H. Darby' handwriting. One day a card was sent through the post to an address in Worcester, Lizzie Knowles' home town. It was signed 'Enoch and Lizzie', and explained why they were unable to visit some relatives. The handwriting was in the familiar style. The police were called, and a search of the burgesses' register of Darlaston District Council revealed that a couple called Enoch and Lizzie Knowles lived in the area.[4] Officers from the investigation branch of the General Post Office in London travelled to the Midlands and combined with the Staffordshire police to put newspapers at the bottom of postboxes near to the Knowles' house. On two successive days Enoch Knowles was observed to leave the house and post cards, which landed on the newspapers and proved to be in 'G. H. Darby' style. The next time he went on one of his missions, this time to the post office, he was arrested. The letter-box was opened and inside were found the last two cards of his career; ironically the intended victims, Mr and Mrs Jones of Low Street

[1] *The Times,* 7 November 1934.
[2] *The Birmingham Post*, 7 November 1934.
[3] Interview with F. Wright, former assistant chief constable of Staffordshire, 1986 (copy in S.C.P.M.).
[4] *The Birmingham Post*, 7 November 1934.

in Cheslyn Hay, were from the parish which had been the object of his original, brooding obsession.[1] Knowles admitted everything, claiming weakly: 'It was all through worry at the works and being upset. I used to get behind in my work and it used to make me that I hardly knew what I was doing.'[2]

In November he appeared at Staffordshire Assizes, charged first with sending communications through the post threatening to kill or murder Mr and Mrs Curtis of Cannock, Mrs Alice Rowley of Wolverhampton, and Miss Leach of West Bromwich, and second with sending letters containing indecent words. A scruffy and forlorn figure, bald, very pale, with bowed back and hollow cheeks, he admitted all the charges and was sentenced to three years' penal servitude.[3] The national press gave the trial full coverage, with a blistering *Daily Express* editorial pouring contempt on Knowles and his ilk: 'The writer of any anonymous letter is an assassin who fires out of the dark. He has not even the courage of his hate.'[4]

In 1934 yet another of the 20th century torrent of articles about George's case appeared in the *Weekly Illustrated*. The author, Bernard O'Donnell, described how on his way to the office in London he sometimes passed George, walking at a fair pace on his way to his own place of business. George, he wrote, was a short, rather thick-set man, with short-cropped greying hair.[5] Inside this George Edalji of middle age there still burned a need to exorcise the ghosts of 1903, and his case was always at the forefront of his and Maud's minds. Soon after moving to Welwyn Garden City they had roped the Welwyn Garden City M.P. into yet another attempt to get compensation for George's wrongful imprisonment nearly thirty years earlier.[6] The dénouement of the 'G. H Darby' story, however, brought the media back in force. The *Daily Express* pulled George out of the cupboard to rake over the ashes of his case, and his gentle, studious-looking face in the accompanying photograph fitted the Conan Doyle image of him perfectly.[7] Then a few months later the *Birmingham Weekly Post* gave him another chance to air his views on the thirty-year 'G. H. Darby' trail and its relation to his own case:

---

[1] *The Birmingham Post*, 27 and 31 October 1934.
[2] *The Birmingham Post*, 1 November 1934.
[3] *The Birmingham Post*, 7 November 1934.
[4] *Daily Express*, 7 November 1934.
[5] Bernard O'Donnell, *Weekly Illustrated*, copy in W. S. L., CB/EDALJI/2 (article wrongly dated 1954).
[6] P.R.O., HO 45/24635, no. 13, 'Shameful Free Pardon Mockers' in *John Bull*, 10.1.1931, and no. 15, letter from Sir Francis Freemantle, M.P., to Home Secretary, 6.3.1935.
[7] *Daily Express*, 7 November 1934.

Conan Doyle at a spiritualist rally

For thirty years it was assumed that to solve the mystery surrounding the Great Wyrley cattle maiming outrages... it was only necessary to identify the notorious 'G.H. Darby' ... Thanks to the alertness of a postal official we now know 'Captain Darby' was really Enoch Knowles who, during the period of his supposed activity at Wyrley, never resided in, and probably never visited that village or knew anything more about it and the crimes he claimed responsibility for than what he read in the papers.

He went on to trawl his memories and his wilder fantasies for some explanation of the traumas and trials of 1903-7. Contemporary theories, he pointed out, had included the idea that the outrages of 1903 had been caused by a great bird, or by a wild boar. The suggestion which he thought the most likely, though still far-fetched, was that the attacker had disguised himself as an animal.[1]

After this sortie into the public eye his pen fell silent, and George and his sister retreated into invisibility. Indeed, an evacuee they received during the War recently gave a curious account of her memories of the Edalji household. At one point, she reported, Maud took her to the back of the house, opened a door and said, 'This is my brother George.' A man sitting at a desk looked up and bowed, and then Maud closed the door.[2]

George may have tried to hide himself away, but he still had one more shock to deal with in his professional life. During a bombing raid one night in 1940 his office was blown up and everything was lost, including the bronze medal and books he had won as prizes as a student.[3] He was forced to practise from someone else's premises, in Argyle Square, and remained there until 1951.[4] Work became very difficult, for his poor eyesight, which has been analysed so assiduously by so many experts and amateurs as a result of his case, deteriorated badly in his last years and at the end had almost completely gone.

It was in this post-war period that Freda Shimmin (née Bagshaw) made contact with her distant relatives. Maud went to visit her in Peterborough, and Freda went once to visit Maud and George. She was however so shaken by the eeriness of the house with its tattered curtains and windows covered in growth, and so frightened by Maud's dog, that she regretted

---

[1] 'The Terror that Stalked by Night', *Birmingham Weekly Post*, 24 and 31 May 1935.
[2] *Daily Telegraph*, 23 September 2006.
[3] Letter from Maud Edalji to Hesketh Pearson, 28 August 1956, Hesketh Pearson Papers, The Univerity of Texas at Austin.
[4] Peter Costello, *The Real World of Sherlock Holmes*, p. 90.

having arranged to stop overnight. George, what's more, was so frail by this stage that it was difficult to have any real conversation with him.[1]

Maud's role, for the second time in her life, was to look after a blind man. One of her tasks was to read to him, and together they groaned about the omissions and inaccuracies in Hesketh Pearson's and John Dickson Carr's accounts of George's case in their biographies of Sir Arthur Conan Doyle. Right at the end of George's life they also had news from across the Irish Sea to discuss; Horace, cut off from his family for nearly five decades, had died in a nursing home in the prosperous suburb of Blackrock in Dublin.[2] George himself went into decline in 1953. In April he underwent an operation, but afterwards, as the nation prepared for the coronation of Queen Elizabeth II, he became completely bedridden. He died a fortnight later.[3]

The end of his life attracted only the slightest attention. The local papers read in Great Wyrley offered brief and inaccurate reports of the death of the community's most famous son,[4] whilst the national papers, which had pored over every aspect of his life in the days of his greatest trials, took no notice of his death at all. 'Guilty or not guilty,' *Roderic Random* of the *Express & Star* once recalled saying after seeing George's behaviour in court in 1903, 'here is a strong man of great possibilities.'[5] The events of George's early life had blighted the career of a man who might have achieved more.

---

[1] Interview with Freda Shimmin, 3 November 2004;
[2] Peter Costello, *The Real World of Sherlock Holmes*, p. 93. The information about Horace Edalji was actually discovered by Michael Harley. The date of Horace's death is given as 1953, but a cutting with the *Cannock Chase Courier*, 19 September 1952 in C.L. gives it as 11 June 1952.
[3] *Cannock Advertiser*, 20 June 1953.
[4] *Cannock Advertiser*, 20 June 1903; *Cannock Chase Courier*, 26 June 1953.
[5] *Express & Star*, 14 January 1907.

BOOK III: A WATCHING WORLD

1. Verdicts

1997. Wading through the Home Office boxes in the Public Record Office. One sheaf of papers after another. But... here, hidden among one set of folders... something completely unexpected... a piece of horse-hide! Horse-hide, roan in colour. This must be it. In my hands I am holding the piece of hide cut from that pony at the scene of the crime on 18 August 1903.[1] The hide from which, Conan Doyle suspected, hairs were transferred to George's coat before it reached Dr Butter the police surgeon. The hide from the pony which is at the centre of everything which has ever been said about the Edalji family.

There is no escape. However much I might believe there is more to the history of the Edalji family than George's sensational case there is no way of getting away from that pony. A conclusion has to be reached on George's conviction. Who was right – George Anson and late 20th century researchers such as Michael Harley, or the Edalji family, R. D. Yelverton and supporters, along with Sir Arthur Conan Doyle and all his admirers?

Stalemate

At first glance, unfortunately, the contents of the Home Office files seemed to make it even more difficult to decide on George's guilt. One major problem was the smoke which poured from the fiery relationship between Anson and Conan Doyle. The dozens and dozens of letters and documents produced by the two men, along with others made available in recent times at the Staffordshire Police Museum, show that there was more to their relationship than has yet been fully revealed. The British public may have salivated at the sight of Conan Doyle as Sherlock Holmes in 1907, but it would surely have positively drooled if it had known about the great man's doings behind the scenes. During 1907 Home Office staff began to use language to describe Conan Doyle and his investigative and campaigning methods which they would never have used in public – in November one groaned about his 'inordinate vanity'. Conan Doyle, on the other hand, began to class Home Office staff as 'insane'.[2] These mutual frustrations could however never match the seething contempt for Conan Doyle

---

[1] P.R.O., HO 144/990.
[2] Sir Arthur Conan Doyle, *Memories and Adventures*, p. 220.

which completely consumed Anson, and this hostility led to a sensationally tempestuous correspondence between the two men which ended with each of them appealing to the 20th century's most famous politician for support.

The relationship had started amicably enough. When Conan Doyle began his investigations in late 1906, Anson was willing to send him some of the information he requested. Indeed, when Conan Doyle visited Staffordshire Anson actually invited him to his home at Green Hall in Stafford.[1] Anson did not however have much faith in Conan Doyle's capacities as a real-life detective, and once the *Daily Telegraph* articles had been published in January 1907 there was no going back. So far as Conan Doyle was concerned the unwavering conviction that George Edalji had been the victim of a gross miscarriage of justice meant that someone must be to blame, and that person was Anson. From Anson's point of view, Conan Doyle, the most famous and one of the most savage of his critics, not only helped to secure a free pardon for a man Anson's police force claimed to be guilty; he also subjected Anson to personal humiliation by blaming him for infecting the Staffordshire police with his racial prejudice and for thus being personally responsible for a wrongful conviction.

It was soon clear to the Home Office what Anson felt about Conan Doyle. 'Is C. Conan Doyle quite mad?' he asked in January 1907. 'There are Popes and Emperors in a Lunatic Asylum. Why not Sherlock Holmes?'[2] Later in the year, after Conan Doyle's case against Royden Sharp had been presented to the Home Secretary, Anson seethed over Conan Doyle's 'utter recklessness and inexactitude as to facts'.[3] In a document produced in October, the Chief Constable went through Conan Doyle's evidence meticulously, pouring scorn on fifty-one points at which he said it was inaccurate.[4] He pointed out, for example, that in November 1892 Royden was at school in Wisbech in Lincolnshire when, according to Conan Doyle, he was leaving poisonous letters at St Mark's vicarage, and that he stayed there until his father died at the end of 1893. Mr Brookes, the postmaster who lived close to the Edaljis, was according to Anson in no doubt that it was George who wrote the letters. As most of the letters were posted through the vicarage door or left on the lawn someone very close to the vicarage, if not in it, must have been responsible. In May 1895,

[1] Michael Harley, 'An infamous Anson?'
[2] P.R.O., HO 144/989 (Anson to Simpson at Home Office, 25 January 1907).
[3] George Anson, 'Sir A. C. Conan Doyle's Allegations', October 1907 (copy in S.C.P.M.).
[4] George Anson, 'Notes on Sir A. C. Conan Doyle's "Statement" of accusation against Royden Sharp', 1907, with additions 1920 (copy in S.C.P.M.).

significantly, the Edaljis received some writing on the inside of an envelope which had been posted to Shapurji several months earlier. The weaknesses in Conan Doyle's detective work bred increasing contempt in Anson, driving him to ask in January 1908: 'Is he an utter fool as well as a knave?'[1]

It was one specific incident which did most to stoke the fires of Anson's rage. The starting-point was a letter from Anson to Conan Doyle at Christmas time in 1906. In the course of the letter he told Conan Doyle about the Edaljis' former sleeping arrangements. Anson believed that Shapurji used to lock his bedroom door, not to stop anyone getting in but rather to stop George getting out for his night-time activities. Shapurji, he told Conan Doyle, 'had the boy to sleep with him. I presume he had good reason.' Three months later he received a letter which shook him to the core. In this letter, Ernley Blackwell of the Home Office reported to him a meeting which had taken place in January at Conan Doyle's request. Present at the meeting were Conan Doyle, Blackwell (Legal Under-secretary), Gladstone (Home Secretary), and Chalmers (Under-secretary of State). During the interview Conan Doyle presented his listeners with surprising news: Anson had accused Shapurji Edalji of 'sodomitical practices' with his son George. This was Conan Doyle's interpretation of Anson's Christmas letter.

On hearing of this development from Blackwell, Anson exploded. Conan Doyle's statement was an 'abominable lie', he said – a phrase he was to use time and again for years. The whole experience tortured him, and he sent the Home Office a full report on the 'abominable allegations'. Conan Doyle had claimed that his friend John Churton Collins knew there had been rumours in Great Wyrley about Shapurji's sodomy with George. Anson did not believe Collins could have known what was going on in Great Wyrley years earlier, and suspected Conan Doyle was using Collins to shield himself. Conan Doyle did write to the Home Office in March to say that he regretted conveying a mistaken interpretation, but he never apologised directly to Anson. After this, Conan Doyle's campaign to prove the involvement of the Sharp family in the crimes of Great Wyrley took over the men's minds, and for the rest of 1907 Anson's criticisms of Conan Doyle were concentrated on his sloppy detective work.

For some reason the Chief Constable's festering wounds burst open again three years later. He wrote to Conan Doyle in

---

[1] P.R.O., HO 144/989 (Anson to Blackwell at Home Office, 26 January 1908).

November 1910, Conan Doyle replied the following day, and a hurricane correspondence of remarkable acrimony followed.[1] By January 1911 Conan Doyle was writing to say that he still believed he had a case against Royden Sharp, and was accusing Anson of discourtesy. Anson fizzed with rage. At the heart of all the pain which Conan Doyle had caused him nothing had hurt him more than what he still called 'the lie'. Conan Doyle, he said, had made a lying accusation to the Home Secretary about him, and then had tried to screen himself by blaming 'that miserable wretch' John Churton Collins for putting the idea in his head; the phrase 'that miserable wretch' was used to express sympathy for Collins, who had been found drowned near Lowestoft in 1908. Anson also suggested that Conan Doyle's case against Royden Sharp was 'arrant nonsense'. Now Conan Doyle cut loose, wilfully misinterpreting Anson's comments on Collins: '... you describe Professor Collins, a man whose boots you are not fit to blacken, as a miserable wretch...' In response Anson simply repeated his demand that Conan Doyle apologise for 'the lie', whilst Conan Doyle retorted that if Anson did not withdraw the accusation of lying the correspondence would be closed. Each man had lost control of himself and, unable to wait for letters to get in the next blow, they turned to two exchanges of telegram, with Anson still insisting that Conan Doyle apologise for 'the lie'.

In a letter of 30 January 1911, Conan Doyle wrote to ask the new Home Secretary, his friend Winston Churchill, to side with him in the battle.[2] He admitted he had said things in 1907 to which Anson had taken exception, but claimed that he had later apologised. Anson, he believed, had no reason for persisting in writing to him about the affair, and the letter allegedly abusing John Churton Collins was unforgivable. Blackwell, in a note to Churchill, gave full details of the circumstances in which 'the lie' had been told, and of its aftermath. He thought Anson genuinely believed that Shapurji used to lock the bedroom door so that George could not go out at night. Conan Doyle, he claimed, had a special reason for deliberately asserting that Anson's letter of Christmas 1906 suggested that Shapurji locked the bedroom door for the purpose of sodomy. It was because he wanted to discredit Anson and further his own cause in the eyes of the Home Secretary.

In his advice to Winston Churchill, Blackwell was at something of a loss. He sympathised with Anson, but felt that the language of the telegram to Conan Doyle was inexcusable.

---

[1] Correspondence between Conan Doyle and Anson, 1910-11 (copy in S.C.P.M.).
[2] P.R.O., HO 144/987, no. 314 (Conan Doyle to Home Secretary, 30 January 1911).

Dismissal or some other action against Anson was however hardly likely. After all, the actions of the Home Office had had the effect of shielding Anson throughout 1907, and Edward VII had actually given Anson the first of his decorations, the MVO, during a visit to Staffordshire in the same year. The Home Secretary was therefore advised simply to write to Anson to ask for an explanation. Anson was unrepentant: he would always use the term 'lie' until Conan Doyle apologised. Conan Doyle kept up his campaign against Anson via his solicitors (Lewis and Lewis, George Edalji's patrons), who sent the Home Secretary copies of the correspondence which had led to the Anson telegram. Anson wrote to Blackwell again, to say that Conan Doyle's 'lie' was aimed at discrediting him. Finally, in March, Conan Doyle's solicitors wrote to Anson to say that all correspondence in future should be directed through them; relations had broken down completely, and Winston Churchill could do nothing to stop it. Conan Doyle still believed passionately in his cause – he wrote to his mother later in 1911: 'I have written to the new home secretary about Edalji... I'll win that case yet.'[1]

He never won, but he also never forgot. In 1913, for example, he wrote the letter to Charlotte Edalji which I held in my hands when I visited Freda Shimmin in 2004; in it he told Charlotte that he was writing a preface to the articles produced by the *Standard* correspondent G. A. Atkinson.[2] In 1924 he returned to the case again, this time in his *Memories and Adventures,* which reveal that his view had not changed in the slightest since 1907.[3] 'If the whole land had been raked,' he asserted with unshaken confidence, 'I do not think that it would have been possible to find a man who was so unlikely, and indeed incapable, of committing such actions.' Nor had he changed his view of the Staffordshire police, the law courts, and the Home Office. Indeed, this view had now been elaborated into a full-blown conspiracy theory: 'The sad fact is that officialdom in England stands together... an unavowed Trade Union... which subordinates the public interest to a false idea of loyalty.'[4] He still argued for Royden Sharp's guilt, and underlined it by rehearsing evidence he had collected on Sharp's later doings: Sharp was given six months' hard labour on one occasion, had been convicted of arson, had three times been guilty of theft, and had once confessed that he had stolen from his mother.[5] So far as George's case was concerned the verdict was clear: 'It is a blot upon the record of English Justice, and even now it should be

---

[1] 2 November 1911, cited in Pierre Nordon, *Conan Doyle,* p. 127.
[2] Conan Doyle to Charlotte Edalji, 29 November 1913 (in possession of Freda Shimmin).
[3] Conan Doyle, *Memories and Adventures,* p. 217.
[4] Sir Arthur Conan Doyle, *Memories and Adventures,* p. 220.
[5] Ibid., p. 221.

wiped out.'[1] It was a verdict which echoed for decades through the pens of many of the dozens of his admirers and biographers – 'a very gentle, perfect knight (Lamond, 1931),[2] a 'brilliant vindication of Edalji' (Pemberton, 1936),[3] 'the incarnation of the English conscience' (Nordon, 1968)[4] – until Michael Harley came to challenge it.

****

Anson's obsession was less public, but he brooded over these painful events for the rest of his long career. His state of mind in his later years is revealed in the memoirs of Sir Herbert Hunter, who was appointed Assistant Chief Constable in 1919.[5] Anson confided that he was tired out, and Hunter himself felt that his Chief Constable was older than his actual years by this time. Anson told Hunter that nothing in his life had caused him more distress than the Edalji affair, about which he had received letters from all over world. Hunter recommended him to try to get the nightmare out of his system by writing it down. Anson took him up on this, and thus produced a batch of documents which provided his final thoughts on the case.

One of the documents was an elaboration of his October 1907 critique of Conan Doyle's case against Royden Sharp.[6] He remained convinced, in 1920 as in 1907, that 'a man must be stark mad to really believe that the "evidence" so far adduced could in any way be sufficient for a prosecution'.[7] Indeed, he signed off his attack with a new side-swipe at Conan Doyle's enthusiasm for spiritualism: the collapse of Conan Doyle's triumphant 'discovery' of Frank Sharp in 1907, he wrote, ended his quest, but 'perhaps he is still pursuing it with the help of other and newer mediums'. He tried to exorcise the pain by sending copies of Conan Doyle's statement and his own contemptuous comments on it to every superintendent in Staffordshire and every chief constable in the country.[8]

---

[1] Ibid., p. 219.

[2] John Lamond, *Arthur Conan Doyle,* John Murray, p. 95.

[3] Max Pemberton, *Sixty Years Ago and After*, Hutchinson & Co., 1936, pp. 243-4.

[4] Pierre Nordon, *Conan Doyle*, p. 122.

[5] Sir Herbert Hunter, 'My Real Life Adventure', unpublished manuscript (copy in S.C.P.M.).

[6] George Anson, 'Notes on Sir A. C. Conan Doyle's "Statement" of accusation against Royden Sharp'.

[7] George Anson, 'Notes on Sir Arthur Conan Doyle's "Statement" of accusation against Royden Sharp'.

[8] Letter from the Chief Constable's office to all superintendents in Staffordshire, 16 June 1920 (copy in S.C.P.M.).

George Anson, Chief Constable of Staffordshire

Kind permission of Staffordshire County Council

Sir Arthur Conan Doyle in later life

Despite all this personal torment, however, Anson's career was not harmed in the least by the Edalji case. He was not only made an MVO in 1907, the year his reputation had suffered the most, but also a CBE in 1925 and (after his retirement in 1929 after forty-one years as Chief Constable) a KCB in 1937. He died in 1947.

Observers

The private fracas and eventual stalemate between Anson and Conan Doyle did not affect the public view of George and his family during all this time. Here the Conan Doyle version ruled the roost until the 1980s. It was not just Conan Doyle's biographers who kept repeating the story. Journalists and feature writers from Cannock to New York revisited the tale of the Wyrley outrages regularly, always using Conan Doyle's writings as their main or only source of information, though often with an attempt at a new slant on the affair. James W. Booth, an American writing in 1949, came up with the succinct 'Elementary, My Dear Corpse!' as the title for his account of Conan Doyle's work on the cases of George Edalji and Oscar Slater (convicted for murder in 1908).[1] David Camelon, on the other hand, writing in *The American Weekly* in 1950, enticed readers with the blockbuster:

> *The Secret Romance of Sherlock Holmes. Sir Arthur Conan Doyle, through his detective work, stands revealed as the model for his famous character. George Edalji knew that Sherlock Holmes* [Conan Doyle], *carrying his bride* [Jean Leckie] *up the stairs, had finally found true love.*[2]

The grip which Sherlock Holmes held over the Edalji story in the UK was reflected by an article in the *Yorkshire Post* in 1983 which declared that a police search in Bedfordshire for a person mutilating and killing horses and ponies brought back memories of a celebrated fight for justice; the headline was 'Sherlock Holmes Link in Hunt for Beasts'.[3]

---

[1] Ronald Burt de Waal, *The International Sherlock Holmes*, Archon Books, 1980, p. 178.
[2] Ronald Burt de Waal, *The International Sherlock Holmes*, p. 178.
[3] W. Clive Davies, 'Sherlock Holmes Link in Hunt for Beasts', *Yorkshire Post*, 11 May 1983.

Conan Doyle believed this photograph of faires to be genuine

Thanks to Conan Doyle, the 1903-1907 period in the life of the Edalji family also inspired writers of fiction. Agatha Christie, who was a teenager at the time of the Edalji affair and read Conan Doyle's detective stories avidly, later incorporated features of Conan Doyle's account into one of her own stories, 'The Cretan Bull'.[1] In this story her famous detective, Hercule Poirot, is called in because a young man, Hugh Chandler, appears to be going insane and terrorising the countryside:

'Even just lately things have been killed,' he whispered. 'All round – in the village – out on the downs. Sheep, young lambs – a collie dog. Father locks me in at night, but sometimes – sometimes – the door's open in the morning. I must have a key hidden somewhere but I don't know where I've hidden it.'[2]

Later in the century Nicholas Meyer created a character based on George Edalji in his novel, *The West End horror, a posthumous memoir of John H. Watson*, which was first published, in condensed form, in *Playboy* magazine.[3] In Meyer's story, George becomes a myopic young Parsi law student from Bombay (the real-life George was certainly myopic and studied law, though it was his father who was born a Parsi in Bombay). This character in the novel is given an incongruous name for a Parsi – 'Achmet Singh', a combination of Muslim and Sikh names. In the totally fictional central story-line, Achmet Singh is accused of murdering an actress, Miss Jesse Rutland. The usual butt of Sherlock Holmes' intellectual superiority, Inspector Lestrade, then takes on the role of George Edalji's real-life adversary, Staffordshire's Chief Constable, George Anson, whilst Holmes, in the role of Conan Doyle, is to be found echoing Conan Doyle's actual fulminations against Anson in 1907: 'Lestrade has built up a neat circumstantial case in which the hideous spectre of racial bigotry plays a large and unsubtle role.'

Dramatists were interested too; a play about Conan Doyle's role in the case was staged at the Victoria Theatre in the Potteries in 1971.[4] As for the broadcast media, the BBC2 television play of 1972 which had sparked my own interest in

[1] Referred to by Richard and Molly Whittington-Egan (eds) in Sir Arthur Conan Doyle, *The Story of Mr. George Edalji*, Grey House books, 1985, pp. 24-5.
[2] Agatha Christie, 'The Cretan Bull', written in 1940 for British and American magazines as one of the *Labours of Hercules*, published as a collection for the Crime Club by Collins in 1947.
[3] Nicholas Meyer, *The West End Horror, a posthumous memoir of John H. Watson*, Hodder and Stoughton, 1976.
[4] Roger Woddis, *Conan Doyle Investigates*, unpublished script, 1971 (copy in C.L.). Performed as a BBC radio play, May 1972.

Conan Doyle's role was not the first of its kind. [1] Remarkably the German television channel ZDF had already entered the field in 1966 with *Conan Doyle und der Fall Edalji*; film and TV star Paul Klinger played Conan Doyle, and white actors took the parts of George, Shapurji and Maud.[2] The 1972 BBC2 programme covered much of the same ground, and with some success: the episode was broadcast in the United States in 1974 with Alistair Cooke as host, and was reviewed in such far-flung publications as the *New Mexican* and the *Tulsa Daily World*.[3] A further play was broadcast on BBC Radio 4 in 1987.[4]

Guilt

Then along came Michael Harley. Here was Rebus not Holmes, completely unimpressed by the 75-year-old image of Conan Doyle perpetuated by a string of writers, the image of a gentle knight in shining armour charging on his horse to the rescue of the helpless victim of a merciless establishment. The gullible Conan Doyle, he said, had on the one hand been taken in by George Edalji, who was certainly guilty of criminal acts, and on the other sullied the reputation of a chief constable whose judgements were much more soundly based than his own.

When I finally got to them I found that the Home Office files did indeed show that there was much to question in Conan Doyle's performance in the role of Sherlock Holmes. One major issue was the question of George's financial problems in 1902-3, which Conan Doyle had simply swept under the carpet. Michael Harley was with Anson in seeing George's 1902 appeal to the M.P. Sir J. B. Stone as evidence that George had a much murkier side than Conan Doyle would admit:

> *I am reduced... to absolute poverty... through having had to pay a large sum of money (nearly £220) for a friend for whom I was surety. I borrowed from three money-lenders... but their exorbitant interest only made matters worse, and two of them have now presented a bankruptcy petition against me but are willing to withdraw it if I can raise £115 at once.*

---

[1] Jeremy Paul, *The Edwardians: Conan Doyle,* unpublished script, 1972 (copy in C.L.).
[2] *Conan Doyle und der Fall Edalji*, first shown on ZDF 29.7.1966. Recording available from ZDF.
[3] Ronald Burt de Waal, *The International Sherlock Holmes*, pp. 389-90.
[4] Roy Apps, *Conan Doyle and the Edalji Case*, unpublished script, 1987 (copy in C.L.).

... I shall be grateful for any aid however small...[1]

Michael Harley saw this story as a cover for gambling debts and a sign that George was in such financial trouble in early 1903 that he might have been driven to desperate measures. His evidence came from Chief Constable Anson: once R. D. Yelverton entered the fray after George's conviction in October 1903 Anson started the behind-the-scenes correspondence with the Home Office which was to last for years, and George's financial position was referred to time and again. Yelverton's weighty submission itself was sent off in December and he followed up this first salvo with dozens more communications, which were to pepper the Home Office for four years.[2] One, copies of a batch of testimonials and letters of support, included a letter from Sir Mancherjee Bhownaggree, the Parsi from Bombay who had become Britain's second Asian M. P.[3]

Already, in November, Anson had started to try to expose the naïveté of Yelverton's efforts by pointing out to the Home Secretary that George was 'in the greatest straights for money at the time of his arrest' and that his arrest 'was a perfect godsend for him'.[4] Later he several times drew attention to a sum of £214 which was deposited in April 1903 for the purchase of land by a client named J. Hawkins of Cheslyn Hay and which was missing by the time of George's arrest in August, evidence of George's dishonesty and desperation to recover from his large debts.[5] By 1905 Anson was sending evidence of a claim against George of £350 from London stockbrokers in 1902, and bankruptcy affidavits against him in 1903.[6] He suspected that George owed money because of gambling on the stock exchange rather than speculating because he was let down by a friend. He also passed on a letter from Horace Edalji, who reported that his brother spent a week in London in February 1903, and noted that George gave no explanation of why he went.[7] In 1907, with Conan Doyle on the trail, Anson wrote again about George's financial troubles, which were caused, he said, by speculation.[8] Michael Harley was equally cynical about the mismatch between George's public persona

---

[1] B.R.L., 370795 (George Edalji to J. B. Stone, December 1902, in 'A Collection of MSS Formed by Sir J. B. Stone').
[2] P.R.O., HO 144/984/112737, no 17, R. D. Yelverton 'Case on Submission' to Home Office, December 1903.
[3] P.R.O., HO 144/984/112737, no 25, R. D. Yelverton to Home Office, 9 December 1903.
[4] P.R.O., HO 144/984/112737, no 5, Anson to Home Office, 8 November 1903.
[5] e.g. P.R.O., HO 144/984/112737, nos 39 and 44, Anson to Home Office, 23 December 1903 and 1 January 1904.
[6] P.R.O., HO 144/985/112737, no 118 (Anson to Home Office, 7 March 1905).
[7] P.R.O., HO 144/989 (Horace Edalji to Christopher Hatton, 6 December 1903).
[8] P.R.O., HO 144/989 (Anson to Home Office, 6 January 1907).

and his private doings. The anonymous letter sent to the Chief Constable in 1907 (claiming that after George lost money in a lawyers' fraud he made a £50 bet with other solicitors that he would rip up six horses, six cows, and six sheep in his father's parish before the end of 1903) appeared to support Anson's suspicions. Michael Harley agreed with Anson that the letter was in George's disguised handwriting.[1]

Anson had other surprises up his sleeve so far as the letters were concerned, surprises which did not come out either in the trial or during the period of outrage over the verdict which followed. One was secretly revealed to the Home Office in 1905, covered in his 51-point demolition of Conan Doyle's case against Royden Sharp in 1907, and updated when he continued his search for resolution on George's case in 1920.[2] In these papers he gave details of an astonishing aspect of the police investigation during 1903: at the height of the reign of terror in Great Wyrley he had himself been guilty of what in our own times is known as entrapment.[3] The 'Lover of Justice' letter in the 1903 series had actually been concocted by a solicitor, C. A. Loxton, the man mentioned by George when he was arrested in 1903. The letter was written under Anson's instructions, and posted in Rugeley by Anson himself. The aim was to trick George into a self-incriminating response. The letter had some features which marked it as different from others in the series:

> George Edalji
> ... I do not like natives. But I think everyone ought to have fair treatment & that is why I write to you because I do not think you have had anything to do with the horrid crimes that everyone talks about. The people all said it must be you because they do not think you are a right sort... If another horse is murdered the people will all say it was you...
>
> A LOVER OF JUSTICE[4]

George handed the letter to the police, and a few days later he sent for Inspector Campbell in order to pass on another letter from Greatorex:

> Littleworth Farm...

---

[1] Michael Harley, *Cannock Advertiser*, 4 November 1983. A copy of the letter is in P.R.O., HO 144/988 ('Martin Molton' to Anson, 7 January 1907).
[2] George Anson, 'Notes on Sir A. C. Conan Doyle's "Statement" of accusation against Royden Sharp'.
[3] George Anson, 'Notes on Sir Arthur Conan Doyle's "Statement" of accusation against Royden Sharp'.
[4] Cited in George Anson, 'Notes on Sir A. C. Conan Doyle's "Statement" of accusation against Royden Sharp'.

George Edalji
... Now dont do anything to Quibell as he only said what
Stanley told him you go tomorrow night to Stanley and
take a thick stick and give him a good hiding, never mind
if you murder him everyone will say you were quite right
in thrashing him as most people here think he and his
father are guilty of the horrid crimes everyone is so
shocked at. Be sure to go to Stanley at once as they are
going to send him to a training ship. It soon caught on
about you murdering the horses because none of the
people think you are the right sort...
Wilfred Greatorex[1]

This letter provides some of the most damning evidence we
have that George was a writer of anonymous letters. Anson
pointed out that it contains references which indicate that the
author must have seen the 'Lover of Justice' letter – variations
on the expressions 'horrid crimes', 'murdering the horses', and
'none of the people think you are the right sort' are common to
both, and the opening 'George Edalji' is different from the form
of other letters in the series. This seemed to provide proof that
George was behind them, and yet on the first day of his trial
Disturnal, prosecution counsel, challenged directly by Vachell
for the defence, said he had no evidence that George had
written the 'Lover of Justice' letter.[2] Anson blamed the defence
counsel for then mislaying the 'Lover of Justice' letter at the
crucial moment.[3]

Anson's other bombshell was his revelation that George's
own brother, Horace, had confirmed Anson's belief that George
had been involved in writing anonymous letters in the 1892-5
series. Anson's information came from a report by P.C. Cooper
about a conversation he had in November 1903 with
Christopher Hatton, son of John and Mary Hatton of Brook
House.[4] Anson believed Horace was prepared to go to the
Home Secretary, presumably to confirm that he had told his
parents that George had been responsible for some of the
letters of 1892-5 and that they had refused to tell Yelverton
about it, and Anson always hoped that Horace would come
forward with more information. Certainly this episode was the
turning-point in Horace's relations with the rest of the family.

---

[1] Cited by George Anson, 'Notes on Sir A. C. Conan Doyle's "Statement" of accusation
against Royden Sharp'.
[2] *News of the World*, 25 October 1903.
[3] George Anson, 'Notes on Sir A. C. Conan Doyle's "Statement" of accusation against
Royden Sharp'.
[4] P.R.O., HO 144/985, no. 124 (police reports forwarded by Anson to Home Office, 1904).

He was clearly convinced about the letters of 1892-5: 'I have always felt very sorry for mater and pater and how they were deceived,' he told Christopher Hatton in his schoolboy style. His family took a different view: 'My people seem awfully wild with me for telling them about George.'[1] The gulf between them was to grow wider and wider over the years, with Horace even giving up his surname, and his aunt and mother each cutting him out of their wills.

The Home Office files also contain the private memo by Home Secretary Herbert Gladstone which reveals that knowledge of Horace's evidence was not confined to Anson and the Staffordshire police. This is his report that in June 1907 Alfred Hazell, M.P. for West Bromwich in Staffordshire, told him that the defence side at George's trial, of which he was a member, were convinced that George wrote two of the letters. They compared them with the handwriting of a crude letter addressed to a maid which they claimed Horace found in George's drawers.[2] Hazell told Gladstone that he had met Vachell again in early 1907, and that Vachell had commented, in reference to the new outburst of anonymous letter-writing represented by the 'Martin Molton' series, 'he's at it again'. Even George's defence team thought him guilty of anonymous letter-writing.

Beyond presenting George's financial problems and the anonymous letters of 1903 as the background to the outrages of 1903 Anson provided the Home Office with new evidence pointing to George's actual involvement in the outrages. First, George was far from being the home-bird he claimed to be: Anson reported on his 'commonly-talked-of habits of wandering abroad late at night'.[3] Second, and more significant, the police, said Anson, started to keep an eye on George in the summer of that year because he was actually seen late at night in a field where an animal was killed.[4]

Conan Doyle was ignorant of some of this evidence and suppressed the rest. Indeed the ideas of the man who believed in fairies were sometimes so far from the truth that Michael Harley had good reason for calling his whole case into question. The 1903 'Lover of Justice' letter, for example, he ascribed to Wallie Sharp, though in fact it was written at Chief Constable Anson's behest. He then went on to claim that Royden was also

---

[1] P.R.O., HO 144/989 (Horace Edalji to Christopher Hatton, 13 December 1903).
[2] P.R.O., HO 144/988 (note by Home Secretary on a conversation with Hazell, 6 June 1907).
[3] *The Staffordshire Sentinel*, 22 May 1907.
[4] P.R.O., HO 144/984, no. 44 (Anson to the Home Office, 15 December 1903).

the 'G. H. Darby' who started pouring out letters after George's trial, though G. H. Darby was actually Enoch Knowles of Darlaston who had nothing at all to do with Great Wyrley. His excited claim in October 1907 that he had tracked down a third Sharp brother, Frank, whom he believed to be the God-Satan of the 1892-5 series of letters, was easily shown up when the Home Office investigated.[1]

But you, Maud, you with your parents, did not need to see the letters pouring secretly into the Home Secretary's in-tray. You may have had too much faith in Sir Arthur's detective skills and in the strength of his case, but that was not the real point, as you all suspected. The overall problem was Anson, Anson and the Home Office, not Sir Arthur. You guessed, almost knew, that once the campaign on George's behalf began in October 1903 Anson was in constant touch with the Home Office, and that he was not really building a more complete and structured case against George. The information he drip-fed to the Home Office was just a series of slurs.

When examined in its entirety Anson's correspondence with the Home Office reeks more of desperation than of conviction. In order to prevent the Edalji campaign from making any headway with the Home Secretary first after Yelverton's intervention in 1903, then during the campaign by *Truth* and finally after Conan Doyle's onslaught in 1907 he dragged up all the dirt he could to tarnish George's name. He did nothing, however, to strengthen the police and prosecution case.

In commenting on the Elizabeth Foster case of 1888 he threw in the nonchalant suggestion that 'I should think she was innocent', thus making it appear that the Edalji family had knowingly accused an innocent person in order to shield one of their own. As the letters have not survived it is no longer possible to compare the handwriting with George's and rule him out as the author, but all the evidence points away from him; Shapurji, in particular, was a man of such strong principle and sense of moral duty that it is hard to believe that he would have covered up for a wayward son and deliberately implicated an innocent person. Anson, however, offered his off-the-cuff verdict without offering a scrap of evidence in support.[2]

---

[1] P.R.O., HO 144/987, no. 297 (Conan Doyle to the Home Office, 7 October 1907, and Home Secretary to Conan Doyle, 11 November 1907).
[2] P.R.O., HO 144/989 Box 1 (Anson to Home Office, 7 March 1905).

He fares no better when his approach to the events of 1892-5 is considered. Examination of the letters in the Home Office files tends to support Conan Doyle's view that the driving force behind the first outburst of letters in 1892 was a feud between boys attending Walsall Grammar School. One of these boys, Royden Sharp, was at odds with two others, Fred Brookes, son of the Great Wyrley grocer, and Fred Wynn. Sharp once told a railway guard that Brookes and Wynn were responsible for breaking a window in a railway carriage, but he himself was found guilty and may well have sought revenge. Sharp was Conan Doyle's 'foulmouth', and although this is difficult to prove one way or the other at this distance, the Brookes family certainly received more of the early letters than did the Edaljis, and Wynn also received two. Even Sergeant Upton himself suspected, for a time at least, that the culprit came from the school. He invested much time in pursuing boys in the Walsall Grammar group, and Fred Wynn later reported that he had travelled several times on the same train. On one occasion Fred Wynn was summoned into the head's study at school to find Upton waiting there to interview him.[1]

Although not a member of the group it is easy to see why George became one of the letter-writer's targets – he travelled on the same trains, and he and his home and family were a focal-point of attention because of racism and tensions relating to the role his father played in the community. A tirade of hatred was eventually directed at the Edaljis, but mainly because George was held to have spoken to Fred Brookes: George was threatened with death if he continued to talk to the 'grocer's kid' and Shapurji was hounded for letting his 'bloody blasted dam bloody currst buger bleeding blasting kid talk to the grocer's kid'.[2] It is difficult to see how George could have played any part in this episode himself, even in support of someone else: the language and the handwriting of the letters are very different from his; many of the letters which arrived in the post had been sent from places well away from the route of his daily journey from Great Wyrley to Birmingham; and the invective poured upon him and his family was so savage that is hard to imagine it being simply the product of George's imagination.

If Royden was responsible for these letters then those produced by a seeming religious maniac, the writer who eventually evolved into 'God-Satan', might possibly have been

---

[1] P.R.O., HO 144/989 (statement to Conan Doyle by Fred Wynn sent to Home Office, 2 February 1907).
[2] P.R.O., HO 144/989 Box 2.

written by one of his brothers. The 'foulmouth' and 'God-Satan' letters have overlapping themes and hatreds, and there are also references to collaboration as in the question 'Do you think that when we want we cannot copy your kid's handwriting?' Here again, though, there is no evidence to support Conan Doyle's thesis beyond his analysis of the letters' content. Using this kind of approach a case might just as well have been built against others – a man suspected by Shapurji, James Morgan, had a wild religious streak, an ability to write in different hands, and a competence in Latin and French, both of which were used in the letters.[1]

So far as Anson's suspect was concerned, Upton's reports from this period prove no connection between George and the letters, the incident of the key or the hoaxes. They do however suggest that the minds of the police soon became closed. Upton's report of 19 December 1892, for example, was written shortly after the key to Walsall Grammar School was found on the vicarage step but before the police knew where it actually came from. He nevertheless reported his suspicion that the owner of the key would be found at George's college in Birmingham. It was on the basis of such wayward claims that Anson indirectly accused George in January 1893 and again in 1895. He even sent these reports to the Home Office in 1905 as he sought to undermine the campaign to have George's case re-examined, presumably in the hope that they would somehow add to the general impression that George had been up to no good for years.[2]

And what do you say Maud? To you the idea that George could have been in any way involved was simply ludicrous. How could he even have afforded to pay the cost of postage for all those letters?

****

Anson's pursuit of George in 1903 was equally blinkered. What did the snippets about George's financial situation amount to? George was in financial trouble in 1902, yes, but there is no evidence to prove Anson's claim that it was the result of gambling rather than of standing surety for a friend. The £214 entrusted to George in 1903 could have been removed by anybody – the police searched George's office the day after his arrest, and after they left the housekeeper found the

---

[1] *Cannock Advertiser*, 29 April to 10 June 1893, passim.
[2] P.R.O., HO 144/985, no. 124 (police reports forwarded by Anson to the Home Office, May 1905).

window open and the cash-box empty.[1] And even if there was anything more sinister behind either situation it does nothing to prove that George was guilty of attacking a pony or even of writing anonymous letters.

As for Anson's suggestion in 1903 that the police started to keep an eye on George because he was seen late at night in a field where an animal was killed,[2] this throwaway line had no other evidence to confirm it. When Anson continued to clutch at such straws in 1907 by reporting that suspicion had fallen on George in 1903 because of his 'commonly-talked-of habits of wandering abroad late at night'[3] even the *Police Review* contemptuously dismissed this as prejudice.[4]

Michael Harley believed that George had a hand in all three letter series – the letters of 1892-5, the Greatorex letters of 1903 and the Martin Molton letters of 1907. The Home Office files contain however no conclusive new evidence from other handwriting experts to bear out the claims of the discredited Gurrin. The only way of challenging the testimony of those experts would be to have modern techniques of handwriting analysis applied to the letters, but this has not been done. When it came to Horace Edalji's alleged claim that his brother had a hand in the first series, the Home Office did not even think them worthy of investigation; one official wrote off Anson's reports on this issue as mere gossip. As for the circumstances surrounding the 'Lover of Justice' exchange of 1903 they were so suspicious that they made the seemingly damning internal evidence of the letters equally unconvincing; D. Michael Risinger has even pointed out that the second 'Lover of Justice' could have been written by the author of the first, Anson's accomplice C. A. Loxton.[5]

The Home Office files do overall suggest that Anson could be forgiven for finding Conan Doyle's methods exasperating. He could not however be forgiven for his own confused pursuit of a man against whom he had no meaningful evidence. In one letter to the Home Office, the month after George's trial, he suggested that George had been convicted almost entirely on the basis of letters, thus accepting that the rest of the police and

---

[1] P.R.O., HO 144/984, no. 28 (letter by J. Hawkins to *Staffordshire Advertiser*, 12 December 1903 + Home Office comment).
[2] P.R.O., HO 144/984, no. 44 (Anson to the Home Office, 15 December 1903).
[3] *The Staffordshire Sentinel*, 22 May 1907.
[4] The Police Review and Parade Gossip, 31 May 1907.
[5] D. Michael Risinger, 'Boxes in Boxes: Julian Barnes, Conan Doyle, Sherlock Holmes and the Edalji Case', International Commentary on Evidence, Vol. 4 Issue 2, Article 3, 2006, p. 55.

prosecution case had been utterly threadbare. He even said that strong proof that George wrote them (the evidence provided by the 'Lover of Justice' exchange) could not be given in court, implying that even the evidence which was presented on George's involvement in the letter-writing was inadequate. Despite all this he pursued his desperate mission to protect his own reputation and that of his police force by undermining the efforts of the Edalji family, R. D. Yelverton, *Truth,* Sir Arthur Conan Doyle and the rest of George's supporters to persuade the Home Secretary that the case against George was a farce.

Indeed in 1920 he made an extraordinary admission: in one of the documents in which in later life he tried to come to terms with the personal trauma caused by the Edalji case he commented on the findings of the Committee of Enquiry of 1907, and in this document he actually admitted that George might not have been guilty of the attack on the pony.[1] He agreed with the verdict of the Committee of Enquiry that although the evidence had not been strong enough to convict George of the outrage he had certainly been guilty of writing the letters. This open admission makes his earlier efforts to discredit George all the more shocking.

It is difficult to see what evidence Michael Harley could have used from these files or from other sources to prove that George as a man guilty of criminal acts. Overall the Home Office files confirm that Conan Doyle, for all his failings, was right to campaign for George's innocence.

Explanations

Conan Doyle was however not yet off the hook. Salman Rushdie's 1980s analysis of British racism, and that of many others, had in different ways from Michael Harley challenged the view that Conan Doyle's crusade could be described as noble. What understanding could the author of the Sherlock Holmes stories, with their traditionalist view of South Asia and empire, have had about the part played by racial prejudice in George's case? Was his onslaught on Chief Constable Anson not that of a self-righteous self-publicist rather than a campaigning hero preaching from the moral high ground? Michael Harley dismissed the suggestion that Anson was racially prejudiced. Who was right?

---

[1] George Anson, 'The Report of the Committee of Enquiry', 1920 (copy in S.C.P.M.).

Again, Conan Doyle's pronouncements contained much unsupported assertion. He produced no explicit evidence of Anson's racial prejudices, nor did he show exactly how it was that they affected the Staffordshire police force as a whole, and yet this was the key to his view of George's case as the British Dreyfus affair. Many biographers and other writers, with no evidence other than Conan Doyle's writings on the case, have offered cruder judgements: according to J.D. Carr, 'Captain Anson was one of those people who thought Black Men less than beasts.'[1] Conan Doyle was also blind to the other side of the coin: if he had celebrated the lives and achievements of the Edalji family rather than merely identifying them as victims his attempts to challenge racism may have been more credible. His knowledge of Shapurji's life, in particular, was superficial, and his suggestion that the only source of tension between Shapurji and his parishioners was his willingness to allow the Liberals to use the National schoolroom for an election meeting in 1892 was absurd.

The Home Office files did make it clear, however, that Michael Harley's defence of Anson's views on race could not be sustained. From the very start the Chief Constable, brought up in an aristocratic family with members who had been at the heart of British imperialism, was disparaging about the Edalji family and its background: 'I remember asking at the time [1888],' he told Conan Doyle in 1906, 'how this "Hindu" came to be a clergyman of the Church of England and in charge of an important working-class parish; he could only talk English with a foreign accent.'[2] It was with attitudes such as these that within a year of taking up his post he had entered the fray over the Elizabeth Foster affair, expressing regret over the part that Sergeant Upton played in securing the maid's conviction. This odd comment suggests that he was already hostile to the Edalji family and may be the start of the 'infection' of his force. Certainly Upton was quicker to home in on George in 1892.

During the events of 1892-5 Anson himself never visited Great Wyrley, and yet he had George in his sights almost from the beginning. His letter to Shapurji in January 1893 set the tone for decades:

---

[1] J. D. Carr, *The Life of Sir Arthur Conan Doyle*, John Murray, 1949, p. 220.
[2] P.R.O., HO 144/989 (Anson to Conan Doyle, December 1906).

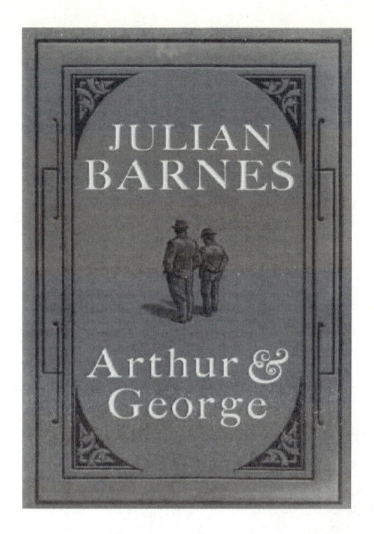

The publication of 'Arthur and George' by Julian Barnes in 2005 gave George Edalji's case a new worldwide fame

Will you please ask your son George from whom the key was obtained which you found on your doorstep on December 12?... I shall not pretend to believe any protestations of innocence which your son may make about the key. My information on the subject does not come from the police.[1]

On the basis of his unnamed source he was able to make accusations from afar. As no action was taken, it is clear that he had no evidence; indeed, one of George's supporters in 1903 was to point out that Anson was so ill-informed that he believed at the time of the key incident that George actually attended Walsall Grammar School.[2] After the three further years of anonymous letters and hoaxes he was still convinced that George was the culprit. In April 1895 he sent his Deputy Chief Constable to tell Shapurji that either he or his son was at the bottom of the letter-writing,[3] and in July he himself wrote to Shapurji to say:

I know the name of the offender... I prefer to keep my suspicions to myself until I am able to prove them, and I trust to be able to obtain a dose of penal servitude for the offender.

Again he clearly did not have the evidence needed to support his preconceived ideas.

Time and again the Home Office and the Staffordshire Police Museum files show the nature of Anson's prejudices. In November 1903, in his first attempts to discredit Yelverton's campaign, he informed the Home Secretary that 'owing to the oriental birth of the convict and of his family' [whatever that meant] it was difficult to get to the bottom of things. George himself he dismissed as 'a worthless scamp'.[4] Four years later he made the perverse claim that the letters of 1892-5 were the work of a boy, George Edalji, possessed with 'a blind fury against his father <u>for being his father & being black</u>' (his underlining).[5] In 1920 he actually blamed George himself for imagining that people were prejudiced towards him: 'It is more

---

[1] Cited by Sir Arthur Conan Doyle, *Daily Telegraph*, 11 January 1907.
[2] P.R.O., HO 144/984, no. 14 (R. D. Yelverton to Home Office, 22 November 1903).
[3] P.R.O., 144/985, no. 124 (Anson to Home Office, 1904).
[4] P.R.O., HO 144/984, no. 5 (Anson to the Home Secretary, 8 November 1903).
[5] P.R.O., HO 144/989 (Anson to Home Office, 7 March 1907).

than probable that Edalji himself felt that all the boys more or less looked down on him because of his Eastern birth.' [1]

Anson was clearly as much affected by the 'stain' as anyone else. Indeed one reason for the wealth and power of his family in Staffordshire and beyond was its history of involvement at the helm of Britain's world-wide imperialism. The profligate Thomas William Anson, who became the first Earl of Lichfield in 1831, saved his family's fortunes in 1819 by marrying Louise Phillips, a West Indian heiress, whose father had made his money out of slavery; although the Earl was a Liberal (he was Postmaster General from 1835-41) and voted against slavery in 1833, Louise supported her father's pro-slavery stance to the end of her life.[2] The Earl's brother, George Anson, was Commander-in-chief of the British army in India at the time of the Indian Uprising of 1857, and a nephew, Augustus Anson, was his aide-de-camp and fought at Lucknow. The Anson family's experiences were woven into the fabric of the British imperial relationship with non-European peoples which helped to create 'the stain' condemned by Salman Rushdie.

It was a big jump, though, to blame Anson's prejudices for all that went wrong in George's case. In terms of modern understandings of racism, Conan Doyle's onslaught on Anson was simplistic; Anson, according to him, was just the bad apple in the Staffordshire police barrel and it was he alone who infected the police apples around him with his racial prejudices. Today we would say that the main problem was the barrel, not the apples. The barrel was rotten, indeed it was held together with hoops made out of negative images of the peoples of South Asia passed on in Sherlock Holmes stories and the like. Today the focus is on institutional racism as much as on the attitudes of particular individuals within institutions. This kind of thinking looked as if it would become mainstream in 1999 when the report of the inquiry into the death of the black teenager Stephen Lawrence blamed institutional racism in the Metropolitan Police for its mishandling of the case. The Prime Minister, Tony Blair, not only endorsed this view but also warned that all our other institutions must fight this disease within themselves too. If this framework is applied to the experiences of George Edalji and his family the conclusion must be that the police, the courts, the Home Office, the Committee of Enquiry and the media were all structurally predisposed to discriminate against the black and minority

---

[1] George Anson, notes on Sir Arthur Conan Doyle's statement on Royden Sharp. .
[2] Clare Taylor, 'The Perils of a West Indian Heiress: Case Studies of the Heiresses of Nathaniel Phillips of Slebech in Pembrokeshire', draft article (copy in W.S.L.), pp. 14-18.

ethnic peoples of the empire and the rest of the world. Anson's attitudes were just typical of those of many. Conan Doyle's condemnation of Anson for infecting his police force with his racial prejudices ignores the fact that the attitudes of both Anson and his police officers were shaped by the same forces.

Poor old Arthur. Michael Harley and Salman Rushdie had between them taken the shine from his crusade. And yet... and yet... this new view was itself one-sided. After work in multicultural education and years of close involvement with the Racial Equality Council in Stafford, the more I saw of the inadequate and inconsistent efforts of white liberals like myself who wanted so dearly to prove our antiracist credentials the more I came to see that there was something in Conan Doyle's campaign which really was noble. Yes, his investigations were flawed. Yes, he might have been at times headstrong and at times naïve. Yes, his ideas on racial prejudice might be seen as self-complacent and narrowly focused in terms of Salman Rushdie's analysis. But at least he did speak out, and he did so with all the passion he could muster. Of how many of his white contemporaries could the same be said? When he started his very public campaign he could not know how much hostility he might arouse through his attack on the prejudices which had been so widespread and so little challenged for so long. How much credibility would the Sherlock Holmes stories have had if Conan Doyle's real-life detective work had been exposed as that of an incompetent amateur? He began with a risky high-profile stand against the might of the establishment and ended by doing more than anyone to fix the Edalji affair in the public mind as the shameful British Dreyfus case.

By the later 1990s, admiration for Conan Doyle was beginning to course through my veins again. Now a sentence in his *Daily Telegraph* articles struck a new chord: 'Until each and all of these questions is settled,' he had written, 'a dark stain will remain upon the administrative annals of this country.'[1] The British Dreyfus case, it seemed, stood in a line of jolts to white majority assumptions which led eventually to the understandings embodied in such later milestones as the Stephen Lawrence Inquiry report. Conan Doyle's campaign deserves a place in the annals of the struggle to make the white majority acknowledge the 'stain upon you all', and to do what is needed to wipe it out.

---

[1] *Daily Telegraph*, 12 January 1907.

Impacts

There was more. Among the torrent of letters about George's case sent to the *Daily Telegraph* in 1907 was one from a Chowry Muthu. This letter reported that 'All India is watching... and for the name and honour of England justice must be done to Mr. Edalji.'[1] With India watching,[2] Conan Doyle may in a small way have strengthened the hand of those who were becoming increasingly critical of British rule, and of the attitudes it had generated in the rulers. This point has been suggested by Shompa Lahiri with respect to Jawaharlal Nehru, forty years later India's first Prime Minister after independence.[3] Nehru was a pupil at Harrow in 1907, learning how to be British, but shortly after Conan Doyle's *Daily Telegraph* articles appeared he commented on the case in a letter to his father back home:

> *I suppose you have heard about the Edalji case and the new phase it has taken here... The poor chap must have been quite innocent and I am sure he was convicted solely because he was an Indian.*[4]

Shompa Lahiri's article setting out the racial implications of the 'British Dreyfus case' suggests that it was the first of several examples of racial discrimination which eventually caused Nehru to become more conscious of his nationality.

So far as British relations with India were concerned, the Great War was a watershed. The trio born in Bombay in the mid-19th century, Shapurji Edalji, Dadabhai Naoroji, and Rudyard Kipling, reached an unlikely consensus on what to do when the British empire went to war in 1914 – they all supported it. Among the cast waiting in the wings for the next act was another threesome, all lawyers trained in Britain: George Edalji, Mohandas Gandhi and Jawaharlal Nehru. In London, it is true, George Edalji swallowed back the pain of his earlier treatment and never challenged the British imperial establishment openly again. His quiet professional life after 1907 did, however, succeed his father's in helping in its own small way to create a wider acceptance that British Asians and Anglo-Asians were not subject peoples but equal citizens in a

---

[1] *Daily Telegraph*, 17 January 1907.
[2] e.g. *Bombay Guardian*, 19 January 1907.
[3] Shompa Lahiri, 'Uncovering Britain's South Asian Past: The Case of George Edalji', *Immigrants and Minorities*, Issue 17.3, November 1998, Frank Cass.
[4] 18 January 1907, in S. Gopal (ed.), *Selected Works of Jawaharlal Nehru*, New Delhi, 1972, p. 16.

multiethnic society. Also briefly back in London in 1914 after his time in South Africa, Mohandas Gandhi, who had in 1888 travelled from Bombay to London to train as a barrister, still saw himself as a loyal British subject. He nevertheless believed a campaign of civil disobedience to be the way forward for the Indian National Congress once the war was over, and soon sailed for Bombay to get his teeth into the new era ahead. Meanwhile in Allahabad, Jawaharlal Nehru, who had in 1907 blamed British racial prejudice for George Edalji's imprisonment, was in 1914 practising as a lawyer after returning from his studies at Harrow, Cambridge and the Inner Temple in London. He took Britain's side in the war too, but was a longstanding nationalist and after meeting Gandhi at the Indian National Congress in Lucknow in 1916 eventually committed himself to the civil disobedience campaign. By 1922 the British had flung both Gandhi and Nehru in gaol, just as they had once imprisoned George Edalji

After World War II the British empire and the Edalji family which it had created passed away in tandem. In 1946, Sir Herbert Hunter, chief hunter of G. H. Darby in the 1920s and 1930s, and Anson's successor as Chief Constable of Staffordshire, went on a mission to the Far East.[1] Whilst in Bombay he went on a drive which had to be escorted because of the threat of missile attack. The mood in the city, as independence approached, was far different from the days of passive acceptance of British control during the 1857 Indian Uprising in Shapurji Edalji's youth; no city had become more committed to the independence struggle than Bombay, the city in which Dadabhai Naoroji and the Indian National Congress had held their first meeting in 1885. It was in 1947, the year Jawaharlal Nehru became first Prime Minister of an independent India, that Salman Rushdie was born in Bombay, though into the Muslim rather than the Parsi elite. Rushdie's analysis of British imperialism is diametrically opposed to that of Rudyard Kipling, born in the same city eighty-two years earlier, in the year before Shapurji sailed to the imperial headquarters. Rushdie's glorious *Midnight's Children*, about the children born two months after he was, 'on the midnight hour' of Indian self-government, describes an India which Shapurji could hardly have foreseen and which, one suspects, Charlotte would have found it difficult to contemplate. In terms of Rushdie's view of the origins and growth of British racism, Conan Doyle and his writings can certainly be seen as part of the problem, and Conan Doyle himself would have shuddered

---

[1] Sir Herbert Hunter, 'My Real Life Adventure', unpublished manuscript (copy in S.C.P.M.).

at Rushdie's TV broadcast of 1983. Conan Doyle's campaign can nevertheless be said to have helped in a small way to create a climate in which analyses such as Salman Rushdie's can have an impact on white British opinion.

2. Shadows

Novel

2005. Easter. In our older daughter's Hamburg flat. She has married a German too. An idle internet trawl. We live in a new world – Edalji information can be accessed from anywhere. I hope for some new detail, though it's unlikely. The vast majority of the couple of hundred articles on George's case now on the net repeat old information derived from Conan Doyle. Many are inaccurate. Some are utterly garbled.

Then the shock. What is this? Julian Barnes? The Julian Barnes who is one of Britain's very finest contemporary writers? That Julian Barnes has written a novel about George's case? *Arthur and George*. On sale in June.

How dare this interloper march in and whisk the Edaljis away? Just because he can write a bit? And how can he know anything about them when there has been no sign of him in the silent archives of Staffordshire or the Public Record Office at Kew? This man is exactly the same age as me, attended the same university... and is now in control of my substitute family!

There is more. The same internet browse reveals another researcher on the trail. In the downloadable *Conan Doyle and the Parson's Son* Gordon Weaver reports in detail on the evidence in the Home Office files and in other sources which no one else has as yet fully made public. George Edalji is back in fashion.

June. *Arthur and George* is out. It certainly looks special. The olive green linen cover with its Edwardian period design looks right to the eye and feels good in the hand. And there they are on the front, George and Sir Arthur, backs turned, engrossed in gentle conversation.

July 26. To London by coach, reading the book. All the way from Victoria coach station to Putney on foot. Thousands of commuters fill the streets as they bustle homewards, some walking with bags and briefcases, some jogging with rucksacks on their backs, some cycling grimly through fuming traffic. It is 19 days since British Muslim citizens bombed three tube trains and a bus, killing fifty-two people. The underground is still half-empty. Britain broods in tortured agony over cosy ideas about the celebration of multicultural diversity.

At Ottaker's bookshop in Putney. Julian Barnes the speaker. It is packed out. His account of the making of his latest novel is remarkable. He only heard of what he too describes as the 'British Dreyfus case' two years ago. Yet after that he acquired not just a grasp of the details of George's case and some of the Edalji family background; he also achieved such mastery over Sir Arthur Conan Doyle's life-story that he can deliver insights of which Conan Doyle's greatest biographers would be proud.[1] He has written his novel within that two-year period too... and been nominated for the 2005 Man Booker Prize on the strength of it.

July 28. Finish *Arthur and George* on the coach home. It's good.

Fact and fiction

The first half of the novel is structured around alternating glimpses, sometimes little more than a few paragraphs long, into the separate lives of Arthur and George, from childhood until the arrival of George's letter on Arthur's desk in December 1906. At some point before that the reader will realise that 'Arthur' is Conan Doyle, but what the connection is with the timid, unknown George is not revealed explicitly until well past halfway. After that the structure becomes more elaborate, with George and Arthur sometimes dealt with separately and sometimes together as their lives become entangled over George's case. Again the last event covered is Conan Doyle's second wedding in 1907, or at least the last event covered in a more or less factual way – there is a dramatic postscript when George is shown attending the séance held by spiritualists after Conan Doyle's death to try and get in touch with the great man.

As one reviewer rightly said, *Arthur and George* is a masterly blend of fact and fiction. Knowing what was coming, though, it was impossible for me to read it as intended. From the start I was itchily pencilling in question-marks, crosses and underlinings about seeming factual inaccuracies, omissions and unsupportable interpretations. A question nevertheless

---

[1] Though some aspects of his portrayal of Conan Doyle have been questioned by D. Michael Risinger in 'Boxes in Boxes: Julian Barnes, Conan Doyle, Sherlock Holmes and the Edalji Case'.

always hovered over the scribbles. Does anyone have the right to challenge the content of a work of fiction for its lack of historical accuracy or for the particular perspective it offers on real-life events, even if it is historical fiction or, as Julian Barnes calls it, 'a contemporary novel set in the past'?

I can imagine that it would be quite obvious to you, Maud. I can see your spirit there in your Welwyn Garden City house right now, penning letters to the author and his publishers:

Dear Mr Barnes

I read your novel Arthur and George with great interest. It is a fine book and I am pleased that you have agreed with Sir Arthur on my brother's complete innocence. Some terrible things have been said about him since my death, and they are all entirely untrue. He never gambled, and he would never use his clients' funds for his own purposes. He was a man who was totally honest, and if his generosity towards a friend in need once caused him some personal financial difficulties, I count that as a virtue.

However, there are some points in your story which I must correct. I know that this book is a work of the imagination but I do not think it right that you should say that my mother was Scottish. She was very proud of our English ancestors and often spoke of the part they played in the Crusades. We have definite proof that one of our ancestors was related to Catherine Howard, the wife of Henry VIII. It is therefore wrong to suggest that we children were half-Scottish, and that our mother had a Scottish accent. As a result of what you have written some reviewers are now saying that my mother was Scottish and other incorrect things.[1] It was our father who many say had a very slight Scottish intonation, but this came from his time with the Scottish missionaries at Mr Wilson's College in Bombay.

The living of Great Wyrley was in the gift of the Vicar of Cannock, not of my uncle the Reverend John Compson, who was my father's predecessor. It was when he fell ill that my uncle strongly recommended to the Vicar of Cannock that my father should succeed him.

---

[1] e.g. P. D. James, *The Times*, 9 July 2005.

You need to check your references to my Aunt Mary Sancta, who was my mother's sister. You speak of her in different places as 'Great-Aunt Stoneham' (page 92) and 'Uncle Stoneham' (page 154).

It is not true that I left Great Wyrley to live with George in London after he received his pardon in 1907. I stayed with my parents in Great Wyrley and spent a lot of time looking after my father towards the end of his life. He eventually turned quite blind and I had to take him from the vicarage to the church for services. When it was time for him to preach I would lead him up to the pulpit. He was a very good preacher and did not need notes.

When he died in 1918 my mother and I had, of course, to leave the vicarage. We went to live in Coalbrookdale. She died in 1924, but was not buried in Shrewsbury, as you say. It was always important for her that she should be buried in the Stoneham family grave at St Mary's in Ketley, which can still be seen to this day. It was from 1930 that George and I shared a house together, and this was in Welwyn Garden City, which is a new town outside London.

There are many parts which you have made up to try to help your readers to understand my family and the life in Great Wyrley better. You say that George went to school in Great Wyrley with the other village children, but we were all educated at home by our parents until we went to Grammar School. The character of Harry Charlesworth, who you say went to school in Great Wyrley with George, is invented, but I suppose you know what is best for your story.

I shall write to your publishers, Jonathan Cape, to ask them to insert an 'addenda and corrigenda' in the next edition, making it clear which points are either inaccurate or made up.

Yours sincerely,

Maud E. Edalji

What is the writer to do about such sensibilities? In the novel there are certainly departures from historical reality which were probably unintended and which can be counted as inaccuracies. So far as the Edalji family is concerned the claim that Charlotte was Scottish is just one example – having been brought up in Edinburgh, Conan Doyle, it is suggested, was galvanised when appealed to by 'a gentle, elderly, female Scottish voice'.[1] Another inaccuracy is put into Chief Constable Anson's mouth when he says that it was Rev. Compson, Shapurji's predecessor as Vicar of Great Wyrley, who passed on the living to his niece's husband; in fact the living was in the gift of the Vicar of Cannock.[2] Sergeant Upton, the police officer on the spot in Great Wyrley during the troubles of 1892-5 is shown as being involved in the 1903 operation, though he had in fact retired by that point.

These inaccuracies do not have great significance for the main issues, but there are some details which do. Some of the geographical references, for example, make the roles of key figures difficult to comprehend. Wallie and Royden Sharp are shown as attending elementary school in Great Wyrley, three miles from their home in Hednesford, a completely different community on the other side of Cannock. This is of some importance for the main story: as Conan Doyle suspected the Sharp brothers of being the authors of the letters in the 1892-5 series, the many knowledgeable references to people in Great Wyrley in those letters need explanation, as does the fact that many of them were not posted but simply left at the vicarage. When Royden Sharp came back to the area in 1902 after his time at sea, on the other hand, he went to live with his mother on the boundary between Cannock and Hednesford, a little more handily placed than their old home for night-time excursions to Great Wyrley for the purpose of slitting open the bellies of horses, cows and sheep – significant if Conan Doyle's accusations are to be believed. So far as the 1903 letters are concerned, the Sharps' Hednesford connection favours Conan Doyle's theory – William Greatorex of Hednesford, supposedly the author of many of these letters, was well known to the Sharps as his father had been the brothers' guardian, and an unpopular one at that. The 1903 letters also show a knowledge of people in the Cannock and Hednesford areas which George Edalji could not have had. For all these reasons it is a little distracting for the story to have Conan Doyle and Major Wood travelling to Hednesford to meet Fred Brookes (who was a native of Great Wyrley) and thence to Great Wyrley to meet the Sharps and Mrs Greatorex (who still lived in Hednesford). In his searching assessment of the degree to which the novel stays close to the historical record D. Michael Risinger has produced a number of other examples of significant distortions.[3]

---

[1] Julian Barnes, *Arthur and George*, Jonathan Cape, 2005, p. 227.
[2] Ibid., p. 266.
[3] D. Michael Risinger, 'Boxes in Boxes: Julian Barnes, Conan Doyle, Sherlock Holmes and the Edalji Case', p. 31.

There is surely a duty or need to minimise the kinds of mistaken departures from historical truth which might mislead or confuse, but what about the sin of omission rather than commission? This is a particular issue in the presentation of some of the characters in the book. The Shapurji of *Arthur and George*, for example, is based largely on the Shapurji of Conan Doyle's writings. He emerges in the novel as a pious, serious-minded Christian, but there is little on his extraordinary career, from boyhood conversion to the lonely life as a missionary among the Warali people, to the tenacious efforts to establish a foothold in the Church in England, and to his appointment as perhaps England's first vicar of South Asian origin. The aspects of his personality which made all this possible – particularly his single-mindedness and even cussedness – do not fully emerge either. This is of some significance, as the more challenging aspects of Shapurji's personality might have contributed to the tensions in Great Wyrley which were the background to the troubles of 1888, 1892-5 and beyond.

As for the Edalji children there are certainly inspired moments in the novel which go beyond existing evidence to suggest ways in which the three may have, thought, felt and interacted. There is a lovely scene encapsulating their possible relationship in which teenage George tries out his cases in railway law on a giggling Horace and an earnest Maud. One key dimension in terms of real life is however omitted, and that is Horace's progress from brooding teenager to family outcast. His attempts to act as informer to the police on George in 1903 are not mentioned, though they are important both in assessing the authorship of the anonymous letters and in explaining Horace's increasing isolation from both parents and siblings.

In the same way the novel is full of insights into the way in which George's mind may have worked. The adult George is shown, for example, as man whose world-picture is shaped by the preoccupations of a lawyer – even the countryside through which he travels on the train is perceived as nothing but a patchwork of potential boundary disputes. There is no attempt however to deal with his thoughts and feelings about the aspects of his career which some have wanted to question, particularly the financial difficulties which threatened to overwhelm him in 1902-3.

Even if the author of a novel of this type is however familiar with every scrap of relevant evidence and uses it accurately it must be admitted that it is almost impossible for a work of fiction to be created within the framework of real-life events without upsetting anybody. There may not actually be any Edaljis around to take issue with the way their ancestors are shown in this novel, but there are others who can. Steuart Campbell, for example, let Julian Barnes know that he was not happy with the way in which his grandfather, John Campbell, the inspector who investigated and arrested George Edalji, is portrayed.[1] The author's response was that in writing the novel he had had a choice of whether to use real names, 'in which case grandchildren were likely to correct me', or invent new ones, 'in which case historians and biographers would do the same'. In Campbell's case, as with many others in the novel, he used the name of a real-life person but invented the actual character of the person. Steuart Campbell is concerned that readers may mistake the Inspector Campbell of the novel for the person his grandfather really was, for there are major differences between the two. So far as the writer is concerned there is no solution to this dilemma.

Does the invention of completely imaginary characters avoid the problem? The life of the invented character Harry Charlesworth holds a number of threads in the novel together. First he appears as George's school-mate at an elementary school which the real-life George, who was educated at home until he went to grammar school, did not attend; this strategy provides insights into the possible values and preoccupations of children and their parents in the Great Wyrley community. Later George invents a sister of the invented Harry Charlesworth to ward off probings about his love life by two Birmingham solicitor friends also invented by the author; this suggests some of George's possible preoccupations as a young man. And then Harry reappears as Conan Doyle's local sleuth, at George's suggestion; here he takes on the combined real-life roles of the two men whom Michael Harley dubbed 'Conan Doyle's Baker Street irregulars', Arrowsmith and Beaumont.

The effect of the creation of this generally sympathetic character is to support Conan Doyle's view of the case. Harry Charlesworth is intelligent (top of the class at school until George gets near enough to the blackboard to be able to read it) and appears trustworthy. Conan Doyle's real-life detectives were a little more problematical – Anson was pleased to be able to point out that Beaumont was later committed to a 'lunatic asylum'. Fiction has twisted the plot in Conan Doyle's favour – and yet the novelist has every right to present one view rather than the whole truth.

---

[1] Personal communication, 22 April 2006.

How has the local community reacted to the novel's portrayal of its past? Many, including former members of my High School history classes in the 1970s and 1980s, have thrilled at the retelling of the familiar story of sensational events full of blood and gore which occurred in well-known locations one hundred years or so ago. Others, on the other hand, have blanched at yet another worldwide media blitz on Great Wyrley's most notorious moment. Rev. Paul Oakley, Vicar of Great Wyrley, spoke for them in an ITV *Heart of the Country* programme, itself inspired by the media coverage of Julian Barnes's book, when he commented: 'I'd like to be the centre of attention for something more wholesome.'[1]

But what would Michael Harley say? There is no doubt that the Michael Harley who first called into Great Wyrley High School in 1983 would have been deeply frustrated at the blessing Julian Barnes gives to Conan Doyle's conviction that George was a dewy-eyed innocent. As D. Michael Risinger has pointed out, *Arthur and George* is a kind of morality play, with George's innocence assumed throughout: this makes any real evaluation of the evidence against George redundant.[2] The novel does touch briefly on some of the issues which Michael Harley was pursuing so vigorously in the 1980s: in an imaginary evening conversation at Anson's Stafford home Anson tells Conan Doyle that there were matters which did not come to court in 1903 – rumours of gambling debts and misuse of clients' funds. This reference is based, however, on just one letter which George wrote to Sir J. B. Stone, M. P. for Birmingham, in 1902; Julian Barnes did not trawl through all those Home Office sources in the Public Record Office which made Michael Harley much more suspicious about the story which George told Sir Arthur. In Michael Harley's hands Conan Doyle would have been more gullible, Anson more professional, and George more manipulative than Julian Barnes makes them. George would have been presented as a man whose financial dealings in 1902-3 were dubious, who was probably guilty of some criminal acts, and who really was the author of the letters ascribed by Conan Doyle to Royden Sharp. As to the mutilated pony, Michael Harley would at least have left the question of George's guilt open. Rightly or wrongly, his novel would have been full of question-marks rather than full stops.

The issues at stake here relate to both research and interpretation. It would be impossible to read all the sources on

---

[1] *Heart of the Country*, ITV Midlands, 10 November 2005.
[2] D. Michael Risinger, 'Boxes in Boxes: Julian Barnes, Conan Doyle, Sherlock Holmes and the Edalji Case', pp. 29-49.

this case in less than two years, but does the writer of historical fiction have to know all the sources anyway? And if Julian Barnes wants to take a particular line on the question of George's innocence does he have to make it clear that not everybody agrees? Any historian writing about this case needs to respond to Michael Harley's evidence, but does the novelist? Historians can only hope that readers do not rely on a novel for authoritative evidence on what actually happened.

1 August. Back to old Great Wyrley haunts. Instead of thirty sets of students' eyes a BBC camera was trained on the window of the famous vicarage bedroom. Interviews in the vicarage grounds followed. After that, former Police Sergeant Alan Walker, another aficionado of George Edalji's case, and I conversed as we walked towards the camera along a path by the railway; the path was close to the route George would have taken if he really was out slashing a pony open on that night in 1903.

Then the road-show moved off to a field near the site of the former Plant colliery, the closest we could get to the scene of the crime. Members of the BBC team were delighted to spot a horse in an enclosure in the field, but would a prestigious television company want its employees wandering about on private land without permission? The decision took about thirty seconds, and soon we were scrambling between rows of barbed wire like boys on a scrumping expedition – a producer, a cameraman, a camera assistant, a sound recordist, a researcher, a former police sergeant with an MBE, and a former head of the local high school's history department. As Alan Walker and I, deep in conversation about the murderous night which made Great Wyrley world-famous, walked through the field towards the camera the horse kept wandering out of shot.

A raid on the BBC van produced the team's ration of five apples, and as the dialogue was repeated time and time again the producer had the task of feeding the horse the apples one by one to try and keep it interested in standing in the right spot. The horse-slasher of 1903 was clearly more adept than we were at keeping animals still.

BBC team filming the window of the famous bedroom, 2005

My shirt already had an oily smudge, perhaps from the bike; the climb back over the barbed wire produced a tear in my trousers; and someone sat on my jacket all the way back to Stafford, turning it into a crumpled mess.

2 August. When I turned up in new clothes for filming at the Stafford Shire Hall, scene of George's trial, the cry went up 'Oh, no! Continuity!', and I was whipped back home to get the previous day's clothes. They remained on in all their grubby glory until the final shots – examining evidence of Royden Sharp's miserable school record at Walsall Grammar School.

October. By this time on the Booker shortlist, *Arthur and George* was everywhere. In dozens of reviews. On the web. In the broadcast media. Featured in the ITV Midlands programme *Heart of the Country*, with more filming in Great Wyrley to back it up. The Man Booker award date got closer. *Arthur and George* was the bookies' favourite. It was chosen as 'Book of the Week' for serialisation on Radio 4. The night of the award arrived. In the build-up two of the three pundits thought it the most likely to win. I was rooting for it. Then the final announcement: John Banfield's *The Sea*. John Banfield looked as surprised as everyone else.

December 25. On Boxing Day ninety-nine years earlier Professor John Churton Collins had found his friend Sir Arthur Conan Doyle 'on fire' with the Edalji case. And it was on Christmas Day 2005 that the BBC first showed *Conan Doyle for the Defence*, to be repeated twice over the next few weeks as part of a bean-feast of programmes about Conan Doyle.[1] The Edalji family was alive and kicking in the 21st century – but still in the shadow of Sherlock Holmes. George was still the focus, and all because of Arthur and now Julian. There are now thousands and thousands of sites on the web which refer to members of the Edalji family, and all but a tiny handful are just about George's case. The *Daily Telegraph* articles of 1907 still make the Edalji family what they are today.

A history

By 2006 Gordon Weaver had published his *Conan Doyle and the Parson's Son* in book form, the only full-length account

---

[1] *Conan Doyle for the Defence*, BBC4, 25 December 2005.

of the range of extant evidence on George's case, based on painstaking research.[1] Weaver's book confirms the verdicts offered by Conan Doyle and Barnes, but goes much further. Conan Doyle at least launched his campaign with some pretence of civility towards Anson: 'Personally I have met with nothing but frankness and courtesy from Captain the Hon. G. A. Anson during the course of my investigation...'[2] Weaver, on the other hand, is merciless. His book is framed by the kind of analysis of British racism offered by Salman Rushdie in his 1983 broadcast, and Anson is condemned throughout not just for racial prejudice but for utter bigotry.

In Weaver's view, moreover, Anson was the ringleader in an unremitting conspiracy in which investigations and proceedings against George were deliberately manipulated and twisted at every turn. In discussing the question of the 'Lover of Justice' letter and the follow-up to it, for example, he claims that a likely explanation for the similarities was that there was a 'set-up'; Anson had both letters sent by Loxton to George Edalji in order to claim that George was the only person who could be responsible for the second letter.[3] Weaver also points to many ways in which Anson might have manipulated court proceedings: he 'almost certainly' pushed the prosecuting counsel at the later police court hearings to connect the maimings with the anonymous letters in order to satisfy his determination to get the 'dose of penal servitude' which he had promised in 1895;[4] he was 'the prime mover' behind the decision to have George's case heard at Stafford Quarter Sessions rather than a higher court;[5] and it was 'highly likely' that he brought his suspicions about George having written anonymous letters in the 1892-5 period to the attention of key prosecution witness Thomas Gurrin.[6] Anson's later claim to the Home Secretary that Horace Edalji had told Christopher Hatton that he suspected George of writing anonymous letters might, Weaver argues, have been an 'Anson conspiracy' to prevent any consideration being given to releasing George.[7]

There are dangers in seeing deception or conspiracy at every turn. Anson himself spent years pouring out negative information about George in the hope that mud would stick, and we must be careful not to do the same. One may wonder

---

[1] Gordon Weaver, *Conan Doyle and the Parson's Son*, Vanguard Press, 2006.
[2] *Daily Telegraph*, 11 January 1907.
[3] Gordon Weaver, *Conan Doyle and the Parson's Son*, pp. 92-3.
[4] Gordon Weaver, *Conan Doyle and the Parson's Son*, p. 115.
[5] Ibid., p. 123.
[6] Ibid., p. 121.
[7] Ibid., p. 326.

whether the Anson who emerges from most accounts other than Michael Harley's had the competence to go beyond haphazard mudslinging to organise any systematic conspiracies. Weaver's dismissal of the case against George is based on by far the most comprehensive and authoritative review of the evidence ever produced. He may be right on the extent of Anson's role, but his is an interpretation of the sometimes patchy remaining evidence, not an open and shut case.

Weaver is also severe in his judgements on the work of Michael Harley. Harley's overall conclusions may be questioned, but his work is nevertheless important. He was the first to show that any full account of Conan Doyle's investigations must acknowledge that they were sometimes blinkered and sometimes sloppy. Not only that, Michael Harley discovered new evidence of great value to other investigators: he produced new insights from interviews with police and members of the last generation of Great Wyrley residents who had memories of the Edalji family; his information about Horace Edalji's later life is important in considering the role Horace played in George's case, as well as in providing a satisfyingly rounded history of the Edalji family as a whole; and he provided a background sketch of Anson's career and personality which may have been too sympathetic but which certainly provided information useful for any account of the Chief Constable's role in the affair.[1] Others who have written on Conan Doyle since, including major biographers such as Martin Booth[2] and Daniel Stashower,[3] have not acknowledged that their question-marks about Conan Doyle's role in the case were shaped by Harley's research.

Conclusion?

The differences between the methods of Gordon Weaver the historian and Julian Barnes the novelist are encapsulated in two differing treatments of one particular aspect of the story, the relationship between Conan Doyle and Chief Constable Anson from first contact to final breakdown. In *Conan Doyle and the Parson's Son* Gordon Weaver explains the deterioration via many pieces of relevant factual information

---

[1] Michael Harley, 'An infamous Anson?'
[2] Martin Booth, *The Doctor, The Detective and Arthur Conan Doyle: A Biography of Arthur Conan Doyle*, p. 266.
[3] Daniel Stashower, *Teller of tales: the life of Arthur Conan Doyle*, Henry Holt and Company, 1999, pp. 259-60.

incorporated into his comprehensive narrative of overall events over a period of years. In *Arthur and George* Julian Barnes uses one imaginary event – Conan Doyle's overnight stay at Green Hall, Anson's Stafford home on 3/4 January 1907 – to do much the same thing. Conan Doyle did visit Anson on 3 January after his visit to Great Wyrley but there is no publicly available evidence that he accepted Anson's invitation to stop overnight. Julian Barnes nevertheless constructs a conversation between the two men in which Anson's barbs and Conan Doyle's growing indignation at Anson's stance leave the men in prickly stalemate after just a few hours, seething hostility just around the corner. The reasons for their increasingly bitter relationship over a period of months and years are telescoped into one night. It is my favourite moment in the novel, a fascinating blend of fact and fiction, and every time I walk past Green Hall in my home town I think of it. The convincing period language and the glimpses into the two men's world-pictures provide vivid insights into their possible thought-processes which no narrative history book could achieve.

And on what were these two accounts based? Gordon Weaver spent four years in England's silent archives, sifting through every document he could find. Julian Barnes, after reading the main sources, visited Green Hall under the guidance of ex-Staffordshire Police Sergeant Alan Walker. They had a look round and then Julian Barnes asked to be left alone. In another kind of silence he sat imagining himself into the Green Hall of January 1907. The scene in the novel was created from a leap of imagination from present into a possible past.

Julian Barnes has revived awareness of the British Dreyfus case in what is no doubt by far the greatest book which will ever be written about it. Historians should be grateful – but they must write the history. As Gordon Weaver has now provided a comprehensive review of the evidence it may appear that there is not much more to be said. The story is still however unfinished. In 2004 the Conan Doyle archive, until then largely inaccessible for the ordinary researcher, was put up for auction at Christie's. Many parts of the archive went under the hammer and there is now a mass of new material for more Conan Doyle biographers to get their teeth into.

**Green Hall in Stafford,
once the home of Chief Constable Anson**

**Vicar of Great Wyrley receiving portraits bequeathed
by Maud Edalji, 1962**

New additions to the Conan Doyle canon are already on the market. In one, the well-reviewed *Conan Doyle: The Man Who Created Sherlock Holmes*, Andrew Lycett only repeats Conan Doyle's account of the Edalji case. He does however add one intriguing detail never previously mentioned, except in Julian Barnes's novel, the suggestion that George Edalji attended the memorial meeting for Conan Doyle held by spiritualists in 1930.[1] I had imagined that this was one of the fictional ingredients of *Arthur and* George, but if George really did strain with the rest of the audience to hear Conan Doyle speak from across the grave that day it is poignant testimony to the fact that, apart from his own family, Conan Doyle had been the most important person in his life.

Sadly, however, Christie's estimated reserve price of £30,000 for Lot 35, the Edalji collection itself, was not reached at the auction and so it was not sold. There are admittedly, passing references to the Edalji case in some of the correspondence published in *Arthur Conan Doyle: A Life in Letters* which includes many previously unpublished letters from the lots which were sold.[2] Edalji researchers must however wait to see if the Edalji collection has anything new and more substantial on the case; with two notebooks, ten photographs and four hundred and twenty-five letters in the collection, including correspondence with F. Arrowsmith and R. Beaumont, the local sleuths who helped Conan Doyle to build his case against Royden Sharp, there may still be new light to shed on the case.[3]

There will certainly be many more tellings of George's tale[4] ... but with Conan Doyle still the hero who will tell the tale of George's family?

---

[1] Andrew Lycett, *Conan Doyle: The Man Who Created Sherlock Holmes*, Weidenfeld & Nicholson, 2007.
[2] Daniel Stashower, Jon Lellenberg and Charles Foley, *Arthur Conan Doyle: A Life in Letters*, Harper Press, 2007.
[3] *The Conan Doyle Collection, 19 May 2004, Christie's* (catalogue), pp 77-79.
[4] Russell Miller, for his *The Adventures of Arthur Conan Doyle*, Harvill Secker, 2008, had access to much of the new material and has a more rounded account of the Edalji case than that provided by previous biographers.

3. Stories

Ripostes

Maud loved that 18th century face, that ancestral face; eyes, hair, complexion, 'so English' as her friend Connie used to say on her visits.[1] Mother had been so proud of the first Thompson Stoneham, too. She even told the Home Secretary so, whilst George was in prison: 'I have a portrait of my <u>great-great-great-great</u> grandfather, who was a judge', she wrote in her innocent, charming style.[2] Now the portrait hung on Maud's wall.

The little house in Welwyn Garden City had been her home for nearly thirty years, almost as long as she had lived in Great Wyrley. George had once lived in the house too of course, but now he had passed on. With Horace gone too, Maud was alone, the last Edalji in England.

She had her pictures to look at, though, as she drank tea poured from that china teapot. They covered the wall of the tiny drawing-room,[3] tugging her daily into her past: the coat-of-arms and portraits of her Stoneham ancestors; mother's treasured portrait of her uncle, the Reverend John Compson; the photograph of father, as a young fresh-faced priest nearly ninety years ago; the family photograph from Easter 1892, just before the troubles began – mother, father, George, Horace, herself, all staring uncertainly at the camera; the photograph of George, a young man of promise. She would go through them proudly with her visitors, explaining who each person on the wall was. And she had the Stoneham family records. And the chest of cuttings on George's case.

There was also a surprise addition to the archive in these years. One day in 1955 she received a startling letter from a London County Council employee. This man had been doing excavation work on the Crystal Palace site, and there he had unearthed something dear to Maud's heart – George's bronze medal, won from the Birmingham Law Society in 1898.[4] It

---

[1] W.L.H.C., 246/38 (unnamed former pupil, 'Queen Mary's High School, Miss Barbara Foxley, and The Edalji Case', undated).
[2] P.R.O., HO 144/984, no. 48 (Charlotte Edalji to Home Secretary, January 1904).
[3] W.L.H.C., 246/38 ('Queen Mary's High School, Miss Barbara Foxley, and The Edalji Case').
[4] Maud Edalji to Hesketh Pearson, 28 August 1956, Hesketh Pearson Papers, The University of Texas at Austin.

transpired that at some point the rubble at the site of George's bombed-out office in Southwark had been removed, and in this way the medal had found its way to Crystal Palace. It was black from the 1940 fire, but the words were still legible and Maud added it proudly to her collection.

As the last Edalji, Maud carried the torch for her brother. In 1956 she started yet again on the campaign to have his case reopened, with a series of letters to the Home Office.[1] Later that year she heard on the radio the voice of an author whose work she had read. It was Hesketh Pearson, one of Conan Doyle's early biographers, to whom she had long intended to write. Out came her pen again.[2] Clearly she had been hurt by Pearson's book: "On P.P. 145-147, in writing of my brother George Edalji," she complained, "you say that 'the family was not popular' & that the villagers felt that they could 'learn nothing from a Parsee'." In response to this unsupported assertion by a man who had never been to Great Wyrley Maud poured out page after page of history in her family's defence. 'My Father gave up <u>everything</u> for Christianity at the age of 11, when he became a Christian...' she wrote, and went on to an account of Shapurji's extraordinary life-journey from Parsi in Bombay to Anglican Vicar in Great Wyrley. Then she went on to inform Pearson that 'I have been to Wyrley many times since my Father was Vicar there, & I always got a good welcome from the people, for, though many who were there when we lived there are now dead, there are still a good many left, & they always speak of my parents & of my brother with real affection.' Pearson, she suggested, should go and talk to them himself. Pearson did reply to her letter, and in response received several more pages of corrections to popular misconceptions about George's case.

Maud was on the march. Three years later her pen was at work again. Pan Books needed to know. Mr Carr wrote well, but there were so many, so many mistakes. A biography[3] of Sir Arthur really should be more accurate. Chapters 14 and 15 were the ones, the ones about George. Even mother's maiden name was not spelt correctly: it was Stoneham, not 'Stoneman'. As for the statements about Parsis, they were based on sheer ignorance: Parsis are not black, nor are they sinister. They are not a native race of India. They are Persians.

---

[1] P.R.O., HO 45/24635, no 18, letters from Maud Edalji to the Home Office, 8.2.1956, 3.3.1956, 28.3.1956.
[2] Maud Edalji to Hesketh Pearson, 28 August 1956, Hesketh Pearson Papers.
[3] John Dickson Carr, *The Life of Sir Arthur Conan Doyle*, Pan Books, 1953.

Mr Carr got so much wrong when it came to George's case. Even though Chief Constable Anson insisted that George stole the Walsall Grammar School key in 1892, George <u>never</u> went to that school. Nor was he sharp-tongued; rather the opposite. He was not sunk in despair in 1903, either; Maud read Mr Carr's chapter to him when the first edition appeared – George was blind towards the end – and he denied that he had been in despair. As to page 188, the idea that George lived in fear of being lynched after his arrest, that was ridiculous; the family had no fear at all of an attack on George, as most people in the parish were on his side. The section on the trial was inaccurate, too. It was wrong to attribute an 'ejaculation' to mother when she heard the verdict, for the family had actually been sent out of the court before the verdict came. Maud and her mother were together when they were told, so Maud knew exactly what happened. These are things you do not forget. As to the later attempts to secure George's release for wrongful conviction, Mr Carr just did not see what was so obvious to them. There was not much point in appealing to the Home Secretary when he, Herbert Gladstone, was cousin to the wife of the presiding magistrate in George's trial, the man who sentenced George to seven years' penal servitude. Surely Mr Carr must see something sinister in the fact that when a Committee of Enquiry was finally established in 1907 one member was first cousin once removed of Chief Constable Anson, the man who had led his police force in the persecution of George for years. It all happened over fifty years ago, but she knew now as she knew then. The whole thing was a police plot against him. George was innocent.

Pan Books must be told. Sir Arthur Conan Doyle, the man who proved George innocent, deserved more than this. Either the Great Wyrley chapter should be corrected or all future editions should contain an errata sheet with Maud's corrections and additions. Maud posted off her demands. She told her friends. She wrote to Mrs Edmunds in Great Wyrley to tell her what had happened. The campaign went on. It was in its sixth decade.[1]

Maud still visited Great Wyrley from time to time, even in her old age. She would stay at the vicarage, visit old friends, and tend to her father's lonely grave in that quiet corner of St

---

[1] Maud Edalji to Mrs Edmunds, 6 October 1959 (with the letter is a copy of her notes on John Dickson Carr's book), S.C.P.M.

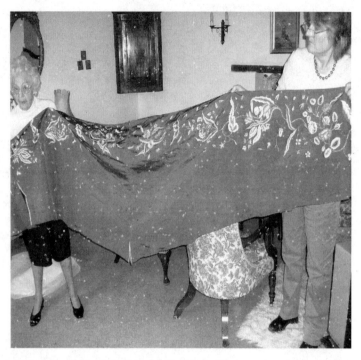

**Freda Shimmin (left) with the piece of a dress which
Maud Edalji claimed to be from an 18th century
ancestor**

Mark's churchyard. In 1961, at the age of seventy-nine, she had the strength and will to return one last time. She was warmly received; as Reverend E. H. Marsh, Vicar at St Mark's, later put it: 'Miss Edalji's life was centred at the parish... when she visited us last year we found her a wonderfully gracious old lady.' She returned home, but by the end of the year was in a nursing home. She died two days before Christmas. Her grave lies next to her older brother's in Welwyn Garden City.

Inspiration

3 November 2004. So here I sit on Freda Shimmin's sofa. Still assimilating first impressions of Peterborough, where elegant modern minarets grace the skyline around the imposing spires of the medieval cathedral. From this sofa in multifaith Britain I peer back into Maud's Welwyn Garden City house, and through that into the windows of vicarages in Great Wyrley and Ketley, and through them towards worlds which have gone.

Freda has shown me all Maud's treasures, all except one. I have been waiting for this. She mentioned on the phone her discovery after Maud's death of a package with part of a dress, an Indian dress, left in a Welwyn Garden City drawer. I cannot fathom this: surely Shapurji would not have brought a woman's dress to England when he came to Canterbury as a student.

Now Freda goes to collect it. When she comes back I am stunned. Out from the packaging pours a long stretch of shimmering green material, embroidered with joyous Eastern patterns. It shines like new, this piece of a dress. And yet with it in the package is a note in Maud's hand: 'Part of a dress worn at court in India by my great, great, great, great grandmother Ruth Swan wife of Capt John Swan and daughter of Robert Thompson. She was mother of Mary Swan who married Abraham Stoneham.'

I shiver in astonishment. Ruth Swan, née Thompson, c. 1680-c. 1758. John Swan, 1670-1729, captain in the merchant navy. Did they travel to India together? Could Ruth really have been to Delhi to the court of the Mughal emperors in the days when the Mughals still ruled over large parts of the South Asia and the British were just small fry flapping around the coastal waters? And if not the Mughal court, then which one? What story went with this dress, seemingly nearly three centuries old?

347

Perhaps family memories were distorted through time. Certainly experts at the Victoria & Albert Museum have not yet been able to place the dress earlier than the 19th century. Whatever the truth, for Maud, for her mother, and for their Stoneham, Swan and Thompson ancestors, however, the family tradition about the dress was the most vivid evidence of its awareness of its age-old connection with India. When Shapurji and Charlotte married in Ketley in 1874 that was just one chapter in the story. And when George's case became world-famous that was just another.

Truths

So what did you see, Maud, as you sat in your little drawing-room sipping tea poured from that teapot?

Which George did you see? George the victim? George the innocent? George the gentle brother outside the George made world-famous by the events of 1903 to 1907?

Who was your mother? Well-loved pillar of the Great Wyrley community? Daughter of the Mary and Thompson Stoneham whose lives filled another vicarage? Descendant of the 18th century Thompson Stoneham of the portrait on your wall? Descendant of the Thompsons, Swans and Stonehams who lived in an age when Muslims ruled India, and the British, still struggling to get a foothold, brought back admired Indian dresses and kept them for generations in their wardrobes and cupboards? Descendant of distant relatives of a wife of the man who established the Church of England? Descendant of Christian warriors who fought against Muslims in the Crusades? Descendant of heathen Anglo-Saxon immigrants from the European mainland?

Who was your father? For 42 years respected Vicar of St Mark's in Great Wyrley? The intelligent, pioneering, remarkable man who was probably the first person from the South Asia to become a vicar in an English parish? The rebellious son of successful Bombay Parsis? Descendant of the Parsis who helped the British build Bombay? Descendant of the Parsis who migrated from Persia to India to escape Muslim persecution? Descendant of the Zoroastrians who were the earliest believers in one God?

And what about the three of you, the children who posed so earnestly for the camera with your parents on the step of your vicarage home at Easter 1892? Who were you? Children of two worlds? Children of many worlds? Or children of one?

The answers are somewhere with you. The Edalji story was not created in the mind of Sir Arthur Conan Doyle. It is made of many stories, and they are all there, somewhere, in your little house.

SELECT BIBLIOGRAPHY

The Edalji family

Yasmin Alibhai-Brown and Anne Montague, *The Colour of Love*, Virago Press, 1992.

George Edalji, *Railway Law for the Man in the Train*, Wilson's Legal and Useful Handy Books, 1901.

Shápurjí Edaljí, *A Gujeráti and English Dictionary*, Trübner, 1863.

Shápurjí Edaljí, *The Brahma Samája*, Free General Assembly's Institute, Bombay, 1864.

Shápurjí Edaljí, *A Grammar of the Gujeráti Language*, Trübner, 1867.

Shápurjí Edaljí, *A Translation of Johnson's 'Rasselas'*, Trübner, 1866.

Shápurjí Edaljí, *The Pand-Nameh, or a Book of Parsé Morality, translated into English from Gujarati*, Trübner, 1870.

Shapurji Edalji, *Lectures on St Paul's Epistle to the Galatians*, Midlands Educational Company, 1879

George Smith, *Life of John Wilson*, John Murray, 1878.

Rozina Visram, Ayahs, Lascars and Princes: Indians in Britain 1700-1947, Pluto Press, 1986.

John Wilson, *The Star of Bethlehem and the Magi from the East: A Sermon Preached on the Occasion of the Baptism of a Parsi Youth 31st August, MDCCCLVI*, Smith Taylor & Co, Bombay, 2nd ed, 1857.

Conan Doyle and the case of George Edalji

Books and articles

G. A. Atkinson, *G. H. Darby, Captain of the Wyrley Gang: an Investigation*, T. Kirby & Sons, 1914.

Julian Barnes, *Arthur and George*, Jonathan Cape, 2005.

Martin Booth, *The Doctor, the Detective and Arthur Conan Doyle: A Biography of Arthur Conan Doyle*, Hodder & Stoughton, 1997.

J. D. Carr, *The Life of Sir Arthur Conan Doyle*, John Murray, 1949.

John Churton Collins, 'The Edalji Case: Its History and Its Lessons', *National Review*, 1907.

Sir Arthur Conan Doyle, *Memories and Adventures*, Hodder & Stoughton, 1924.

Peter Costello, *The Real World of Sherlock Holmes*, Robinson Publishing, 1991.

A. J. Cronin, *Great Unsolved Crimes*, Hutchinson, 1935.

Shapurji Edalji, *The Case of George Edalji*, The United Press Association, 1905.

Richard Lancelyn Green, *The Uncollected Sherlock Holmes*, Penguin Books, 1983.

Michael Harley, 'An infamous Anson?', in *Staffordshire History*, 2, Spring 1985.

Charles Higham, *The Adventures of Conan Doyle*, Hamish Hamilton, 1976.

Stephen Hines (ed) and Steven Womack (introduction), *The True Crime Files of Sir Arthur Conan Doyle*, Berkley Prime Crime, New York, 2001.

Shompa Lahiri, 'Uncovering Britain's South Asian Past: The Case of George Edalji', *Immigrants and Minorities*, Issue 17.3, November 1998, Frank Cass.

John Lamond, *Arthur Conan Doyle*, John Murray, 1931.

Paul Lester, *Sherlock Holmes in the Midlands*, Brewin Books, Studley, 1992.

Andrew Lycett, *Conan Doyle: The Man Who Created Sherlock Holmes*, Weidenfeld & Nicholson, 2007.

Compton Mackenzie, *On Moral Courage*, Collins, 1962.

Russell Miller, *The Adventures of Arthur Conan Doyle*, Harvill Secker, 2008.

Pierre Nordon, *Conan Doyle*, John Murray, 1966.

Roger Oldfield, *The Case of George Edalji*, Staffordshire County Council, 1987.

Hesketh Pearson, *Conan Doyle: His Life and Art*, Methuen 1943.

Daniel Stashower, *Teller of tales: the life of Arthur Conan Doyle*, Henry Holt and Company, 1999.

Ronald Burt de Waal, *The International Sherlock Holmes*, Archon Books, 1980.

Jennifer Ward, 'The Letter Writers of Wyrley', text of talk to Police History Society, 1994 (copy in W.S.L.).

Gordon Weaver, *Conan Doyle and the Parson's Son: The George Edalji Case*, Vanguard Press, 2006.

Richard and Molly Whittington-Egan (eds): Sir Arthur Conan Doyle, *The Story of Mr. George Edalji*, Grey House Books, 1985.

R. D. Yelverton, 'In the matter of George Edward Thompson Edalji', 1903 (copies in C.L. and P.R.O.).

Television Documentaries

Conan Doyle for the Defence, BBC, first broadcast 25 December 2005.
'Scene of the Crime', *ITV Forensic Casebook,* ITV, first broadcast 24 November 2008. Series reshown as *Forensic Casebook with Matthew Kelly,* 2009.
Heart of the Country, ITV Midlands, 10 November 2005.

Unpublished plays

Roy Apps, *Conan Doyle and the Edalji Case,* broadcast on BBC Radio 4, 1987.
Alexandra Becker and Rolf Becker, *Conan Doyle und der Fall Edalji,* Dokumentarspiel, ZDF, broadcast on 29 July,1966.
David Edgar, *Arthur and George,* first performed at Birmingham Repertory Theatre, 2010.
Tony Mulholland, *Conan Doyle's Strangest Case,* broadcast on BBC Radio 4, 1996.
Jeremy Paul, *The Edwardians: Conan Doyle,* broadcast on BBC2, 12 December, 1972.
Roger Woddis, *Conan Doyle Investigates,* performed at Victoria Theatre, Newcastle-under-Lyme, April 1971, and as a BBC radio play, May 1972.

INDEX

A

Aberystwyth, 48
Akers-Douglas, A., 81
Aldis, James, 99, 105, 106
Alibhai-Brown, Yasmin, 202, 203
Anson, George
  Barnes, Julian, 330, 338, 339
  career, 96, 288, 305
  Edalji, George, case of, 60, 76, 81, 82, 95, 100, 105, 106, 114, 128, 130, 137, 210, 260, 269, 297, 302–5, 307, 309–22, 345
  Conan Doyle, conflict with, 297–301
  family, 96, 106
Anson, Louise (née Phillips), 1st Countess of Lichfield, 321
Anson, Patrick John, 5th earl of Lichfield, 76
Anson, Thomas Francis, 3rd Earl of Lichfield, 96
Anson, Thomas William, 1st Earl of Lichfield, 321
Apps, Roy, 308
Arrowsmith, F., 78, 111, 113, 332, 342
Atkinson, G. A., 285, 301

B

Badger, Henry, 37, 38, 39, 42, 80, 222
Badger, Maud, 80
Bailey, Henry, 159, 168, 173, 243
Balfour, Arthur James, 81
Barnes, A. W., 61
Barnes, Julian, 338–41
Barrie, James M., 104, 116
Beaumont, R., 111, 113, 332, 342
Beck, Adolf, 102, 104, 268
Benson, Richard Meaux, 167–69, 169, 170, 245
Bhownaggree, Mancherjee, 139, 149, 309
Birmingham, 25, 31, 44, 45, 48, 63, 78, 90, 94, 129, 135
Birmingham University, 104, 250
Blackpool, 101, 112

Bolton, 176, 178, 179, 182, 209
Bombay
  administration, 152, 154, 189
  churches, 149, 160, 162
  colleges, 143, 145, 162, 166, 243
  economy, 147, 178, 229
  Hindus, 151
  Muslims, 151, 187, 324
  origins, 146
  Parsis, 25, 146, 175, 200, 203, 309
  population, 187
  schools, 149
  Towers of Silence, 144, 281
Booth, Martin, 90, 338
Boycott, Richard, 246
Brahmo Samaj, 153
Bridgetown, 38, 44, 49, 67, 113
Bromsgrove, 23
Brookes, Fred, 94, 97, 98, 112, 113, 314, 330
Brookes, William, 38, 94, 298
Browell, Charles, 251
Bruton, William, 58
Buchan, John, 136
Bungay family, 37, 38, 39
Burford, 143, 160, 163, 169–70, 171, 172, 173, 176
Burgess, John, 169, 170
Burton-on-Trent, 37
Butter, John Kerr, 38, 59, 61, 277, 297

C

Calcutta, 146
Cambridge, 193, 200, 250, 324
Campbell, John, 42, 46, 47, 56–59, 59, 61, 65, 76, 81, 114, 310, 332
Campbell-Bannerman, Sir Henry, 108
Cannock, 38, 43, 59–62, 62, 93, 95, 111, 112, 114
Cannock Chase, 117
Catherine of Braganza, 146
Charles II, King, 146, 187
Cheslyn Hay
  animals, 39
  anonymous letters (G. H. Darby), 290
  anonymous letters of 1903, 45

Greatorex, W. A., 112, 113
Greatorex, Wilfred, 43–48, 109,
    111, 112, 113, 129, 130, 310,
    311, 316, 330
Green, Elizabeth, 38, 62, 79
Green, Harry, 38, 62, 63, 64, 67,
    68, 70, 78, 79, 113, 286
Green, Richard Lancelyn, 76, 131
Green, Thomas, 38, 39, 62, 79
Greensill, John, 236
Grier, Macgregor, 78
Guinness, Robert, 172
Gujerat, 145, 146, 187
Gujerati, 146, 150, 152, 153, 157,
    175, 179, 243, 246
Gurrin, Thomas, 61, 65, 67, 102,
    109, 268, 316

H

Hardy, Sir Reginald, 44, 64, 69,
    81, 102, 107
Harley, Michael, 128–32, 138,
    152, 200, 259, 260, 262, 273,
    293, 297, 298, 302, 308–10,
    312, 316, 317, 318, 322, 333–
    34, 338
Harrison, H. A., 65
Harrow, 323, 324
Hart, Jack, 38, 113
Hathaway, Edward, 172
Hatherton, 1st Baron, 216, 217
Hatherton, 2nd Baron, 240
Hatherton, 3rd Baron, 44, 64,
    115, 217
Hatton, Christopher, 255, 262,
    263, 309, 311, 312
Hatton, John, 32, 59, 212, 220,
    221, 235, 236, 242
Haug, Martin, 152, 166, 175
Hawkins family, 37, 221
Hawkins, F. W., 281, 282
Hawkins, J., 309
Hawkins, Thomas, 251
Hazell, Alfred, 262, 312
Hednesford, 43, 45, 46, 78, 94,
    99, 109, 111, 225, 330
Hereford, 273
Hobson, David, 49
Holmes, Joseph, 38, 39, 78, 259
Holy Trinity (Oxford), 100, 171–
    72, 174, 176
Hong Kong, 146
Hopkins, Gerard Manley, 176,
    179
Hornung, E. W., 116

Howard, Sir Ebenezer, 283
Hughes, William, 38
Hunter, Herbert, 287–88, 302,
    324
Hussain, Syed, 144, 150–51

I

Indian National Congress, 253,
    324

J

Jack the Ripper, 43, 44, 207
Jayes, John, 62
Jerome, Jerome K., 104, 116
Johnson, Samuel, 153, 154
Johnson. Lindsay, 111
Jowett, Benjamin, 166

K

Ketley, 22, 23, 24, 98, 116, 177,
    194–98, 200, 202, 230, 233,
    256, 282, 329, 347, 348
Kingsley, Charles, 97
Kipling, Rudyard, 69, 137, 156,
    233, 256, 274, 323, 324
Kirk, Charles, 156, 157, 158, 163,
    173
Klinger, Paul, 308
Knowles, Enoch, 288–92, 313
Knowles, Lizzie, 289

L

Lahiri, Shompa, 323
Lancashire, 172, 177, 182
Landywood, 31, 32, 37, 39, 70,
    240, 241
Lawrence, Stephen, 321, 322
Leckie, Jean, 90, 116, 305
Ledgard, George, 156, 157
Legge, Augustus, Bishop of
    Lichfield, 259
Lester, Paul, 131
Lewes, 77
Lewis, Robert, 58, 68
Lewis, Sir George, 77, 104, 107
Lincolnshire, 99
Little Baddow, 186, 187, 190,
    189–91, 193, 265
Littleton family. *See* Hatherton,
    Barons

359

Liverpool, 23, 24, 108, 112, 135, 176, 180, 181, 182, 200, 259
Livingstone, David, 153
London, 43
Loxton, C. A., 57, 310, 316, 337
Lucknow, 321, 324
Ludlow, 60
Lunt, Susannah, 92
Lycett, Andrew, 342

M

Macaulay, Thomas Babington, 148
Mackenzie, Compton, 106–7
Magee, Annie, 273, 282
magi, 245
Markew, Joseph, 56
Marley, Bob, 138
Mason College, 94, 104, 250
McNeile, Hugh, 180, 182, 183
Meredith, George, 104
Meyer, Nicholas, 307
mixed marriages, 24, 230, 282
Montague, Anne, 202, 203
More, Jasper, 77
Morgan, Hollis, 114, 115
Morley, John, 189
Much Wenlock, 77, 98, 230, 258, 282
Mughal emperors, 148, 347
Müller, F. Max, 166, 167, 169, 175
Munich, 166
Munro, David, 24, 235, 236
Muthu, Chowry, 323

N

Naoroji, Dadabhai, 139, 149, 157, 200, 205, 209, 252, 273, 323, 324
Nauroji, Dhanjibhai, 150, 151, 152, 154
Nehru, Jawaharlal, 21, 324
New Bury, 176, 177, 178
Nightingale, Florence, 166
Nordon, Pierre, 107, 285, 302

O

Oxford, 163–74, 197, 243, 245

P

Pahlavi, 150, 152, 166, 175

Palmer, William, Dr, 246
Parsis, 23, 25, 60, 107, 143–51, 157, 158, 176, 187, 200, 203, 205, 209, 228, 229, 252, 255, 274, 307, 309, 324, 344, 351
Pattenden, Rosemary, 268
Paul, Jeremy, 113, 308
Pease, Pike, 108
Penkridge, 60, 217
Pentonville Prison, 82
Persia, 145, 150, 245, 348
Poona, 203
Powell, William, 37

Q

Queen Mary's High School (Walsall), 31, 185, 216, 255, 283

R

Read, Tony, 91
Rider Haggard, Henry, 136–37
Risinger, D. Michael, 316, 330, 333
Robinson, Charles, 61, 62, 67
Rogers, William, 251
Romer, Robert, 106
Rost, Reinhold, 159, 161, 162
Rugeley, 220, 248, 310
Rugeley Grammar School, 78, 225, 246, 247, 250
Rushdie, Salman, 135, 137, 138, 191, 317, 321, 322, 324, 325, 337
Ruskin, John, 166

S

Saklatvala, Shapurji, 25, 139
Salisbury, 3rd Marquess of, 81, 139, 168, 253
Sambrook, Albert, 115
Scott, Kenneth, 91
Selwyn, George, Bishop of Lichfield, 171, 210, 227
Shaftesbury, Lord, 195
Sharp, Frank, 302, 313
Sharp, Louise, 111, 112
Sharp, Peter, 111
Sharp, Royden, 94, 111–14, 285, 298–301, 302, 310, 311, 312–15, 321, 330, 333, 336
Sharp, Wallie, 111, 112, 312

Shaw, George Bernard, 268
Shimmin, Freda, 22, 83, 197, 292, 347
Shropshire, 23, 77, 192, 216, 258
Simeon, Charles, 195, 197
Smith, F. E. (Lord Birkenhead), 108
Society for the Propagation of the Gospel, 156, 157, 158, 162
South Africa, 70, 79, 113
St Augustine's College, 157, 159–63, 170, 173, 176, 243
St Clement's (Toxteth Park), 176, 183
St James' (New Bury, Farnworth), 177, 178
St John the Baptist (Burford), 170
St John's (Cowley), 168
St Leonard's (Bromley), 206
St Levan, 176, 201
St Mark's (Great Wyrley), 23, 24, 26, 31, 32, 48, 62, 76, 78, 115, 131, 198, 210, 214, 215, 217, 220, 223, 226, 229, 231, 233, 235, 240, 243, 251, 256, 259, 262, 281, 286, 298, 347, 348
St Mark's (Liverpool), 180
St Mary's (Ketley), 23, 25, 98, 177, 192, 200, 201, 202, 209, 210, 256, 282, 329
St Thomas (Toxteth), 181–83
St Thomas's Cathedral (Bombay), 137, 156
Stafford, 60, 61, 63, 77, 96, 103
  prison, 64, 77
Staffordshire
  animal attacks, 42
  armed forces, 229
  courts, 64, 102, 217, 290
  landownership, 216
  mining, 217, 251
  police, 38, 42, 96, 100, 103, 131, 137, 247, 289, 297, 298, 301, 312, 318, 321
  Potteries, 256, 307
  schools, 136, 271
Staffordshire-Worcestershire canal, 38
Stanley, Herbert, 70
Stashower Daniel, 338
Stoker, Bram, 116
Stone, Sir J. B., 129, 260, 308, 309, 333
Stoneham, Abraham (1693-1752), 189, 206, 347

Stoneham, Abraham (1778-1851), 190–91
Stoneham, Catherine (née Morley), 189, 190
Stoneham, Charlotte. *See* Edalji, Charlotte
Stoneham, George Thompson, 190, 191, 192, 229
Stoneham, Mary (née Compson), 23, 98, 192, 193, 197
Stoneham, Mary (née Swan), 347
Stoneham, Mary Sancta, 22, 23, 25, 77, 78, 98, 192, 200, 201, 230, 258, 266, 282, 329
Stoneham, Thomas, 189
Stoneham, Thompson (1809-1877), 23, 98, 189, 192, 193, 200, 230
Stoneham, Thompson (c.1732-1780), 187, 189, 192, 193
Stoneham, William Phillip, 192
Suez, 158
Swan, John, 347
Swan, Ruth, 189, 206, 347

T

Taylor, James, 156, 157, 161
Thomas, Ernest, 39
Toxteth, 117, 135, 143, 176, 183, 201, 202, 205
Trevor-Roper, Hugh, 138

U

Upton, William, 93, 94, 95, 97, 98, 100, 314, 315, 318, 330

V

Vachell, C. F., 64, 65, 67, 68, 262, 311, 312
Vaz, Keith, 139
Victoria, Queen, 21, 152, 195, 205, 256
Visram, Rozina, 25, 138, 139, 149, 197, 207, 253

W

Wacha, Sir Dinshaw Eduljee, 151, 253
Wadia family, 146
Wales, 25
Walker, Alan, 132, 334, 339

Walsall, 31, 38, 44, 57, 117

Walsall Grammar School, 43, 45, 94, 95, 99, 105, 109, 112, 314, 315, 320, 336, 345

Waralis, 154, 155, 156, 157

Ward, Jennifer, 131

Wellington, Arthur Wellesley, 1st Duke of, 138, 156

Welwyn Garden City, 21, 22, 83, 185, 264, 283, 290, 328, 329, 343, 347

West Indies, 81

West, E. W., 152, 166, 175

Wharton, John, 106

Whitehouse, Mary Ann, 98

Whitehouse, Walter, 49, 65, 68

Wilberforce, Samuel, 167, 169, 173, 177, 195

Wilberforce, William, 156, 195, 197, 224

Wilson College, 153, 161, 243

Wilson, Arthur, 106

Wilson, John, 143, 144, 145, 149, 150, 151, 152, 154, 156, 170, 243

Woddis, Roger, 307

Wolverhampton, 48, 70, 93, 115, 117

Woods, Alfred, 90

Woodward, Herbert, 183

Wootton, Fred, 45, 97

Wootton, Thomas, 37

Wootton, William, 50, 58

Wynn, Fred, 94, 112, 271, 314

Wynn, William, 38, 94, 271

Y

Yarmouth, 114

Yelverton, Roger Dawson, 44, 45, 46, 47, 48, 63, 76, 77, 78, 79, 81, 92, 98, 99, 100, 104, 158, 248, 250, 258, 262, 265, 266, 268, 297, 309, 311, 313, 317, 320, 352

Yonge, Reginald, 23, 24, 181, 183, 200, 202

Z

Zola, Emile, 103, 104

Zoroaster, 145, 147, 152, 203

Zoroastrianism, 145, 150, 167, 175, 203